The World
by the Tail

The World
by the Tail

Brooke Negley

To Antoniette & Mitia,
Have fun together,
Brooke Negley
9-23- 2000

THE **WATERCRESS PRESS**   San Antonio 1999

Revised Edition

A *Watercress Press* book from
Evett-Geron Associates, San Antonio, Texas

Cover design by Paul Hudgins

To order more copies:
call toll free
1-877-653-6936

Additional copies may be ordered from
Brooke Negley

4210 Colonneh Trail
San Antonio, Texas 78218

Library of Congress Catalog Card number 99-71051
ISBN 0-934955-38-7

For Janie—
who started it all

Prologue

At one point in every person's life, there is a choice to be made: to be or not to be a dog person. As parents have been known to say, "Having a dog is a big responsibility." It's one thing when they are adorable puppies— and I have yet to see an ugly puppy—it's another thing when they are gnawing on my Gucci shoes or the upholstered furniture; and they have to be fed and watered every day. Not to mention exercise, shots, teething, worming, grooming, training, check-ups, and the inevitable bills.

When I was growing up in San Antonio in the late fifties, my mother had two dachshunds, Bruno and Gretchen, a matched pair of black-and-tan, well-tempered, and extremely cheerful hounds. I will always remember their perky ratty tails wagging sharply, like little birch whips. They were a delightful duo. Of course, I never had to feed or water them; in fact, I hardly ever saw them as I was riding my bike or roller skating too fast for them to keep up on their Vienna sausage legs. Anyway, they loved Mom the most.

Within a six-month period, Bruno died of hepatitis and Gretchen was poisoned in the neighborhood. My mother's grief was quiet, a solo grief, and I could not help her at all. She said she never wanted another dog as long as she lived. At that point, I believed her. And I was surely not considering a man's-best-friend life if it could cause such sadness.

With Bruno and Gretchen there was born in Mom an awareness of what it was like to have a warm beast by her side, to scratch soft ears, to be held in such high esteem, and to be so blatantly rewarded for such simple feats as coming through the door. Mom was never to lose that feeling of being loved. She was set, molded for life. A dog person.

But for six years her desire for another dog remained dormant, during which time I was even more oblivious to her feelings as I was living in Switzerland, going to the school Candice Bergen went to, skiing the same slopes as Hayley Mills, teaching David Niven and William F. Buckley how to do the Madison. Glamour, glamour, glamour. Life was good for this teenager. But life was not real. It was like a gorgeous movie still. A picture I was not in. I was simply the photographer.

And in that sixth year, my mother broke her vow and everything came bounding to life. With an impulsive and startling gesture on her part, she changed the course of our lives.

Although I first thought the impulse a careless one, even slightly inconvenient, it was to change my life even more than Mom's. As Yogi Berra said, "When you come to a fork in the road, take it." And my lucky day was the day Mom did just that.

Brooke Negley

San Antonio, Texas
1998

The World
by the Tail

One

Ah, yes. Another postcard. "Having a wonderful time, wish you were here. Love, Mom." And lip prints. Big red lip prints after the signature. She always kissed her correspondence, and it had become her trademark, along with the informant message. A drawing of a thatched-roof cottage was on the stamp and in the upper left corner it read, "The Manor House, Moretonhampstead, Devon." Turning the postcard over, I stared at a magnificent stately home, landscaped with dark green rhododendron bushes, smothered in flamingo pink blooms, and a never-ending, rolling green lawn.

"Wow," I said out loud, standing alone in my room. I smiled at the latest postcard, tapped it on my hand, and gazed around me. It was 1968. I was 21 years old, living in the Alps in Gstaad, Switzerland, in a chalet that my mother, Nancy Holmes, had rented. Six years earlier, we had moved from a booming neighborhood in San Antonio, Texas, where subdivisions were taking over wide-open spaces and we were starting to lock our doors. Mom decided to move us when she asked my brother, Pete, if he had done his homework and he replied, "I'm aimin' to," and worse, he was bragging that he was going to buy a pickup truck. I, on the other hand, kept answering Mom with, "I reckon." "Have you made your bed?" "I reckon." "Have you brushed your teeth?" "I reckon." Mom was a single, gutsy woman, a classy woman, strapped with two hick children.

When I was two and Pete was three, our father, Bud Thompson, a suave and sexy bomber pilot, graduate of West Point, and my mother, a suave and sexy model, first American to model for Balmain in Paris after World War II, were divorced. I had already lived

1

in two states, Virginia and New York, by the age of two, when Dad was gone from our lives and my mother married my stepfather, Chris Holmes, moving us from New York to San Antonio. I liked Texas instantly. Horses, big sunsets, jackrabbits, rodeos, tamales. We lived in San Antonio during Mom's nine-year marriage to Chris. But with a sad divorce from him and the fear that we could become rednecks, Mom packed us up and sent us to boarding schools to broaden our horizons. She sent us away and then came to us, renting a chalet in Gstaad as home base while she worked in Europe. Four of my teen years were spent at a finishing school, Ecole Montesano, in Gstaad, and two of Pete's were at the boys' equivalent school, Le Rosey.

That day in 1968, I was alone. Pete had been in Vietnam for a month and Mom was in Devon. I stood holding the postcard, missing my jet-set mother and worried sick about my big brother. I needed some company.

The phone rang. I scooped it up, jumping at the infrequent noise.

"Brookie, you've got to come see this place," Mom said, with no salutation. "Did you get my postcard?"

Her previous postcard had come from South Africa. The picture was of a camel, a desert, a sparkling blue sky. "Having a wonderful time, wish you were here. Love, Mom," it said. Big red lip prints.

"Yes, Mom, but are you in South Africa or Devon?" I asked, guiltily aware of how unretentive I had become of her whereabouts. I excused myself by remembering how much she had to travel. Mom was working for Columbia Pictures as a photojournalist, spending her life on exotic locations, taking pictures of movie stars, living on a big expense account, returning to Gstaad on occasion. She went places I could not pronounce, much less find on the map. A couple of times a year, she flew back to America to sell some photos freelance to American magazines, to help publicize Columbia's films, and to make a name for herself.

"I'm in Devon, South England," she replied, "and I want you to come. I'm in a funny little town called Torquay." She pronounced it

Tor KEE, which annoyed me because I knew I couldn't spell or find it.

"Never heard of it," I said blandly, as tractable as a goaded bull. Looking back, I wonder why she ever asked me anywhere.

"I have booked you on Thursday." The connection was crystal clear and her enthusiasm was genuine. "The flight leaves Geneva in the morning for London, then you take a train from Paddington Station to Newton Abbot and change for Torquay. You'll be crazy about it here," she ended. She had had years of experience trying to get me to behave and be grateful but I was a normal, common, selfish, and totally ungrateful daughter. Mom smartly played right around me.

"Oh, gee, Mom, I don't know. The first snow could come any day now . . ." a poor feint. It was only September and my job as a ski instructor in my old boarding school did not start until December.

"Come on, " she cajoled, "I'm tired of being alone." And wasn't that just how I was feeling?

I bit my lip and studied my chewed nails. "Fine," I said, not giving up much.

"Goody! Bibbings, my driver, will meet the train at Torquay and carry your bags to the Imperial Hotel. It's right across the street from the station."

"Mom, I can carry my own bags," I fussed. Mom could not seem to understand that I was never going to dress as well as she did. I favored a poor, beatnik look and therefore traveled light.

"Nonsense. He'll be there. Bring me some warm clothes. I have two scarves on my head as we speak. This weather goes right through you. Bring everything warm you ever had." She hung up as suddenly as she had rung up.

"Bye, Mom. Nice talking to you. Sure, see you. Right. Day after tomorrow." A little late to become a chatty Cathy. I put the silent phone back in its cradle.

Walking over to the window, I leaned my head against the cold pane and watched a herd of beige-and-white cows grazing calmly in the near meadow. My thoughts backed up to two years earlier, remembering when Pete decided not to finish his last year at George-town University in Washington, D.C., but to join the army. He told me that President Johnson had convinced many a young man that there was a noble objective: to save the poor little Vietnamese from Communism. He spent six months as an enlisted man, six months more at Fort Sill, Oklahoma, where he graduated a second lieutenant from OCS. Because he spoke French, he spent his next six months at Fort Bragg in North Carolina, in Special Warfare Training, an officer on TDY (temporary duty). As so many boys had been drafted, the facilities on the base were overrun and Pete ended up alone in a small house, paid for by the army. I joined him for his first two weeks, to get him settled and play housekeeper, cooking and doing laundry. It was not easy for me to grasp that my twenty-three-year-old brother was going to be sent off to Vietnam instead of hanging out and getting drunk with college buddies. He went on from there to Fort Bliss in El Paso, Texas, for six months where he played tapes through the night and learned military Vietnamese. He had six more months of training and went off to Vietnam in September, 1968, for a year's "tour." A war tour. Looking back, it was like a bad dream and it played out just as quickly. Like Mom, Pete was now in a country I knew nothing about. He was training Vietnamese troops up in some mountain village I could not pronounce. I figured his mountain village was not as pretty as my mountain village. Magazine and news-paper pictures showed a colorless country, a soggy land, and teenage boys looking like they were playing war games.

Pushing the window open, I sat down on the red-checked win-dowseat and felt the sharp, cold air dart into the room, accompanied by the great smell of cow manure. Thank heavens I liked the smell as it was certainly the country's primary perfume. The season was changing, one of my favorite changes in Gstaad, as any change was thrilling after San Antonio's mere two seasons. All the animals were astir, preparing their nests and dens for hibernation. My life was a fantasy. My mother's life was a fantasy. My brother's life was a nightmare. I tried to keep my hopes up that he would come home safely, and the only way I felt useful was to write him every day. Mom and I talked about our fears on occasion, and I knew she was sending Pete many a postcard with big red lip prints every chance she got.

I sat down at the thick wood dining-room table and finished a letter to Pete, trying to write about something other than what a grand life I was living in a neutral country. I sealed it and walked into the village. In September, mountain villages like Gstaad and other resorts belonged to the peasants. The air was thick with the odor of cow manure as the farmers began to move their cows from grazing the upper pastures in the warmth of the summer sun to the lower barns. They used the main street, coating it with a runny manure and producing ammonia that was practically visible in the air. That, and the huge bells around the cow's necks, clanging resoundingly, had to be the reason the fall was not much of a pedestrian season. After six years of living among the Swiss, I had concluded that they were very simply a basic breed, different from any that I had ever met: hardworking yet stressless, humorless yet happy.

Walking through the village to post the letter, I started getting excited about the trip to England. I had to admit that whenever I went anywhere with Mom, it always turned out to be quite an adventure. As young as I was, I felt I had lived a long time with a mother so energetic and social. Another admission, but one I jealously kept to myself, was that I was proud of her. In what I saw as a man's world back in 1968, Mom stood out very bravely, and made an impressive living. I was glad I had allowed her wishes to stampede me into going and, if nothing else, the trip would give me new material for my letters to Pete.

Two days later, dressed in a navy blue turtleneck and jeans, wearing my favorite, broken-in and highly polished brown cowboy boots, and carrying a flannel-lined waterproof jacket with a thick red scarf, I flew to London. Having always been an athletic girl, especially after years of skiing, I was now solid, strong, full of myself, and had never once been accused of being feminine. Toting two canvas duffel bags filled with foul-weather gear and a fine stack of colorful Hermes scarves for Mom, I made my way like a linebacker to British Rail at Paddington Station, bumping and pushing frailer people out of my way. Finding the proper track was a breeze, inasmuch as public transportation in England is the Brits' main means of passage, they have made it simple. Signs told me which track, which stairs, which tunnel. There were even helpful people who knew the answers to any question a foreigner might like to ask. Fluent in French from finishing school and bringing Spanish with me from Texas, I felt very secure in Europe, and I was sickeningly impressed with myself.

Waiting to depart for Newton Abbot and Plymouth, the shiny silver train hummed efficiently on Track 4. I threw the bags on the train's platform, climbed aboard, and took a seat in an empty car. The seats were upholstered in a scratchy red material, but were clean and otherwise comfortable. We pulled out of London smack on time at five o'clock. A man and woman settled at the other end of the car, a middle-aged couple. He read a London newspaper and smoked a filterless Gaulois. He was a beefy man, with few illustrious features other than yellow, stained teeth. She was slight, gentle, quiet. She sat, pretty hands folded in repose in her lap, staring silently at them, looking as if she wished they, at least, would talk to her. The train ride to Newton Abbot would be about two hours and I bet myself that he would never turn and speak to her.

As Mom had trained us to learn what we could about our whereabouts, I got the Blue Guide to England out of my backpack and turned to the chapter about Devon. It told me about the great patchwork quilt area of southwest England, part of the West Countree, abounding with cliffside farms, rolling hills, foreboding moors, semitropical plants, and fishing villages that provide some of the finest scenery in England. Devon, a land of jagged coasts, with the red cliffs in the south facing the English Channel. In south Devon, the coast from which Drake and Raleigh set sail, a tranquil life prevails, and on the bay-studded coastline of north Devon, pirates and smugglers used to find haven. How romantic. I looked outside at the landscape, just as the light faded, imagining cliffs and water where the countryside I saw was flat, fantasizing that this was where Daphne du Maurier wrote *Frenchman's Creek.* I fell asleep dreaming of the Frenchman, the smell of a pipe, and me, as Dona, unfurling an immense cloak of dove-colored cut velvet to reveal a silvery-gray silk frock, ruffled skirts underneath to give me a sensuous swish, my bosom enticingly exposed. Dreaming I was feminine was the best I could do.

When I woke up at 6:45, it was already dark and the lights were on in the train. The train was still whipping along and my quiet traveling companions were gone. I picked up my book and learned that Newton Abbot was a busy market town and railway center, close to a large and popular resort, Torquay. Elizabeth Barrett Browning had made a long convalescent stay at Torquay from 1838-41. The birthplace of mystery writer Agatha Christie opened onto twenty-two miles of coastline and eighteen beaches. I had never thought of England as a place to swim, like the south of France, or Texas, because I had always imagined it a cold, gray country.

The door was opened and the conductor came in, looking back and forth from seat to seat, touching them to keep his balance. It looked as if his heavy, black wool uniform had been tailored just for him, and that the shiny gold buttons rising to his chin made him hold his head high. A jaunty red cap topped him off like a cherry.

"Next stop, Plymouth," he said as he went past me.

"Oh, Plymouth. How lovely. How long before we get to Newton Abbot?" I asked him.

"Newton Abbot, Miss?" he repeated. "You have missed Newton Abbot, Miss." He smiled. Another smoker. He had ten discolored teeth at least, and they were all showing.

"Missed it?" I stared at him, insultingly, as if *he* had failed a

7

geography course.

"The train will arrive in Plymouth in thirty minutes . . . after a ten minute wait, it returns to London, back through Newton Abbot at 7:55. You will just have a little jaunt to Plymouth," he said, formally, clicking his heels and bowing to me. "I would be delighted to check on you and make sure you disembark in Newton Abbot this time if you would like, Miss."

"Will I be able to get a train to Torquay?" I asked, annoyed as hell.

"One leaves right away for Torquay, Miss." Tipping his red cap, he exited.

Not feeling nearly as cocky as I had earlier, I cupped my hands against the window and watched my shadow crash speedily along on the ground outside. I could not make out anything about the country-side; it just seemed ominous. I was covering a lot of ground and my shadow was touching parts of Devon that were instantly forgotten and not in the slightest way permanent. Off in the distance bright, yellow squares of light shone from windows, but I could not see the outlines of any houses or pubs; they might well have been as grand as Tara for all I knew.

I picked up my backpack and made my way to the buffet car, bought a cucumber sandwich, a bag of chips, and a Coca-Cola. At 7:15, the train settled at the station in Plymouth. I waited, smelling the salt air, looking out the window at what appeared to be a ghost town. The only activity was a huge, white-faced clock on the wall, ticking away the seconds, slowly. I realized my mistake had cost me over an hour, would have Mom worried, or mad, and the driver, Bib-bings, was probably pacing angrily at the station. Two people got on the train but did not come to my car. The conductor blew his whistle, then yelled, "All aboard."

As the train picked up speed and headed north, back to London, I ate my sandwich and chips and thought about my life. Ironically, I thought, I wasn't really on the wrong track, just slightly askew. At twenty-one, living in Europe, I had no real connections other than to my roaming and hardworking mother, and to my brother fighting an alien war in Vietnam. I wondered if the whole sports and jock thing was what led me down the road less traveled. When I was younger, back in Texas, Pete used to bet his friends I could throw the football farther than any of them. The fools put their money on the ground and Pete would hand me the ball and say, "Here, Kid, show 'em." Each time I threw the football farther than any one of them and Pete collected his money, I had one less chance of getting a date. With all the money he was piling up, Pete was the one who took me to the movies. Most recently, in boarding school, Montesano girls and Le Rosey boys would get together to dance at the Hi-Fi club after the Thursday afternoon combined ski races. I stood alone, a wallflower. One boy, Jeff Werner, had the guts to ask me to dance. I led, of course, and asked him why he had had the nerve to ask me to dance. He replied that it didn't really bother him that I always beat him in the ski races. The others, it bothered. But I was not the kind of girl to giggle and feign helplessness. It was not my style and I was beginning to get a very virginal outlook on life. Some day, somewhere, somehow, someone or something was bound to accept me as I was. I could hope for it.

Trying to settle down, I read my book and discovered that Dartmoor National Park covered 365 square miles and its core was Dartmoor proper, 300 square miles, that had once been a royal forest and was still sometimes called by that title. The characteristic gray "tors" that crowned many hills were actually piles of granite, broken and weathered, looking oddly like the ruins of human habitation. The slopes beneath the heights were covered in gorse and heather, while the low-lying country was spotted in tracts of dark peat and dangerous bogs, marked by bright green grass. The moorland provided rough grazing for a semi-wild breed of Dartmoor pony and for cattle and sheep, some of which, like the ponies, were pastured there all year round. Remembering what meticulous care I took of my horse, Playboy, many years ago back in Texas, blanketing him in the winter, putting pine tar on his hooves every week, filing his teeth, worming him, I found it amazing that animals were left on these seemingly harsh moors to simply fend for themselves.

I turned the page to a picture of Dartmoor Prison, a massive and eerie-looking stone building, housing "hardened criminals." The long-term prison, together with the unfriendly contours of the landscape, the treacherous bogs, the frequent mists and penetrating rain, all contributed to the forbidding reputation of the moors. All the eerie references made me feel very much alone. I read that the moors' grimly romantic atmosphere had been well evoked by Conan Doyle's *The Hound of the Baskervilles*. I shivered. Grimly romantic. What if I got off the train in this terrifying place and could not find my mother? So what if I spoke three languages and could throw the football farther than any of the wimpy boys I knew? I was still a young girl all by myself. I resolved at that moment that I would get myself a huge dog. An Irish wolfhound, perhaps. Hey, a bull mastiff. An intimidator. Dogs were allowed to go anywhere in Europe. In trains, in restaurants. I was going to find a big dog and never feel this alone again. That's all that my life was missing. A great big dog.

At 7:45, I arrived for the second time at my first destination. The conductor stuck to his word and came to remind me, grinning toothily. With its minimal lighting, Newton Abbot looked less inviting than Plymouth. I smiled at the conductor who was throwing my duffel bag off the train, ready to help me disembark. I stepped daintily into the dreadful dreary night as renewed thoughts of pirates, hounds, and prisoners crept into my mind.

Peering into the night, suddenly and surprisingly incapable of taking a simple step forward, I reached back instinctively for the security of the train. The conductor took my trembling hand.

"The train for Torquay is right across the track there, Miss," he said kindly. I was happy for the strong touch of his warm hand and the pleasant tone in his voice. A disgusting feeling of femininity swept over me. He flicked the hand I wasn't clinging to in a hapless gesture and said, "You can not miss it." Now, in Texas, when someone says , "You cain't miss it," you're lost for four days . . . the third left after the second right, past the second deer blind, over yonder hill, beyond the big tree, beside the third water trough. I was surely doomed.

Releasing his hand and squinting in the direction he pointed, I saw the train.

"Go ahead, Miss. You can do it," he said, gently discharging me.

Turning and puffing up as best I could, I dragged my bags of foul-weather gear and my guide-book-inspired terror along with me.

"Good night," the conductor said.

"Good-bye. Thank you," I spoke. Possibly my last words. I would have traded places with that conductor and his discolored teeth in a New York minute.

Two minutes later, the train for Torquay pulled out and I was on it. Another deserted train. Why were there no people anywhere? Thirty minutes later the train arrived in Torquay and Bibbings was not to be found. Across from the station, blanketed in a soft fog, lurked an ugly, sharp building that I prayed was the Imperial Hotel, but feared was Dartmoor Prison. At 8:20 in the evening, it was so still, it could have been 2 A.M. Only three lights were on, looking like laser beams shining into the closed-up night. I trudged up to the entrance. It had a single lamp over a dark black, shiny door. A rusty chain hung down, and when I pulled it, I heard a bell jangle faintly somewhere in the depths of the hotel. I waited impatiently, shifting from foot to foot, and was about to ring the bell again when the massive door opened slightly. Expecting the hounds of the Baskervilles to jump out and eat my face, I was relieved to just barely make out a young lady in the gloom.

"I want my mother," I cried.

The door opened a little more.

"She's staying here. Nancy Holmes?" I hoped.

Opening the door and becoming much less ethereal, she said, "She's been worried sick waiting for you. You're late." She appeared to be awfully young to be reprimanding me.

"Well, er, ah, I kinda missed the station." Feeling stupid was not how I had wanted to end the evening. I had a quick vision of my bull mastiff, Brutus, by my side, and felt somewhat heartened.

"Ah," she replied.

She turned and I followed her through the dark foyer into a lordly room, lined ceiling to floor with books, the smell of their leather bindings reminding me of the tack room back in Texas. Two brass floor lamps lit the room and curled over dark-green leather wingback chairs ticked in brass tacks. At one end of the room, a welcome blaze flapped and hissed and crackled in an enormous walk-in fireplace. A tall vase on a round table in front of the bay window was filled with magnificent multicolored gladiolas reaching for the ceiling, and a backdrop of crimson curtains, heavy and thick, outlined the flowers like a Georgia O'Keeffe painting.

Pointing down a dark hallway and handing me a cold, heavy key, the girl said, "Room 122. My name is Charlotte. I'll be bringing your breakfast in the morning."

"Thank you," I said, looking at the small, moon-pale girl with childlike blue eyes, wisps of brown hair curling around her heart-shaped face. Only her cheeks were rosy, embers from the English climate stoked by the fire. She wore a long, warm, brown dress with a starched white apron, and as she moved across the room to put a huge log on the fire to burn through the night, she glimmered like a moth in the firelight.

The key in my hand looked like a medieval weapon, and with it I felt secure. I proceeded to the room, turning back to say goodnight to Charlotte and seeing her graceful disappearance down another hallway with the warmth and light from the fire clinging to her departing figure.

By a tiny yellow and gold-stained hall light, I found room 122 and unlocked the door. My mother was sound asleep in a huge bed, breathing fitfully like an asthmatic in a fog. She had left the bathroom light on for me to find my way.

"Brookie, is that you?" I heard her voice.

"Yes," I whispered, "it's me."

She turned her back to the light and her snoring resumed.

"Good night," I said, leaning over her, and, feeling the loneliness of the moors again, I pulled the big wool blanket over her shoulders.

I slipped into my red flannel pajamas, brushed my teeth, and turned off the light. Making my way barefoot across the soft carpet in the dark, I stepped up to get in the one large bed with my mother and snuggled under a fat and fluffy comforter. I fell asleep seeing red lip prints on a postcard, and dreamed of a great big dog licking my face.

Two

A rap on the door woke me. I lay still under the covers, reaching into my mind to sort out where I was. Dark, cold, big comforter, nice smell.

"Come in," I heard my mother's voice only inches away, and remembered. Moors, prison, big dog.

I drew myself up against the chubby pillows and said, "Hi, Mom, how's it going?"

Mom switched on her light, wrestling for a moment to remove a black sleep shade and pulling out a few strands of premature white hair in doing so. I was always amazed how nice my mother looked in the early morning; fresh, clear-eyed, her gray hair soft and shaped. "It's always important to have nice shape to your hair," I had heard her say over and over again. She was proof. I must have aggravated the heck out of her.

"Ouch! Good morning," she said. "Sorry I couldn't wait up for you."

"Don't worry. I fell asleep and missed the change."

Charlotte entered the room bearing a fancy silver tray loaded with hot coffee and tea, mounds of steaming breads, pastries oozing raspberry jam, cakes dark, rich, and moist, and crammed with fresh apples and oranges. She set the tray on a squat table and crossed the room to draw open the curtains. But outside it was still black dark.

"Everything looks delicious," Mom said. "Thank you, Charlotte."

Mom threw the covers back, slipped into a white terrycloth robe, and, before she headed to the bathroom and shut the door, she managed to tell me we had to be packed and downstairs by 5:30 because we would be moving to the Manor House in the afternoon from the set location. It dawned on me that the forbidding Imperial Hotel, even though it was lovely and cozy inside, was not the Manor House of the postcard. Goody.

I watched Charlotte move lightly about the room, straightening the curtains and perking up dark pink tulips in a vase on the side table, and I realized she was only about my age. But something in her manner said things could be left safely to her. She was in place. This girl had already done more for other people in the dark morning hours than I had done in my whole life! I felt spoiled and ashamed. It was a checkpoint for me, but one whose lesson I had shed by 5:25 when Mom and I were downstairs standing at the front door.

The dawn was chilly and misted with dew as we loaded into one of the three dented vans filled with film crew. Inside our van, ten nondescript people were chattering, laughing, getting organized, highly active, asking each other if someone had remembered tissues, and announcing a general consensus that they hoped it wouldn't be as cold on the moors today.

Having no idea what these people did in connection with the film, but not recognizing any stars, I crossed my arms and felt let down. I had come a long way assuming Mom was working on some fancy, highfalutin movie with big stars. Should have asked. On top of that, outside the van, a slow, drifting grayness rolled over the low, empty hills, making me feel like I was on a big, silent ship out to sea, surrounded by crew mates who all knew each other and were not in the least bit interested in me. Things looked dismal, with little hope of improvement, so I decided to be annoyed with Mom.

"Nancy, is this your daughter?" A handsome man turned around right in front of us. I wiped the ugly look off my face the minute I saw his sparkly blue eyes and thick, unruly reddish hair.

"Oh! Good morning, David. I didn't see you there. Yes, this is my Brookie." Mom loaded a camera as she spoke. "Brookie, this is David Rook, author of *The White Colt*, the lovely book about a boy

15

and a pony. We're very lucky to have David helping on the film."

I smiled at him, coyly, mysteriously, deeply sensuously. I hoped. "Hello there, David," I said, dropping my voice to a sexy rasp.

"It is certainly a pleasure to meet you. Your mother hasn't stopped talking about you for two days." David reached back with both hands and looked at me very nicely. Quickly, hoping he wouldn't notice my bitten nails, I put my hand in his. His hands were warm and his eyes were such a blue . . . dare I say, Hawaiian blue? Freckles danced on his cheery face, and I felt a flush come to my cheeks as he let go of my hand.

"The pleasure is mine," I said, desperately sorry I hadn't taken two minutes to put on a little blush, eyeliner, mascara. Something.

"Nancy, she's as beautiful as you said," David declared, a talented charmer.

Me, beautiful? Hold on a minute. Me? Beautiful? I had an entirely different image of myself: a jock, a smart ass maybe, but a beauty? I don't think so. I blushed to my little frozen feet.

"What are we shooting today?" Mom asked David, noticing as a mother would that I had been struck dumb while she loaded the second of four cameras. She carried 75 rolls of black and white film, assorted lenses, caps, and four cameras in a heavy bag. Was it possible that she had needed me here to carry her camera bag? Whatever. Fine by me. David was dishy.

"Philip finds the pony stuck in the bog," David answered.

"Oh, please don't tell me," I blurted, adding, "I haven't read the book," with a meekness I hoped was disarming. Next, I would try purring.

David delved into a big, green duffel bag and handed me a copy of his book. Speechless for a second time, I turned to it for help and read the jacket flap. It was the story of a young boy named Philip, who lived with his parents in a Dartmoor village. Through a series of mishaps, but nobody's fault, the boy had stopped speaking. His frustrated parents thought it hopeless, but the doctors told them he could talk if he wanted to. Philip found a white pony on the moors, a white

16

pony in a herd of brown ponies, and the boy and the pony instantly recognized a common need in each other. But the pony was wild and free. Philip, withdrawn into a private world, dependent on no one as yet, reached out to an old retired army officer who shared a deep and consuming love of the moors. As the boy, the colonel, and the pony built up a life together, the boy started to speak again, curiously calling the pony by his own name, explaining to the moorman that he and the pony should have the same name because they were alike in that they were different.

I gulped, a sap for animal stories. When I was young, Mom had given me all the Black Stallion books, which turned me into an avid reader. But the Christmas I was ten, she gave me a book called *Black Gold*, a tragic and true story about a racehorse who broke his leg on the track and still finished the race. I cried so hard that I decided Mom must not have loved me, as I was sure I was going to die of a broken heart. *The White Colt* had all the makings of another tear-jerker, and after all these years, I wasn't sure I wanted to set myself up again. On the back of the book there was a picture of David with a little bird on his shoulder. I was in awe.

We had been driving along for thirty minutes in consistently brutal weather, across barren, open land separated only by cattle-guards that whirred each time we crossed one, and occasional white cottages, standing ghostlike on deserted hillsides. Spongy, bright green grass rolled down the vast hills, ending as one with the roads. Sheep were lying around, sleeping everywhere, owning the roads. Long-haired, rusty red cattle moved as if in slow motion. I saw a herd of shaggy ponies outlined in the dull skyline. I thought of our Texas cowboys and how well they cared for their animals. But ranching was their livelihood. I could not imagine foremen on horses checking the herd out here, nor did I have any idea what these wild and woolly animals were used for. Road signs saying, "Don't feed the animals" seemed unnecessary: the creatures looked as taboo as the landscape.

Our van turned onto a narrow road with raggle-taggle rock walls on either side. A small, whitewashed stone barn stood on a rise

17

covered in clumps of cinnamon-colored ferns and large, wet, round rocks. The drivers pulled over and stopped, turning their headlights off as the dawn's light strengthened. The crew jumped out from every door energetically and headed for their places like busy stockbrokers on a Monday morning at Wall Street.

"This is where you're shooting?" I asked David. We appeared to be in the middle of flat-out-nowhere.

"This is it. Bill's Bog," said David. He turned a full circle slowly and beamed. "It is perfect!" He wore a peacoat over a thick, navy blue turtleneck and mustard-colored corduroys, and he acted like a kid who had just been set loose on a playground. He seemed charmingly unaware of his appeal.

I looked over the moor as low clouds like tattered gray blankets streamed across the sky in unending procession, dropping a wet veil of soft rain that crept into every pore. Within thirty seconds I could tell that my thick tights under my corduroy pants, T-shirt, turtleneck, red plaid flannel shirt, heavy-duty jacket, and wool scarf around my neck, were no match for this weather. It was the foulest of days, but as I watched the crew set up mist machines and stabilize cameras on tripods, organizing a movie scene, a tacit thrill ran through me. I felt I was a lucky girl. Here was my newest adventure.

Raising the collar around my scarf and shaking my hair to fluff it up, I pulled on my gloves and sauntered over to Mom. "I think David is kinda cute," I said.

"Yes, dear," she replied, busy with her own job. On duty and taking pictures.

A brown van, "Royal Society for the Prevention of Cruelty to Animals" written on the side, slid into a muddy track and stopped. Two passengers got out.

"Michael St. John, at your service," a little man bowed ever so slightly to David as they shook hands. David was attaching suspenders to a shapeless pair of army green waders he had put on, which covered him all the way up to his chest.

"Gertie Standish," said the second passenger, a tall, toothy woman with bright red cheeks. Her long, brown hair flew every which way and she tried to keep it in place with one hand, shaking David's with the other. She wore a thick, beige turtleneck sweater, and bright red suspenders held up her oversized waders. "It is the most perfect day for the shoot," she stated.

David was introducing himself and slapping Michael on the back, nodding his head to Gertie when a hearty round of handshakes started all over again as a huge man in a fox hat and a beaver coat joined the group, introducing himself as Dick Sarafian, the director. He looked like a great Himalayan bear, the kind of man I would want to use as a windbreak if it got any rawer. Next, a top-heavy, blue horse trailer pulled up and two men got out, galoshes flapping. More handshakes all the way around. A shiny, red fire truck parked and four handsome firemen joined the group, proper English manners oozing all over the place. The little isolated hillside had become a center of activity, reminding me of a small town in Texas at rush hour. I backed away as each new ring enlarged the circle. Mom was snapping pictures like crazy and I wished I was more involved, or even useful, in all the action.

Circling the scene, I watched as the lights were turned on, highlighting Gertie's red suspenders, the firemens' dark blue, buttoned coats and yellow oil pants, and shone directly onto a green patch of grass . . . Bill's Bog, which looked out of place in the otherwise brown and gray terrain. A colorless area when we arrived, it had been transformed into something like a big top for Barnum and Bailey's Circus.

One of the young men driving the horse trailer, Jeremy, I remembered him introducing himself, opened the back of the trailer and climbed in. Slowly, a small, mud-splattered pony backed down the ramp with Jeremy at his head, chirruping to him. Almost white, with an underlay of ochre, mane standing defiant, his forelock swept aside to reveal two eyes of palest blue.

All at once, the chatting stopped. Everyone knew what was to be done and they went into action. The firemen waited to see if they were needed to squirt water for the mist machines, Gertie put on a jacket, Mom changed a lens, and David and Jeremy held on to either side of the pony's halter and led him to the edge of the bog. Sarafian watched the men setting up his scene. The pony snorted and stopped, locking his front legs. His head popped up, jerking the two men a couple of inches off the ground. Jeremy moved around to the pony's hindquarters as David waded into the soft bog, holding firmly onto the halter rope. Both men clucked and cooed to the pony, gently trying to persuade him to get in the bog.

Realizing David was sinking into a consistency like thick soup, as I had read, ground that had no substance, I found myself clenching my cold hands and holding my breath. The Dartmoor pony was instinctively terrified of that bog, as quarter horses in America are afraid of quicksand. The poor pony stood as still and firm as an Easter Island statue while David continued clucking from below, and Jeremy tried pushing from behind, both trying to move him into that muddy hell. I looked around for Gertie, wondering if she was paying attention. Not far away, she was explaining something to Sarafian, gesticulating wildly, but neither pair of their eyes ever left the pony, so I gathered all was well.

When the pony started trembling violently, darting back and forth sideways, securing his position six inches out of the bog, I cringed in horror watching his terror and confusion, his natural instinct pitted against his trust of man. Taking my eyes off the ghastly sight, I looked for Mom. She was staying out of the way, moving around, photographing everything. She didn't look worried about the pony either. As she struggled by me, her big rubber boots sinking in the mire, I watched her in awe. My amazing mother, the high-fashioned woman that she was, dressed in rubber and oil cloth, a waterproof poncho to protect the cameras, her boots thick with mud. Still she wasn't completely graceless. Topping it off, she sported a Hermes scarf, one that I had brought her, a flowers-of-England design bursting with yellows, reds, blues, and greens. My mother, a woman far from adverse to hard work, a divorced woman who somehow actually made divorce look good. At that precise moment I was acutely aware how lucky I was to carry her bags.

She caught me staring at her and said, "Don't worry, Gertie is here from the R.S.P.C.A. to make sure nothing happens to the pony."

I smiled in gratitude.

I turned back to see that the struggle had turned the bright green patch of grass to an oozing mud pit, and the men had actually managed bogging down the pony. It was done so calmly, so kindly, with no whips or kicks or shouting.

The poor animal was frantic, his ears straining back, eyes wide, nostrils flared, and breath coming in great gasps of effort. He was sunk deep in the mire, his quarters no longer showing. David was up to his shoulders in the ooze, at the pony's head, cooing to him. The pony's terrified pale-blue eyes stared at David as he breathed calmly and slowly into the pony's nose, an old horse-lover's trick to gain the animal's trust. Soon the pony was responding to David's presence like a small child hugging his mother after a horrifying moment of being lost in the endless aisles of a supermarket, and he quieted.

The director shouted, "Get Mark out here!"

A beautiful young boy about ten years old with messy blond hair emerged from a trailer. He was dressed in dark jeans tucked into tall mud boots, a brown parka over a thick, cable-knit sweater. With his head down, he listened intently to the director for a few moments and then went over to the edge of the bog. He waved at David who tipped his chin to Mark and slowly made his way behind the pony's neck, out of the camera's eye.

Raising his hand and looking around at his crew, Dick Sarafian reminded me of a quarterback calling signals at the line for a big play.

"Ready?" he cried. "Let's roll it. Action, Mark!"

Mark got down in the grass and mud and crawled on his belly, pulling himself along on his elbows, struggling to get to the pony fifteen feet away. The poor beast, sunk to his neck, now was deadly still, his nose clogged with the black mud, his jaw barely above it. He had closed his eyes. My hand fluttered to my mouth and my heart

21

beat so loud I thought Sarafian would hear it. Everyone was stone-cold silent and I thought the pony was dead and no one else had figured it out yet.

Again my eyes found Gertie. She was 100-percent focused on the procedure, unblinking. I hoped she wasn't one of the people who said they knew everything about horses but couldn't even ride. I had to believe that David, invisible at this point, knew what he was doing also.

There was an eerie, cold little wind that seemed to gather momentum, whipping around our clothes and cameras. The whir of the movie cameras was the only noise. The thirty-odd people who had been working in a frenzy, were frozen and motionless as Mark reached the pony, caressed his nose, and, after a long breathless moment, rested his head in the mud and started to sob. Just when I thought maybe he thought the pony was dead, too, Mark lifted his head, mud and tears smearing his face, and he pulled on the halter. Grimacing, his mouth contorted, a faint noise came out of him.

"Phh . . . Phh . . . Ph . . . Phil . . . ip," calling the pony by his own name, "do . . . don . . . *don't* give up!"

The pony's eyes remained closed and, almost sick to my stomach, I was convinced they had let him die for the shot!

Mark begged again, then dropped his blond head back in the mud. Not a move. Dick put his hand up for continued silence. I don't think anyone else was breathing either. Suddenly, the pony opened his beautiful eyes and snorted. Mud splattered from his nose and he started to push forward toward Mark, plunging like a great fish. Mark pulled on the halter and cried, "C . . . c . . . ome on, Phil . . . ip!"

The pony made little progress and gave up. Gertie signaled to Sarafian, who yelled, "Perfect! That's just brilliant! WRAP IT!"

Gertie blew her whistle and jumped into action to get the pony out. The hillside erupted into activity. Mom never let up with her camera as Sarafian reached down and plucked Mark out of the bog. He gave him a big bear hug and told him he was superb. Gertie drove the R.S.P.C.A. Rover to the edge of the bog and Jeremy threw David a rope. David wiggled back one last time to circle the pony's rump with the rope, pushing it down as low as he could get it, and chucked it back to Jeremy. Jeremy attached the halter rope and the rump rope to the front of the Rover and ever so slowly, Gertie backed the truck up, and the pony's limp body was dragged out of the bog. David held on to his tail for his own way out. It looked like some wild mud wrestling championship of the world. The pony was brown and mushy, lying on his side, exhausted, but I could see his sides heaving. David squatted down by his head, patting and coaxing him again, this time to get up. I could hear Gertie telling David he would be fine, that he was out of the bog before he could give up. I wondered if that meant the pony's heart would have stopped if he had been too scared. I recalled that quicksand had the same effect. All of a sudden, the pony popped up, onto his feet, like out of a hypnotic trance, saved by something beyond him. I jumped up and clapped spontaneously and heard the crew going into it at the same time. David rubbed the pony's face and looked like he was whispering something to him.

This was why I was here. The movies. I half expected the pony to take a bow and pick up a paycheck. But Jeremy loaded him into the trailer, and he and Gertie whisked him off so suddenly I wasn't sure it had all happened.

The combination of Mark's acting, David's passion at work with the pony, and my own roller-coaster feelings of the scene and reactions to the vast emptiness of the moors, left me with a big lump in my throat. I was fighting back tears when Mom bumped me on the back and said, "Aren't you glad you came?"

Three

As the crew worked quickly to wrap up and put away lights, cameras, cords, and wires, I bounced on the spongy tundra-like ground to shake the accumulated water off me and then trudged to a small knoll. Wanting to cheer up and feeling unneeded, I watched as fitful gusts of wind allowed the sun to peek through clear holes in the leaden sky. Circling around like David had earlier, I was amazed to find that I could find no point of reference. And then, off in the distance, looming gravely in the rolling mist, I saw an austere, well-proportioned gray stone building.

"Dartmoor Prison," David said from behind me, as he pulled his hood up.

"You're clean!" I said.

"The nice part about waders is that you can take them off and be all clean underneath," he said, with a short bow. "Ta-da."

His lips were blue, his ungloved hand shaking as he lifted a battered, gray camp cup.

"Cognac?" he offered.

"Good idea," I said. Of all the great times to shock the system. A nice burning jolt. "David, that was a very touching scene." I coughed a little and handed the cup back.

"We're very lucky. That shot could have taken all day. The weather held, ghastly, as we needed it." David took another sip. "Not to mention Mark was brilliant and the pony was amazing. Lucky, very lucky." He babbled and shivered.

I actually opened my big mouth and said, "You were terrific." I was real close to batting my eyelashes at him.

It left me embarrassed and David speechless. He drank more cognac. I turned away. As part of my mind kept thinking what a smashing fellow David was, I squinted to make out the dark steel bars on the windows of the prison, and thought of Alcatraz. Ominous and monumental, both prisons actually were escapable, but each had its own form of security: Alcatraz had its shark-infested waters, whereas Dartmoor Prison, as my guidebook had told me, could boast that no prisoner had yet survived after escaping because they either went mad roaming the moors or were swallowed up in the bogs. I imagined the men immured there, like in *The Man in the Iron Mask*, the dungeons packed with horribly treated, decaying, dying convicts. Not a single sign of life came from the prison, not a puff of smoke, not a whimper.

I shivered, pulling my coat up around me. David, taking my age into consideration and hence understanding my crush, behaved like a perfect gentleman and stood closer to me, offering his warm pockets for my cold, red hands. I slid my hands into his pockets and felt oddly comfortable. I had not made a fool of myself. Yet. Silence is so romantic, I thought, for the moment not feeling the need to say a word.

"Your mother is beckoning," David said.

Mom was waving at us to come. Behind her, the crew had quickly and efficiently broken camp and the only remaining evidence was Bill's Bog, which would return to its natural green camouflage state after the next drenching rain, to become an invisible trap for prisoners or anyone not familiar with the moors.

We joined Mom who told us Sarafian was happy with the shot and the rest of the day was free. Thoroughly drenched, yet still persuasive, Mom coaxed David into borrowing a four-door, low-riding car from a crew member to get us to the nearest town to dry off and have lunch.

By two o'clock, the sun had won its bid for the day as we drove in to the small, cobblestoned, red-roofed town of Tavistock and parked on the main street. A noble old church with an Elizabethan clock on the northern side reigned over a genuinely quiet and quaint town. Shops lined each side of the main street; an art gallery, library, pharmacy, clothing store, all with their doors wide open, yawning into the warming day. An active pack of rosy-cheeked women were shopping for the evening meal, their string net bags filled with green apples and cheese, lettuce, carrots with their tops on, fat white potatoes, and thick slabs of meat from the butchers. It was a working town. No frilly, touristy shops, just the bare necessities. Before credit cards and indulgence. These people were happy living within their means.

David steered us through a heavy, scratched-wood door with a brass lion knocker, into the pitchy and smoky interior of the Red Lion Pub. Mom and I were the only women other than the portly and busy waitress. Under the curious gaze of a lively group of men smoking pipes, drinking dark beer, and throwing darts, we sat at a corner table. A stone mantel arched around a fierce fire crackling in an enormous hearth, making the smoke-filled room airless and very manly. I wanted to reach for some sudsy ammonia. Oak beams, linen-fold paneling and wall paintings had me thinking I could look over and see the Pirate, seated at the window, smoking his pipe, a loaded pistol on the table before him. A creaking stairway and narrow winding passage led to the restrooms, on changing floor levels. Not yet accustomed to English terms, I was intrigued when David ordered bangers and beans for all three of us. I wanted to believe he was completely fascinating, my pirate, but I was somewhat let down when the waitress brought plain old pork 'n' beans.

Invigorated by lunch, we made our way down the sunny side of the main street. I got the feeling that the wonder of medieval charm persisted in this town, too strong to be spoiled by progress. In no hurry, we stopped to look at fat, tumbly Corgi puppies romping in the window of a cheerful, well-cared-for pet shop called "The Pompous Poodle." About to mention to Mom that I wanted to get a great big dog, my mind sidetracked to conjuring up that big dog from the back of the shop and I started screening a vision of David and me roaming the moors with a rugged hound, when I heard Mom ask, "What's a

Jack Russell Terrier?" She was squinting at a handwritten note on a piece of paper taped to the window.

"Small dogs, infinite amount of trouble," David answered immediately.

"And who is Peter Tavy?" Mom asked.

"It's a village, about 25 kilometers up the road. Why?" David peered suspiciously at Mom.

"Have you ever heard of a Jack Russell Terrier?" Mom looked quizzically at me.

"No."

"Let's go see. We have the time. We have the car." Mom turned 10,000 watts of charm on David, who appeared to be a little annoyed that Mom had yet to acknowledge his information.

"Nancy, are you looking for a dog?" David asked.

"I am," I replied bravely. "I want a great big one."

"Not really. Just curious," Mom said, gaily. "It will be an adventure."

My turn to not be acknowledged.

We drove north out of Tavistock on the A386, with tors rising on either side of the road as we climbed up along the boundary of Dartmoor Forest. David drove like a madman as the road wound its way through miles of beautiful hills covered in lush, wet, green pastureland. The low, gray clouds were rolling back in and the sun, like a lamp in need of rewiring, flashed on and off. Rolling around in the back seat moaning, I was not yet comfortable on the left side of the road. I thought I would pass out the few times that we met motorists coming the other way and David pulled over from the middle of the road, squeezing the little car against a high hedge of brush. We were passing so close I could see the nose hairs of the other passengers. Mom, normally an active and verbal participant in the passenger seat, or the back seat, or from the trunk, seemed so calm in front of me I thought she had fainted.

"David, have you ever had a Jack Daniels?" Mom asked after one of our near-death encounters.

"Jack Russell," he corrected. "No, but many of my friends have them and they tell me outrageous stories. They're well known in England. Neat little packages of ferocious stuff. I would never consider having one. You'd have to be mad!"

David was gripping the wheel and clipping along with a new vigor. I hoped Mom would stop asking him about this annoying breed of dog.

I tried another tact, asking "How big are they?"

"Like a Westy, or a Norwich," he replied and stepped on the gas in a straight-away.

I was considering how little help that information was when, finally, I thanked God, we skidded to a stop in front of a white farmhouse that sat neatly on the side of a hill. It had a thick thatched roof and window boxes full of leggy, red geraniums. Rose bushes along the side of the house were dropping petals that seemed to be as big as saucers. A fox-red barn stood to the right, bursting with hay that spilled out into the muddy yard. Cows, goats, cats, and horses were part of the backdrop of the farm; groups of children in rubber boots and soaked clothes were laughing and playing in the open courtyard, unhindered by mud and weather. An expansive woman stopped pitching hay and watched us. She wore an Irish knit sweater, and her tweed pants were tucked into generic wellies.

The three of us emerged from the car and walked up the cobblestone path.

"We would like to see the Jack what'sits," said Mom.

The woman gazed at us curiously and said, "We only have one bitch left, but she really isn't a good one."

The children had gathered and were giggling. I figured they were sort of startled to see anyone as fancy as my mother with her Hermes scarf and bright red lipstick. I thought I counted seven children, but they seemed to be multiplying and with their constant movement, I might just as well have tried to count a flock of birds flying in a high wind. They were all tangled up, like badly cast fishing lines, holding on to one another and circling their mother. Maybe she was running a day care. Waves of laughter came from these layers of arms, legs, muddy wellies, mussed-up hair, and rosy-cheeked children.

"Well, thank you," David said. "We'll be off." He reached for Mom.

Three fat chickens hustled out of the barn, flapping and squawking. On their heels, a round pink pig, like an extra big serving of cotton candy, ran a few feet, crashed through a little white picket fence and fell into the vegetable garden, staying there. A goofy Great Dane puppy stopped in the doorway and surveyed us, but we were not his main concern. Strangely, he trembled as he nervously looked from side to side, his uncut floppy ears slapping him with each thrashing turn of his head.

"Most peculiar," my mother said. "That looks like a breed I already know."

"That's a Great Dane, Mom," I said, "a very big one. My kind of dog."

Just then a tiny black-and-white puppy walked nonchalantly around the side of the barn, sniffing the ground, dismissing us with a mere glance. She stopped, one tiny paw poised, and stared at the Dane. She licked her lips. Fascinating, I thought. She was looking at him like *he* was the hors-d'oeuvre. She was no bigger than a Texas cockroach.

"That's the bitch," said the woman. I hated that word anyway, but the way she said it made me think she didn't like the harmless-looking little creature.

The Dane squealed and took off. The puppy lunged after him, and by the time the Dane had reached his second uncoordinated stride, she had caught up to him, locking her teeth into his back leg. He bellowed like a mating sea lion but she held on.

The children burst into a chorus of laughter.

"You might keep looking," the woman said. "There are more litters up the road in Mary Tavy."

"Excellent idea," David said, trying again. "Come along, Nancy."

"How much is she?" I heard my mother ask.

"How much is she?" David and I asked at the same time.

I couldn't believe it!

The woman said, "She's a fiver."

I saw my mother rifle around in her purse and pull out a crispy, pink five-pound note. Queen Elizabeth's face stared out regally, or was she smiling? The woman took the money, saying nothing. The exchange, in 1968, meant that for $12.00, Mom was the proud owner of a tiny Jack Russell terrier. And as far as I could tell from the screams around the other side of the barn, Mom's peculiar purchase was presently dismembering a Great Dane.

"How do we catch her?" inquired my mother, calmly. "Brookie, close your mouth. You too, David."

The children scattered in all directions, chortling and whooping up a storm. They seemed to know something we didn't. After a series of leaps and bounds and mud sliding, children running into each other, falling down and holding their bashed heads, four of them came forward, proudly, white teeth showing through the mud, gingerly holding out a yapping, bespattered puppy.

Standing there in the muddy yard, my mother looked too sophisticated to handle anything other than the financing, and David was making noises like defective plumbing, so the children's eyes landed on me. I was the one standing with a look of sheer stupidity on my face, and I said nothing as they handed the puppy to me.

Bouncing in my arms like a Mexican jumping bean, it was apparent that the puppy was black and white with tan trimming around her mouth, head, and eyes. She began to make ear-piercing, wailing noises because the Dane had come wearily back into her line of vision and dropped. I put my hand over her mouth, which was no bigger than a half dollar, to get her to stop the racket but this only infuriated her and she nipped at me and renewed her war cry. The noise was one that I could only imagine coming from Dartmoor prison when a prisoner was being stretched on the rack. I had never heard a dog scream before.

"Don't hurt her," my mother commanded.

Hurt her? My jaw dropped in disbelief. I was the one about to become hearing impaired.

"You take her," I said, longing to let Mom deal with her. I didn't like her. She was trouble. I wanted a big, quiet, helpful dog. One to take care of me. But by now the Dane was probably taking his last breath.

"We'll go home now," Mom announced in a fine queenly tone, ignoring my request as she walked down the wet, grassy path to the car. "Thank you very much."

The woman watched us go, her gaze calm, as she leaned on her pitchfork. No names had been exchanged in the transaction, just a dog.

I held the frantic puppy as far away from me as I could and slumped into the back seat. As we pulled out, I looked out the back window at the woman and her dirty, healthy, perfectly sane family which was going back to its routine. The deal was probably not going to change *their* lives, but I got the distinct feeling it would be changing *ours*. How deeply, I could not imagine.

Four

David was at the wheel again, with Mom, the new dog-owner, perched proudly next to him. I was riding in the back seat as overlooked as an unknown second cousin, stuck with the odd little beast who started popping from the back up to the front, and from the front to the back, using me as a springboard. It was cute the first three times, then the novelty wore thin. Truth be known, for my whole life so far, I had been wanting my mother to love me best, to validate me, so to speak. Now I was going to have to compete for her attention with four pounds of personality. Validate *me*! Obviously, this little "bitch," as the woman so crudely called her, was not in the same dire need of being validated. Bottom line, it wasn't that I wanted to be nice to my mother, I just didn't want her to like anyone else more than me, no matter how I behaved. What I deserved was a swift kick in the pants. Still, I sat there, rolling around with my tiny rival, contemplating a jump out of the speeding car for attention, and thought how I would bang my head on a rock wall and wander years on the moor, an amnesiac. However, thinking about Mom, David, and the puppy living happily after made me take my hand off the door latch.

"Russell, Russell," Mom said, "we should be able to think of a very clever name to go with Russell."

"Our author, Bertrand Russell," said David.

"That was a man, this feisty little thing is a girl," Mom said, trying to pat her as she bounced by. Mom's coordination not nearly as acute as the puppy's, missed her by a beat each time.

"Jack Russell. Mmm. How about Jill Russell? You know, Jack and Jill? You'll have to get a male," David said. Good God, they were already talking about another dog! And I thought he didn't like these little troublemakers. I was not having fun.

"She doesn't look like a Jill, does she, Brookie?" Mom said. "Why are you so quiet back there?"

"Mom, the dog is a psycho. She's jumped back and forth twenty-eight times so far. Doesn't that irritate you?" I growled. God only knows it would have irritated her if I'd been doing it.

"Isn't she marvelous? I haven't had a dog in years," Mom went on. A dog? This wasn't a dog, this was a piranha! She had just eaten a hole in the back seat with her needle-sharp teeth and lethal jaws.

"How about Jane Russell? Now, there was a classy actress," David said. Jane Russell. That was it. I knew it the minute it came out of his mouth.

"I love it! Jane Russell! She was beautiful, too," Mom said.

It had come down to Jane Russell. And I had wanted a Goliath, a King Kong, a Mack truck.

David drove in his normal manner, reminding me of being on Mr. Toad's Wild Ride at Disneyland, for the next hour until we reached the Manor House in Moretonhampstead. Arriving at dusk, we went through massive stone gates and down a long and winding gravel pathway, bordered by emerald-green grounds manicured as well as a golf course. Rhododendron bushes bursting with flamingo-colored flowers, glowing like neon in the first darkness, grew as big as trees along the way. At the bottom of a rolling hill, a silver pond spread across the land, the size of a big ice-skating rink, with swans and ducks shaking and wagging their tails.

At the end of the drive, golden lights in the windows cut into the impending dark, and together with the drenching fog, the Manor House loomed like a jack-o'-lantern. It was so gigantic it seemed out of proportion with the entire country. *This* was Mom's postcard.

"They won't let this crazy dog stay in this grand hotel, will they?" I hoped out loud.

"Gracious me, Brookie," David said, "the English prefer pets to the patronage."

Swell, just swell, I thought. We entered the front hall, which was bigger than a football field, and checked in. The concierge noted that Janie, who had wisely chosen Mom to carry her, was a "fine specimen." I thought specimens were in laboratories. Mom regained her queenly air with the concierge's remark, and Miss Russell sat calmly in her hands, behaving like an angel, looking down at me. I felt like a big mutt.

David went off to his room and we were shown to ours, agreeing to meet for dinner in an hour. My ungrateful jealousy dissolved when I saw our suite. Two queen-sized beds with great, puffy down quilts filled most of the bedroom. Dark green-and-maroon brocade draperies matched the quilts and a wingback chair, all trimmed in navy blue ticking. Bright brass sconces decorated the blue walls and an oil portrait, possibly a Hans Holbein, brooded over the room. Walking into the bathroom, I could feel the heat from the fluffy white towels hanging on a heated rack. Enamel and gold fixtures sparkled on a grand iron-clawed tub sitting under a stained-glass window, and there was a marble sink the size and shape of a bird bath.

Mom tipped the porter, who also complimented her on her new pet. Remembering how David seemed to warm to Jane Russell during the afternoon, I felt resentful and jealous again, fully aware that even the dog was more feminine than I was. It was time to make an effort.

While we freshened up, Janie ran through the room like a Secret Service agent searching for missing plans, sniffing the corners and darting under the furniture. When she ran out of steam and fell asleep in Mom's Louis Vuitton suitcase, we tiptoed out, closing the door gently behind us.

"Do you think she'll be all right?" Mom asked, looking quite elegant in black pants and sweater and a bright Hermes scarf with a pink rose pattern that matched her lipstick exactly.

"Mom, I'd want her covering my back in a barroom brawl," I said. "She'll be fine."

"You're sure?"

"I'm starving. Let's go." I swept a hand in the direction of the lobby. "Remember, we're having dinner with David?" I remembered! I had pulled myself together as best I could with what I had to work with, putting on a short black skirt, Mom's baby blue cashmere sweater, black hose, and low suede heels. Borrowing Mom's makeup and washing and fluffing up my long brown hair, I was feeling better about getting in touch with my feminine side when we met David in the grand foyer. The man who could easily have taken first prize in a mud-wrestling championship earlier was now elegant in a pale pink Oxford shirt, navy-and-white striped tie, double-breasted blue blazer, gray slacks, and shiny, brown tasseled shoes. He offered an arm to Mom and an arm to me, escorting us gallantly to dinner. I felt like a princess and stood up straight, breathing slowly, head held high.

The dining room was gigantic, typical English, 1800s, high ceilings with thick oak beams and elaborate wood paneling. Portraits of men, women, dogs, and horses, along with landscapes of the countryside, hung all over the walls. Two giant glass chandeliers, softly lit, hung overhead. We sat at a candlelit table in the middle of the room, surrounded by men in tweed coats, starched shirts, and knit ties, hair slicked back, and women in dresses, heels, shawls, and hats, hair neatly coiffed. The sheer elegance, the chivalry and glamour of the scene had long since passed out of the States.

Devouring roast beef and Yorkshire pudding, fresh brussels sprouts, and chocolate soufflé for dessert, we were quite a step up from our lunch of bangers and beans. We listened to David's tale . . . the history of the Jack Russell terrier.

He told us that in 1819, while an undergraduate at Oxford, a young parson named John Russell was taking a walk one morning when he came across a milkman with a small terrier on his milk cart.

The parson had wanted a dog to hunt with, small enough to fit in his coat while he rode and gutsy enough to tackle a fox or a badger in its hole. He bought the terrier on the spot, and named her Trump. She turned out to be the most energetic and courageous little dog who went to ground "in a wink" and could retrieve a badger or a fox twice her size. Trump was the ancestor of the parson's legendary strain of terriers. Since the parson had basically invented the breed, they were named for him. An obsessive hunter, in 1832 he became vicar of Swymbridge and at the same time Master of the Hounds. By the late 1850s, Parson John Russell was one of the leading breeder/dealers of terriers in the West Country.

When I asked David how he knew so much about the breed, he told us with a smile about friends who bred them. Once while visiting them in Wapsworthy, he saw their Jack Russell, Patches, trot off down the road in the morning to hunt on her own, returning around noon, covered in blood and with a new patch of hide missing. This behavior had earned her the name. Eventually, Patches killed every fox and badger within a five-kilometer radius of their home. David laughed heartily, mumbling something about a girl like that.

I could be like that. "Quite right. Kill the little suckers," I said.

"What on earth has come over you?" Mom asked.

I could feel the blood go out of my head. Had I said that out loud?

David grinned at me and continued. The Jack Russell was the most popular breed in England, and Ireland, too, for that matter, and a good Jack Russell was fourteen inches at the shoulder, fourteen inches long, rough or smooth coat, tan and white, black and white, or tri-colored. The tails were docked on the second or third day to about three inches, the width of a hand, so that when the dog went to ground, the master could grab him by the suitable little handle, pulling him out of the hole with the fox at the other end.

As the evening passed, David kept talking, his face alive and his eyes bright, his voice deep and rich, and I became even more enchanted with him. But I did it silently. No more blurting out. He rode horses, he had two kestrels, called sparrow hawks in America, Violet and Schroeder, two owls, Blink and Hoot, and an otter named Mansfield, who burped. David made a living by writing and drawing. He was renowned for a cartoon character named Arbuckle, the fat mouse. He loved his sister, father, mother, saw them often, and was not married. I was hopelessly infatuated.

"Janie is perfect!" Mom declared, bringing me back to a more frustrating reality.

"She *is* a beauty," David admitted.

"I bet Parson John Russell would have been proud of Miss Jane Russell if he'd seen her dissect that Great Dane," I said, faintly aware that I was smiling, thinking of that scene.

"Parson Russell was a bit of a cad, for lack of a nicer word," David said. "When he held the dual role of vicar of Swymbridge and Master of the Hounds, the bishop of his diocese accused Russell of poor behavior when he refused to bury a child on a Wednesday under the pretense that there should be another day of mourning for the family, when in fact it was because it interfered with the fox hunt."

"That's awful," Mom said.

I got the feeling the little dog was about as impersonal as her inventor.

"You have it all in front of you," David said, arching his bushy eyebrows.

My mother summoned the waiter and ordered steak tartare.

"Mom, didn't you have enough to eat?"

She'd been through enough roast beef to gag a timber wolf.

"For Janie," she said, grandly.

She never gave me steak tartare, I whined to myself.

"Now," David declared, "the Russells make one fatal mistake."

"What's that?" Mom asked.

"They choke on raw meat," I said.

"Hush," she reprimanded.

"They go to ground digging for badgers and foxes, rabbits, whatever the case may be, and then they dig in."

Neither Mom nor I understood or responded, so he continued.

"They dig and dig, piling the dirt high outside the hole behind them, closing themselves in and eventually suffocating. It is absolutely imperative to take a shovel along with you when you venture out with a Russell."

A young waiter with excellent posture bowed to present the steak tartare to Mom on a silver platter garnished with parsley.

"Tell me you're joking, Mom," I said, seeing the raw pink scraped steak.

"I'm going upstairs to feed Janie," she answered, as she rose and motioned for the waiter to follow her.

David and I stared at each other as she departed.

"She's starting that puppy off on the wrong paw," he said.

"I get the feeling Miss Jane Russell will be sleeping in my bed," I said.

"Speaking of that, it is getting late. We have another early call tomorrow morning." He rose, pulled my chair out, and walked me to the great hall.

"Good night. Thank you for a lovely day," I said.

David tipped into a half bow. "It was my pleasure. See you in the morning." Lifting my hand, he kissed the back of it.

I watched my lucky hand, and curtsying said, "I look forward to it." If he had pulled out a pipe at that moment, I'd have calf-roped him on the spot.

Upstairs, Janie was daintily finishing up the last of her raw steak and Mom was leaning on the tub, running her hand through the water. She looked out of proportion next to the immense enameled bathtub.

"Hey, Mom," I snickered, watching Janie reject the parsley, "aren't you going to make her eat her vegetables?"

"It will be good to have a nice, clean puppy, won't it?" she asked.

Janie saw the plush white towel trailing from Mom's hand, seized the end of it and tugged, growling ferociously. Mom got down on all fours to play tug-of-war. Janie, all four pounds, bumped backwards with a grip like crazy glue. Mom swung her around the room giggling and enchanted. Through the eyes of jealousy, I had to admit the puppy was very cute. And so was Mom! I hadn't seen her play like that in years.

While Mom was fluff-drying her after the bubble bath, I said I'd take Janie out for a walk before we went to bed. My better nature told me I might want to try a little bonding with the dog. We didn't have a collar or lead, so I detached a thin leather strap from Mom's purse and hooked it around her neck. She immediately hit the deck, spread-eagled, like an ungainly frog. When I tried to pull her, she started to gasp and spit. Apparently, this clean and poofy little princess did not want to go out, and she became very vocal about it. One thing for darn sure, I didn't want to see any of her dinner come up. Bond with the dog, my *tokus*.

Mom barked at me, "Pick her up and stop being so cruel."

Removing the leash, I jerked Janie up off the floor, making her squeak, which fortunately went unnoticed, and carried her downstairs, subduing a fierce desire to throttle her. When we reached the lobby, she launched herself away from me as if she wanted to be the first English astronaut and dashed out the door.

The concierge smiled at me and said, "She's a beaut."

"Isn't she though," I replied, my smile fixed.

I went outside. "Janie," I called, not too loud in the dark. Using the inadequate light shining from the manor, a few faint lights in the garden, and a full moon, I found my way down a hill covered in grass as smooth and even as corduroy. At the bottom there was a pond, black and shiny as tar, highlighted with the swans and ducks floating gently and silently on the water. I inhaled the sweet, cold air and listened. It was pin-drop quiet. There was no sign of Janie. Mom was going to kill me.

Not worried yet, I looked back up at the Manor House from

window to window, hoping to get one more sighting of David before he went to bed. It was an enormous structure and very dark. No luck.

I called for Janie, searching everywhere, getting more worried, colder, and madder every second. Having thought I would only be outside for a moment, I hadn't worn my coat and the night was surely cold. As I was starting up the steps to ask the concierge for a flashlight, the beastly reason for all my woes fell in beside me, keeping perfect step as I headed into the Manor House. Trying my best to ignore her for fear of kicking her, I suddenly realized a foul stench was coming from her, like raccoon or duck poop. It smelled wet. Bending down to wring her neck, I discovered that her slender throat was precisely where the smell was most pungent.

When we entered the room the odor hit Mom.

"What on earth have you done to her?" Mom asked acidly, putting aside her *Life* magazine which she was reading in the depths of her warm bed.

"What did I do to her?" I echoed, holding my nose. "What do you reckon: I dragged her outside and through a big pile of caca on purpose, Mom?"

Between the smell and my slipping back to "reckon"-ing, I thought Mom might have a seizure, so I hurried Janie into the bath again. As I washed her neck, I found myself beginning to mutter like David had earlier in the day and I imagined him, sound asleep, not suffering through a first night in the life of a Jack Russell terrier. I squeezed Janie's throat until she gagged.

When Janie was all dried off and only faintly smelly, Mom got out of bed, pulled on a flowing teal blue satin robe, and fixed a place for Janie to sleep in the bathroom. Spreading the *Herald Tribune* on the floor, Mom said, "You pee here," pointing optimistically.

Watching the expression on Mom's face and then the one on Janie's, I knew the dog was going to out-dumb my mother. To my total astonishment, Mom put her red cashmere sweater, the red cashmere sweater I had had my eye on for years, on the bathroom floor. She then placed Janie on the sweater, bid her a cheery goodnight and pulled the door closed.

I got into my snug bed silently, now painfully aware that Mom was more interested in Janie than me. For a short while it was quiet, except for me growling to myself, but then we heard a high-pitched wail, a sound I thought a female eagle would make if deprived of her young. I hoped it was just someone escaping from Dartmoor Prison.

"That's that dog!" Mom screeched, picking up the *London Times* and rolling it up as she flung open the bathroom door. Standing mightily over Janie, she shook the paper in her face and said, "If you think you're going to get away with that kind of behavior when I've gone to so much trouble to make you comfortable . . . you don't know who you're dealing with, my little pet."

Go Mom. Maybe I'd get the red cashmere sweater after all. I sat up to get a better look at the action. Mom slapped the paper, CRACK! against the bathtub. And again, crack! "No more of that," she commanded and slammed the door shut. Now, this she had done before with me.

Janie started to scream. Louder than ever before. Mom looked at me like it was all my fault.

"What did I do?" I yelled over the ruckus.

Coward that she was, Mom conceded defeat and released the hound from hell who dashed around the room on her victory lap and tried to jump on the beds that were about four feet too high for her. She bounced up and down as though made from trampoline material.

"What spirit. What charm," Mom said, adoring her yet again.

And so well dressed, I mused. I half expected my mother to tell me that she had always wanted a daughter just like her.

Mom, acting as if I should be as thrilled as she was, gaily dumped Janie onto my bed. Janie smiled at me, panting, leapt onto a fat white pillow, circled around twice, then curled up in the middle, sighed, and closed her eyes. Mom got back in her bed, turned out her light and said, "Sleep well, you two."

I scooted down to give myself room to put my head on another pillow and turned off my light. Closing my eyes, I did not say goodnight. Granted, I needed to lighten up, but I didn't think the red cashmere sweater fit Janie that well. Of course, at that time, it never dawned on me that in the course of one day, Janie had been more fun than *I* had been in years.

Five

During the last ten days of filming, I read and enjoyed *The White Colt* and, on the side, became Janie's dog handler. I spent hours trying to train this very independent creature and surprised myself by actually liking it. Janie had a quality about her that was infectious: she loved life. She always seemed on the verge of a breakthrough discovery, a new horizon, a new relationship. Her vivacity and interest brought out the best in people, even stodgy, spoiled me. I was much more interested in her outlook than my self-centered one. As for training her . . . I wouldn't have known how. She reminded me of Bob Hayes, the running back, No. 22, for the Dallas Cowboys, who didn't like the huddle or instruction, so the coach told the quarterback, Don Meredith, to "just throw him the ball." Like Bob Hayes, Janie was a natural.

The star of the film was actor John Mills, who played the old colonel. The most gracious English gentleman I had yet met, he and his wife, Mary, an author, and their son, Jonathan, who worked with the crew, were all staying at the Manor House. There was a closeness and warmth and everyday ease about the Mills family that I loved. The daughters, Juliet and Hayley, were working in America and dearly missed. This was a family packed with talent.

During those days, the cast and crew produced their movie on the moors with the sun coming and going, the wind and mist ever changing, and the wild animals keeping an eye on things from an aloof distance. Mom took dozens of rolls of film, following the story through to its climactic and happy end I'm relieved to report. It would be released as *Run Wild, Run Free* within the year, and I could hardly wait to see the scenes I had been privy to. I got to do odd jobs, unpaid but helpful, like fetching tea and coffee for Sarafian, or winding up lighting cords, carrying Mom's camera bags formally, even taking pictures. We all became a big extended family, eating lunch provided by a caravan that came to the location every day, bringing hot baked potatoes, ham-and-cheese sandwiches, chips, and sweet pies to be covered in fresh Devon cream. We drank bitter lemon and lots of hot tea. Janie was in the big middle of it all, with everyone knowing her name and calling her over for a pat and a cheer. She was a little social butterfly.

In the evenings, we ate together in the big dining room, in shifts, sitting at whichever table needed to be filled. Afterwards, we descended deep in the basement to the game room to play snooker, a billiard game resembling American pool. The game room walls were wood-paneled to the middle, the upper half upholstered in a red plaid tartan. A pair of enormous deer heads stared at one another from each end of the room. Four sets of dark red leather chairs with coffee tables were arranged under a row of thick-glassed, multi-paned windows opposite a monstrous fireplace. It was pure British stuffy, but I had come to love it.

After snooker, cards, or backgammon, we found our way down the hallway to the dark Manor House night club where we danced to the new Beatles hit, "Hey Jude," Dionne Warwick's "Say a Little Prayer for You," and Herb Alpert's "This Guy's in Love with You."

I developed a huge crush on David, following him every chance I got, listening intently to every word and eventually realizing that he was an old independent soul, happily unattached and destined to stay that way. Gads, he reminded me of Janie!

The day *Run Wild, Run Free* wrapped, Mom took the young star, Mark Lester, on a train to London for the opening of *Oliver*, another Columbia film. Mark had made *Oliver* almost a year before, playing the title roll, in which his unbelievably touching performance was about to make him an international star. David's life also took him flying off like one of his kestrels. My heart went pitter-patter thinking about him and we promised to try and keep in touch. But I pined shamelessly when he left.

Beyond my guidebook's information, I had first-handedly experienced a new place that I loved and knew I would never forget. The morning Mom packed up her cameras to go to London, I faced, to my dismay, a separation from Janie. The thought poked its way into my gloominess that I was lucky to lead such a life and to have such an extraordinary mother showing me the way. I had lots of material to write to Pete and, after all, I had met famous film stars. But ironically, in spite of her diminutive size, Janie turned out to be the brightest and biggest of all the stars. I no longer wanted a brute of a dog, I wanted a dog just like Janie. She was the most intriguing animal I had ever met and I was crazy about her. I did not want us to part, to lose each other—like Pete, like David. My life suddenly seemed to be a series of too many good-byes and too many uncertain reunions. The voids were almost tangible.

I left for Gstaad on a dreary misty morning, one to match my mood. The train ride from Moretonhampstead to London was hardly memorable as I was so miserable in both look and outlook. I missed being on the set, I missed my new friends, I missed Janie, and Mom. I took the underground from Paddington Station to London Heathrow and for the first time in two weeks saw the sun shining solidly as the plane flew over France and into Geneva. On the approach, the view from the airplane showed the ordered loveliness of the landscape unrolling beneath me, and the mere physical beauty of Switzerland, as always, amazed me. The signs at the airport were in four languages: *bienvenu*, *willkomen*, welcome, *bienvenidos*, and people around me were gabbing in many other languages I didn't understand. The happy cacophony made me feel welcome.

Throwing my duffel over my shoulder, I followed the simple signs from the airport downstairs to the train station, taking the four o'clock to Lausanne. For thirty minutes the tracks skirted along Lac Leman, clear, clean, cold, the water the color of blue glass. In Montreux, I changed to the M.O.B.—Montreux Oberland Bernois—for Gstaad. I loved the strong and neat little Swiss train with its spotless windows, and watched intently as we wound through picture-book villages of wood chalets placed neatly along narrow, cobbled streets. With fat red geraniums tumbling out of every window box, they looked more like opera settings than habitats. I opened the window and let the cool air lap at my face, feeling brighter as the little train chugged up the track. The train traversed laboriously back and forth up the vertical mountainside until we reached the high pastures where the valley leveled out and where I could see the jagged march of the Alps exposing themselves, purple and white, against a kingfisher blue sky. Emerald green pastures were occupied by cows, goats, peasants, dogs, and great fat Swiss cats, flicking their tails, torturing trapped mice with their patience—half the fun before turning them into the evening meal.

As I looked out the window watching a fantasy world unfold on a chugging television screen, I wondered if I would ever want to go back to Texas. I had had so many happy times in Switzerland. But naturally there were painful memories, too. No one my age will ever forget where they were on November 22, 1963, when Kennedy was assassinated in Dallas. Of the 100 girls at Montesano—Swiss, French, Belgian, Italian, German, Spanish, Brazilian, and eight Americans—I was the only Texan. Just 16, I was devastated and shamed by that horrid event, and strange as it may seem, the wind was blown out of my proud Texan sails. Living in Gstaad gave me a place to hide, as I was hiding now, five years later, more grateful than ever to be out of the States, with Pete in Vietnam. When I'd been in New York to see Pete off in September, I'd had the dreadful misfortune of watching the five o'clock news show pictures of dead Vietcong being piled high by Vietnamese and American soldiers, then doused in kerosene and set on fire. American television had an all-new approach: explicit, show-em-everything, sideshow coverage that made my blood run cold. I knew I didn't want to see any more, and one of the great benefits of living in Gstaad was that there was no television in the chalet.

Three stops before Gstaad, in no hurry to get home to an empty chalet, I got off the train and had dinner at the station in Chateau d'Oex. Over the years, Mom and I had discovered that each station had a *restaurant de la gare*, with fresh delicious food. We had often hopped on the next train out of Gstaad, getting off at whichever station we decided on, dining at a new restaurant each time, enjoying the scenery as we came and went. Even though Mom and I traditionally ordered whitebait covered in lemon, *pommes frites*, and *salade*, this time I chose *eminé de veau à la crème avec rosti*. The meal couldn't help but cheer me up.

The night was clear and cool, dark and quiet at 8:30 when I took the last train to Gstaad. It was a twelve-minute ride and there were no other passengers. The Swiss were tucked into their chalets, the cows in their barns, the cats curled up in the hay. After a long day of traveling and a final ten-minute walk to the chalet, I returned to my former misery, dragging my bags behind me and dreading the emptiness of home. I missed my brother. I missed David. I missed Mom. But mostly, I missed the daft enthusiasm of that high-spirited little dog.

Turning the lights on as I entered the chalet, I saw a postcard sitting on the side table. I smiled at a picture of a litter of Jack Russell puppies, turned it over for the message, "Having a wonderful time, but we miss you." Red lip prints and, for the first time, a *paw print*!

Six

After a long and lovely steamy bath, I put on a thick, navy flannel robe, sat in the sun in my favorite windowseat drying my hair, and wrote to Pete. I pushed the window open to breathe in a snootful of cool changing air that was laced with that fine aroma of manure. Summer had passed and fall was on top of us. A multitude of grasses and flowers were reaching up to the sun's rays, trying to store heat for the winter.

Chalet Schaufelberger was a two-story, four-bedroom pine-wood chalet. It sat at the bottom of the Eggli, a mountain sloping smoothly right into our back yard. A stream, bursting at the seams with the Diablerets glacier's summer melt-off, ran along one side of the property. The force of the water tumbled huge rocks around, making noises like muffled thunder, night and day. On the other side, a rickrack larch fence separated us from a working farm.

Surrounded by a dozen cows moonily chomping and staring, my neighbors cleared the field of its final yield. The sturdy father wore brown work pants so old they looked like velvet, a white shirt with suspenders, and well-broken-in leather boots with new red laces. He cut the grass with a scythe, thrashing back and forth, swinging to his own rhythm. His *zaftig* wife wore a flowered dress, white bonnet, and low-cut clunky work boots as she deftly raked the cut grass into long rows. Three children, two boys and a girl, all typically blond and messy, were dressed like miniature versions of their parents. Their job was to bundle the grass and stack it around a tall wood pole, and in spite of the fact that they danced and darted around throwing fresh green grass on each other, the stack grew with each handful, mixed with dandelions and wild daisies and aster.

I tried to imagine the life all the farmers and their families would be living in two months' time when the snow came again. They would be closed up in barns together, twenty or thirty cows hibernating in dirt-bottomed stalls on the ground floor, their warmth and odor rising to the living quarters above where the family would be snuggled in for the five long, cold winter months, only going out for work or school. I decided the fireplaces burning upstairs all day for cooking must have cut the fragrance at least a little. Each morning early, in the dark, the farmer would feed and milk his cows, then clean the barn. A mixture of hay and manure would go into a well-worn wheelbarrow and be taken outside and dumped in a dredged-out hole. After the last snow—and each farmer knew instinctively when that was—the farmer would fill the wheelbarrow with the brown runny mixture from the hole and make several trips to the pastures to spread the slop methodically over clean white snow. This was my least favorite vision of Switzerland. Layers of manure and snow would lie dormant until the thaw when the blend would melt and fertilize the grass. I could already imagine the early morning hours, Gstaad blanketed in a steamy, ammonia-laced cloud that would linger in the valley adding to smoke from the fireplaces until the sun rose and burned it away or the winds pushed in through the valley. Winter would be on us surprisingly soon.

As my neighbor buckled an enormous bell around the thick neck of one of his milk cows, I wondered why on earth she didn't fall over with the weight of it. But the cows loved their bells and there was a pecking order for them; the bigger the bell, the older the cow. The farmer knew each cow, even in the dark, by the sound of her bell.

The clang of the bells made me think of Pete and how he loved them, unless he was Katzenjammered the morning after several bottles of good Swiss wine. I had an instantaneous feeling, a pang, that for that moment, he was all right. He had written several letters recently, but there was a frightening gulf between us. Writing him every day was the one thing that kept me from feeling he could slip away. We had always been so close. I could actually say he had been the only male representative in my life up till then. He did the heavy lifting for me and was even proud of me. When we ended up in Gstaad together, the tradition of his bragging about me continued, this time about my skiing ability, to all his classmates. He, however, did not make bets any more, but I still had no dates. Watching Pete ski, on the other hand, was quite a thrill. He was a terrific skier, well, let me put that differently . . . he was a unique skier.

I moved across the room to the window looking out on the Wispillen, remembering a race he did on that mountain one year, the Rita Hayworth cup. I had survived my downhill run in the same race, and stood at the final schuss to watch how he handled a little bump fifty yards from the finish line that caused my finish to be anything but pretty. I had crossed the line backwards, on my ass. I saw Pete coming, No. 36 that day, his Morty Sills silk scarf flapping behind his dented white crash helmet, his weight slightly more uphill than down. He got down in the schuss position and he was really clipping along when he hit the bump. I will never know how he managed to do a complete front flip, land on his feet, and cross the finish line in third place. He did fall after and slid up to the base of a pine tree. As each competitor crossed the line, an enthusiastic young Swiss boy was there to hand out hot apple juice. He rushed over to Pete, tripped, and landed on top of him. By the time I skated on my skis up to them, steam was coming off of the two and they were hopping up and down, yelping the same words in two different languages. The boy fled. When the burning stopped and Pete got the snow out of his long johns, I asked him how in the world he did that flip and he simply replied, "I meant to do that."

The mountain was green now, no lift running, a few cows grazing in the sun. Here I was, living in a tranquil Swiss chalet, going on glorious shoots, reading by the fire, and there Pete was, existing in a war-ravaged world I had no means of understanding.

In finishing a three-page letter on thin blue air mail stationery, I told him that Mom was bringing Janie to me. Mom was going to work on a movie called *Castle Keep* with Burt Lancaster, Scott Wilson, Patrick O'Neal, and Astrid Herren. It was set in Yugoslavia, and it seemed Mom had some silly qualms that Yugos would kill and eat Janie. Fat chance. I had a vision of Janie redecorating the lives of those people behind the iron curtain. Realizing that she would have to go into quarantine for six months if we wanted to get her back into England, I gathered that Gstaad was to be Janie's new base of operations.

The girls drove in on a gelid Friday afternoon. Janie jumped right out of Mom's flashy, new red Volkswagen Beetle and ran across the field to bark at the cows. Janie was twice as big as when I last saw her, and a tuft of white hair grew around her neck. The cows regarded her, as only cows can do, witlessly, chewing their cud, slowly, with bits and pieces of grass hanging out, not in the slightest riled by the little noisemaker. When I hugged Mom and mentioned Janie had gotten a lot bigger, she bragged, "And she's smarter than a tree full of owls!"

Now that I liked Janie so much and my jealousy was under control, I said, "Look at her! She's beautiful! She must weigh five pounds."

Janie shot into the chalet just as though she knew her home already.

The chalet was immaculate thanks to our Swiss-German housekeeper, Edwig. She was a hard worker and arrived slap on time like a Swiss train. But she was as disgruntled as a little javelina and rarely smiled. By midmorning, however, she was singing and whistling. This baffled me until it dawned on me that she might be a drinker. Mom always locked up the wines and whiskies when she'd go away, since company constantly came and went, drinking the chalet dry, so I couldn't figure out for the life of me what Edwig was getting into that cheered her up so conclusively. Her bland, brown hair was disappearing and the stiff, gray hair replacing it had a way of standing up in different directions, giving her a slightly crazed look. She spoke mostly Swiss-German, or shall I say, spat Swiss-German. All Swiss speak a minimum of two languages, Swiss-German and French, and most of them three or four others, adding English and Swiss-Italian. Edwig and I communicated in French when we wanted to understand each other. Otherwise she spoke Swiss-German and I assumed she was annoyed because there is nothing about the language that makes you feel you're not in trouble.

When we heard a sudden yell from Edwig, Mom and I ran into the kitchen to find her perched up on the counter, pointing and blabbering at Janie who was sitting perkily on haunches at Edwig's feet, wagging her tail and panting a happy, "Hello, Hello."

Mom picked up Janie and said, "*Edwig, voilà. Eso est Janie.*" Mom bypassed all the language barriers by communicating in an assortment of foreign words and gesticulating wildly. She stuck Janie in Edwig's face.

Janie coughed and curled her little lips back at Edwig. Mom pulled her away and said, "What is that God-awful smell?"

"*Das ish nicht gut,*" Edwig spluttered, dropping off the counter fretfully and straightening her apron.

"I don't think she likes dogs," I said.

"How could anyone not like Janie?" Mom asked, kissing Janie's nose. Janie humored Mom by licking hers back quickly, then wiggling wildly until Mom put her down.

Edwig said, "*Thppft,*" or something like that, and a mean expression pinched her face. She left the room, shuffling angrily in her old chunky shoes, the only pair I had ever seen her wear, with heels that were mashed for comfort. She expectorated something in Swiss-German. Nope, she sure didn't like this dog.

"By the way, Mom, I think maybe Edwig's drinking."

Straightening an oil painting of the chalet in winter, she replied, "She drinks lighter fluid."

That struck me dumb. "I'd be pretty thick to believe that one," I said, repudiating the explanation.

"Well, fine. Are you buying the booze for her?" Mom asked.

"No way. There is no booze in this house," I retorted, indignantly. I had yet to drink any delightful Swiss wines without being sick for two days after and I looked down jealously on those who could.

"Okay. You ask her if you want to. Just don't light a match!" Mom left the room to unpack.

Lighter fluid, I murmured to myself. Now I'd heard everything. I had a vision of Edwig cooking a juicy turkey: when she opened the oven door, the chalet blew to smithereens. But then I stopped, bewildered: here we were in a land of excellent wines and beer flowing on tap at every corner, and Edwig was drinking lighter fluid! It made me feel terrible that I knew so little about her. Maybe I would just make myself useful, keeping an eye on Janie until Edwig learned to like her. And I'd keep the other eye on the oven door, just in case.

Before the first snow, Janie and I had become big-time buddies and I no longer felt like a lonely Maytag repairman. We went hiking in the day and she got to know the lay of the land. The days were still; sometimes the sun shone, mostly the skies were colorless, waiting to change into winter. In the evening, I built cozy fires and sat in the living room, writing to Pete and reading. Janie staked out a spot on the daybed, keeping me company in her own independent way, sleeping in a harvest moon glow, twitching in her dreams. I had heard that puppies grew as they slept. Janie grew into a compact machine, built like Mom's Volkswagen Beetle, sturdy, balanced, economized, with an extra added feature—the cutest little speckled belly. She enjoyed a nice rub, at her convenience.

The nights were peaceful, the village empty of foreigners, and the air frigid, preparing us for the season to come. Letters from Pete described the soggy, moldy monsoon season in Vietnam. When I read that he was suffering from moldy feet, guiltily I took my clean feet in plush wool socks down from the stool where they were propped up in front of the sparkling fire. I had always had a tendency to over-empathize with, even live for, characters I read about. Reading of the Joads in *The Grapes of Wrath* many moons ago, I lost eight pounds because I couldn't bear to eat while they were all living off coffee and dust, nearly starving.

Switzerland was pure and polar, Vietnam soggy and depressing, Texas probably was experiencing eighty-degree weather, overcast, and hinged with humidity and mosquitoes. Here again, I told myself, I was the lucky one.

That fall, Mom kept up her peregrinations, taking pictures, working on different venues, not often knowing when she could get home. She had hired Edwig to clean Tuesdays and Fridays as she always wanted the place clean to come home to, stating that I could not be relied on to keep it up myself. I was somewhat affronted, demurring modestly however, for fear she would try me out. Besides, I had my unwritten, self-imposed commission—to appease Edwig on her cleaning days by taking Janie on our longest hikes. On top of that, I bought Edwig a bottle of L'Air du Temps perfume. She was touched and thrilled and her bilious disposition altered miraculously. But not for long. With or without lighter fluid running through her veins, Edwig did not like Janie. And it was no wonder. The days she came to work, steeped in the perfume, Janie sneezed melodramatically, over and over again. That left Edwig with no choice but to stand in the doorway, disdainfully sending us off with a snap of her dust rag, directing potent fumes in short explosive puffs as she yapped at us incomprehensibly. Janie and I were stunned to our shoes and saddened that someone didn't like us much. I personally think she needed to go somewhere and get her psychological knots untied.

Seven

In Texas, we know that spring has arrived and it will not freeze again when the leaves come out on the mesquite trees. In Switzerland, spring arrived when Monsieur Wursten, the florist, put window boxes of fat, screaming red geraniums on the balconies of every shop and chalet. The day he delivered our six boxes, Janie came into the chalet with white feathers stuck all around her muzzle and matted blood on her chin and chest. How strange, I thought, how strange. Worrying she could be cut somewhere, I turned her upside down to inspect. Hating that violation of her dignity, she growled at me savagely.

"Don't you dare," I said, holding her down. I evaluated the situation: she was not cut, it was not her blood, they were not her feathers.

"Janie, are these *chicken* feathers? What on earth have you done?"

She flipped back over nimbly, ignoring me. Edwig materialized and stood arms akimbo. Seeing Janie decked out in a bloody boa, she spat out a few curt lines with unusual venom. Not in French. She went off hastily in one direction, Janie in another, while one white feather floated down and came to rest on the blue-and-white needlepoint rug Mom had brought back from a trip to Greece. I could only extrapolate what somebody's chicken looked like.

A few days later, I was sitting peacefully on the red-checked cushion in the window writing to Pete, when Janie entered the room wearing a fresh outfit of blood and feathers. I grabbed her. She pulled out of my viselike grip by snapping at my wrist. I knew then that I'd have to see about this. My burning look scarcely fazed her.

Next day when I got up and let her out, I quickly dressed in my jeans, a turtleneck, and a sweater, and followed her. It was early morning, and the town lay in shadow. The sunlight slanted butter-cream on the snowy peaks at the end of the valley. I wore tennis shoes, tiptoeing like a burglar if she stopped to smell anything, or I hid behind milk carts, buildings, or lamp posts. She never looked back. She obviously didn't suspect I might be as clever as she was. I felt this was the Swiss version of Wile E. Coyote after Roadrunner.

The road wove up between vast, verdant-flowered slopes and charming antique chalets, dark brown from age. The air was bracing, like a slap of Aqua Velva in the face, and as I reached a good high point I looked around me. Here in the mountains, I had such a sense of space—the vastness, the sharpness, the contrast of sky, mountain, trees—I felt I could own the soil up to the sky. But remembering my mission, I tried to catch up to Janie, who, not distracted by natural wonders, moved casually at a steady and determined pace.

Puffing around a bend, I saw her boldly enter an old wood barn. The whole uphill side of the barn was piled high with flawlessly stacked firewood; Swiss perfection, even in stacking wood. A black-and-white cat, seeing Janie, scampered silently up a home-made ramp, finding safety in the living quarters above. In the barn, some thirty chickens were going nuts. It reminded me of the day we got Janie in Peter Tavy . . . and now she was plunging into the fray, a small checkered firework, lighting her own fuse.

I rushed into the barn, hoping to catch her before anyone heard the commotion, but she had turned back and, crashing into my leg, jumped around me and took off out of the barn. I looked into the cool interior and saw a stocky farmer waving a pitchfork, through a veil of chicken feathers. In a husky voice he hollered some of the same words I'm almost certain I'd heard come out of Edwig's mouth. He was in a fury, pointing the sharp fork at me with one hand and hold-ing up two fingers with the other hand. His face was as red as a tur-key gobbler's.

"*Je suis désolée, M'sieur,*" I said, instantly angry that I was the one taking the heat for Janie's behavior. Raising my hands in a calming gesture and whipping up a cheerleader smile from a large and phony stock, I backed apologetically out of his barn.

I sprinted all the way down the hill and slid into the chalet, running smack into Edwig who was sucking the last drops out of a green gin bottle. She hiccuped in succession about a dozen times. I didn't own that problem. It was enough to have to deal with Janie.

Janie was already napping on the couch, in front of the fire. When I stabbed at her with the fire poker, she woke up. Blocking her escape by grabbing her two front legs, I stared her in the eye and said, "I might mention, my pretty little pet, that that farmer is going to kill you if he catches you on his property again. Do you hear me?"

She jerked loose, lay back down, and turned her back on me.

"You know, Mom is not here to save your little neck. Are you listening to me?"

She yawned.

I threw a pillow at her and left the room. It annoyed me enormously that when, at last, I had found someone to run around with, that someone was more trouble than a $5 home perm.

Following her again two days later to the same barn, I heard the squawking before I could catch up to her. Inside, Janie had both paws on a lifeless bird and was pulling at the breast, too busy to notice that she was in the sights of the farmer's fat, big-barreled musket.

"Run, Janie!" I screamed. "He's going to kill you!"

The farmer lowered the gun and started hopping up and down, bellowing like one of his bulls. Janie held her ground, too delighted with her kill, too arrogantly impressed with herself to be worried about a stumpy Swiss on the verge of cardiac arrest. Picking her up with the chicken corpse locked in her jaw, I had to slap her face hard to get her to let go. Putting her down, I drop-kicked her out of the barn and we ran together for the road so fast I almost ruptured myself.

Back at the chalet, I slammed the door behind us and went for her throat with both hands. Her tongue hung out of her head and her eyes bulged. I imagined the story I would tell Mom:

"The happy hunting ground, that's where she is. I couldn't get there in time—he shot her right between the eyes. It was terrible, Mom. Poor little thing! Let's get a big dog this time." Man, I was fickle.

I released my grip. She tumbled away from me.

Edwig was standing in the doorway, grinning like the Cheshire Cat, saying, "*Ja vohl!*" as she staggered back to the kitchen.

From then on, either I took Janie out on a long rope, or she was locked up whenever I left the chalet. For the next two weeks, all went well, if only because she couldn't open doors . . . yet.

One evening, I went to dinner with the Woods, friends of Mom's she had asked to keep an eye on me. I don't remember Mom asking anyone to keep an eye on the real troublemaker, Janie. The Woods lived in Rougemont, two train stops away. Len Woods was a tall, gangly fit man who wore horn-rimmed glasses and looked like an extremely intelligent hawk. He had graduated from Dartmouth, mastered several languages, and was now retired in Rougemont with his equally intelligent wife, a beautiful Spaniard named Mariuca. They lived in a converted barn on a slope facing a breathtaking rocky mountain called the Videmanette. The barn section below had been redone into small bedrooms, stuffed with clover green-and-white checked feather *bodens*, soft pillows, and multicolored crochet blankets. Mariuca had obviously enjoyed perfecting the concept of "cozy."

In the upstairs living room, watching the sun set on the mountain, we had our dinner by candlelight as the night turned on. An enormous vase of homegrown red roses filled the room with vibrant color and an incredible redolence. Mariuca made paella, one of her many specialties, and we ate while the fire crackled and Charles Aznavour sang to us in a smoky voice from the record player.

Perhaps to get it off my mind, I told them about Janie and the chicken crisis, acting out the squawking part. Len told me it sounded like the name of a new rock band, Janie and the Chickens, then he leaned back in his chair, closed his eyes, and placed the tips of his fingers together, as if praying. I looked at Mariuca .

"He's thinking," she mouthed the words, her huge, brown eyes sparkling. She set a tray of miniature pastries on the table in front of us. I hoped Len would keep thinking while I ate all of them.

But he opened his eyes and cackled playfully, clapped his hands, then rubbed them together. His face seemed to grow longer, and when he burst out laughing, he threw his head back so far I could see the gold fillings in his back teeth. Stuffing the fifth pastry in my mouth, I watched him, thinking he must have been on a different page. Janie and the chickens was not *that* funny!

"*Bon!*" Len shouted. "I have just the ticket for Mademoiselle Jane Russell," he said, pointing at me with a long, freckled finger. "Mariuca, you remember how well it worked with our Luki? Brookie, our St. Bernard hasn't touched a chicken since!" He laughed again, his hand caressing his jutting chin as he savored the memory.

"Oh, Lenny! You wouldn't try that on another dog?" cried Mariuca. "Remember, this is Nancy's beloved Janie."

"Better yet!" he shouted.

"Try *what*?" I was most curious.

"I will tell you tomorrow. I'll be at your chalet at 9 A.M. *Ne t'inquiéte pas*," he said.

"Yes, Len," I said, an uneasy feeling creeping into my bones. Never mind—whatever his chimerical scheme, it probably couldn't be as bad as the Swiss farmer blowing a hole through Janie with his army-issued musket.

Promptly at 9 A.M., Len arrived. He wore comfortable old navy blue corduroys, slack at the knees, a red turtleneck, and a navy blue

V-neck sweater. His hair was slicked back and his skin had a sunny tint from exercise and red wine. He could have been a Spanish grandee. Edwig opened the door for him. Already slightly sauced and swimming in L'Air du Temps, she liked what she saw on the doorstep and took the pose of a hooker.

In spite of her condition, Len thought it wise to include her in our efforts. In perfect Swiss-German, he made Edwig promise to do the simple job of letting Janie out of the chalet at nine o'clock sharp the next morning. More than agreeable, believe me, she looked like she was about to try and lock lips with him.

"Where's the farm?" Len asked.

"Five minutes up the hill," I pointed.

"Let's go," he said.

When I asked if I should bring Janie, he answered, "No, good God, this is the preliminary groundwork for her cure. She's not to know what we're doing."

Preliminary groundwork? Len was taking this far more seriously than I had intended. Then I remembered Mom telling me that he was a decorated war hero . . . in demolitions! He was such a commanding figure, I couldn't get up the nerve to ask him just what it was that we were doing as we double-timed up the hill. Much less could I catch my breath.

When we arrived, the farmer was standing in his garden, leaning on his pitchfork as if he were waiting for us. I wondered if he had been on guard for the last two weeks. Len went right up, extending a hand, and introduced himself, and carried on a conversation in superb Swiss-German. I never understood one word except "boom," which Len kept repeating wildly, making a big circle with his hands. The farmer listened sourly in the beginning, then his expression changed to a not-too-often-used grin. By the end of the explanation, he was slapping his thighs and laughing rather cynically. Then the two men thumped each other on the back and shook hands in a roaring good humor.

Business finished with, Len came over to me, wiggling with

delight. Putting his hand on my shoulder, but still not explaining any of his antics, he guided me downhill. When I looked back, the farmer pointed at me, and when I waved good-bye, the Swissy, recently so stolid, broke into a guffaw.

"Len, what is going to happen?" I demanded to know.

"If I tell you, you won't bring the dog," he said. "By the time Edwig lets Janie out tomorrow morning, you need to be right here at the farm with me." He stopped for a moment, thinking. "But don't let Janie see you."

"Should I come armed or with a stretcher?" Any clue would do. "Len, please tell me what you're going to do."

"*À demain*," he saluted, formally, and walked away whistling.

My curiosity almost got the best of me. For distraction, I focused on Janie the rest of the day, taking her to the village, leashed, and for a short hike along the bottom of the Eggli. We passed the trout farm and the lumberyard, following the usual paradigm. Back at the chalet, I fluffed up the fox throws and started a fire to warm her. I fed her tuna and rubbed her ears, cooing to her in a loving and pitiful voice. She had to know something was up but she went along with the offerings.

In the morning, the mountains were gleaming like metallic green knitting needles, the sky was a beautiful butterfly blue with a soft breeze fanning from the west. Earth and sky were propitious; a good day for our adventure. But I felt terrible about the furtive and impending "event." Maybe Janie wasn't such a bad dog, maybe she'd grow out of murdering chickens. But I pictured Len up all night, plotting and planning over top secret papers, and knew it was too late to call him off.

Janie didn't hear me when I opened the door quietly and sneaked out downhearted, without her . . . my last look at her as she lay asleep and innocent in her favorite spot.

I sprinted up the hill to the farm. Len was already there in baggy camouflage pants tucked into laced-up boots, and a white pullover.

He was leaning down, hammering a stake into the ground. The farmer rummaged around in a bulging camouflage bag lying at Len's feet and pulled out a fully feathered, dead chicken. Len stuck the chicken up on the stake. The farmer rummaged around some more and pulled out a pair of pliers and handed them to Len with relish. Len attached two wires to the limp chicken. I approached them warily.

"The explosive chicken," Len greeted me. He stood and rocked back on his boots as if nearly bowled over with pride.

"The *what*?" I asked, incredulously.

"*Hinterur hooterur goom phlu*," the farmer said, distinctly.

"This has never failed and I haven't lost a dog yet," Len declared.

"You mean, you're not going to kill her?"

"*Mais, non.* Rudy here doesn't want her dead either, he just wants her to stop killing his chickens. He can hardly wait to see her go up."

Go up? She was gonna go up?

"Edwig will have let her out by now," Len said, checking his watch. Rudy accompanied us, with his new permanent grin, as we followed the wire to a square black box at the side of the barn. Len motioned for us to crouch down out of sight.

"We are now ready," Len whispered, then said something in Swiss-German to Rudy and the two men snorted. Rudy said something to Len and the two laughed again. Rudy then gave me the thumbs up and a big smile. They had bonded, making me wonder just how difficult the life of a turncoat could be.

Two seconds later, Janie came around the corner at top speed. With an earsplitting battle cry, she pounced on the chicken. Len slammed down on the handle of the box at the exact moment when her mouth closed on the prey. The feathery decoy exploded with a tremendous BOOM and the impact threw Janie three feet into the air! She did a flip and landed solidly on all fours, covered in chicken skin, feathers, blood, and two little chicken feet. She stood there, stunned.

I thought the noise had pierced my eardrums, and, in a delayed reaction, covered my ringing ears and worked my jaw. Closing my eyes, I wondered if I should have trusted Len's demolition skills so implicitly, but when I opened them, Janie was still alive. I chuckled to myself with relief, covering my mouth so neither side heard me.

"Bingo!" bellowed Len. He and Rudy collapsed in gales of laughter, congratulating each other. World War II had never produced a more perfect or satisfying mission!

The smoke settled, but still Janie did not move. She was spread on all fours, her tongue out. Her brown eyes had gone dead flat, unblinking, and her breathing was slow. She was alive, but she had been bested. Looking the two grown-up men squarely in the eye as if she was committing them to memory for revenge, she pulled her legs close under her, included all of us in a final searing glance, and trotted off towards the chalet. I had never seen a more dignified departure.

Len and Rudy slobbered all over each other, and Rudy's plump wife emerged from the barn to hear their instant replay rendition. She looked and smelled as though she had been baking bread. She listened, wiping her hands on a worn white apron, her gimlet eyes squinting brashly upon them as though they were ridiculous children.

As Len packed up his bags for his next demolition mission, I thanked him spuriously and waved good-bye to a giggling Rudy, who, if I wasn't mistaken, was being led into the house by his ear by his humorless wife. Maybe she wasn't so keen on the overhaul of his personality. I made my way slowly back home.

When I entered the chalet, Janie was lying once more on the fox throws, with Edwig shouting and brandishing a soup ladle over her bedraggled body. Edwig's sputtering efforts fazed Janie not at all, as it was evident her hearing had not yet returned. Her back was turned to Edwig, and she appeared to be resting quite comfortably.

Knowing I was one of the last people Janie wanted to see right then, I retreated to the windowseat and began a letter to Pete.

"Mom is going to kill me this time for sure. The dog is deaf as a post, but WOW! You should have seen how high she blew!"

I desperately wished Len and Rudy would go over to Vietnam and take care of Pete.

Eight

Occasionally in the fall, pernicious storms peculiar to Switzerland known as the föhn—a mixture of wind and bursts of rain—pushed through the valley whipping across the mountainsides, snapping trees in half. The wind wasn't cold; it was hot and heavy, a kind of pressure cooker heat that was slow and deadly, so pudgy I felt I could poke a hole in it. With an approaching föhn, the local atmosphere was one of dread and misery, loaded with confusing anticipation. Rumor was that more suicides occurred during a föhn than at any other time. I had thought that nothing could rattle the Swiss and found it hard to believe that in this beautiful, gentle, hardworking country, people were not exempt from depression and madness.

The word "Gstaad" means, the "coming of valleys." Seven valleys feed into Gstaad and our chalet was situated within view of four. Janie sat in my lap in the windowseat as we watched the wind blast through the Feutersoey valley, bowling over everything in its path. I will never forget the sound of hundreds of trees cracking and snapping. It lasted about two hours. When I no longer felt we could be blown over like an old shed, or drenched, I escorted Janie out of our battered but undaunted chalet to survey the havoc. She no longer bolted for the farm up the hill since the chicken incident, and strangely enough she became more attached to me. Maybe her hearing hadn't come back completely and she was using me. Who knows.

Emerging into a new, raw, kinder air, Janie and I were unaffected emotionally by the föhn for different reasons: I hadn't suffered through them all my life and found the atmosphere spooky, even powerful, whereas Janie . . . nothing ever got Janie down.

Deciding to take a walk into the village, I grabbed Janie's red leather collar and leash, decorated with gold charms of Swiss cows. She liked her collar, I think she thought it was pretty spiffy. Unless we were going on the train, I didn't bother to put the leash on her because she had acquired the maddening habit of feigning death, spitting and choking and dropping to the ground in front of passersby if I ever dared to pull ever-so-slightly on it. Today I carried the leash.

We made our way to the PTT—Post, Telegraphe, Telephon—a little building attached to the train station, where we mailed a letter to Pete, personalized by Janie's paw print from a black stamp pad. The village was bustling as shop owners cleaned up the leaves and branches the storm had left for them on the sidewalks.

I found it next to impossible to bypass the *pâtisserie*; every day but Sunday, Oehrli Bakery made light, flaky pastries, rich, berry-filled doughnuts, and great steaming loaves of bread. Before sunrise, roly-poly shop girls placed the steaming breads and doughnuts on racks in full view in the street windows. As if that was not enough advertising, the double doors were left open so the air could cool the pastries, emitting a fragrance that waved its way through the village, up the hill to the chalets, drawing inhabitants to the shop like Texans to Lone Star beer. I bought a warm raspberry doughnut and ate it as we crossed the street to the butcher's. Powdered sugar floated down the front of my dark green sweater, reminding me of the colors of the slopes in winter.

"*Bonjour, Janie et Mademoiselle Brooke. Quelle jour terrible!*" Monsieur Zurcher, the butcher said, raising his arms and swatting a stiff broom down valley in the direction of the departing storm. He was a neat man wearing a clean, crisp white apron. A solid, square jaw was set in his jolly pink face and his eyes shone like bright blue marbles. The storm had not had a morbid effect on this Swissy.

I nodded my head up and down and smiled, saluting him with the donut and a small flurry of sugar.

Hustling into his immaculate shop, he returned with a brown

paper sack containing a few goodies. "*Pour Janie,*" he said, squatting down. Janie rested her front paws on his leg and reached up to lick his chin. Here was someone she had been wise enough to butter up from the first day.

"*Merci,*" I said. As Janie followed me away, I heard Monsieur Zurcher telling his neighbor, Monsieur Werner, who owned the clock shop, about the "*poulet claque!*" Monsieur Zurcher had supplied the dead chicken to Len and recounted the explosive chicken saga with great pride, as if he'd been on the mission.

At Pernet, the village grocer's, I bought an Italian sausage, a small cut of Gruyère cheese, a bottle of apple juice, and a bar of Lindt Excellence bitter chocolate to put in my backpack. We turned left at the Rossli Restaurant where the farmers had gathered. It was Wednesday, market day. Thirty-odd farmers had brought their cows down from the pastures very early in the morning, missing the storm, to sell and buy others. The farmers were now at ease, holed up in the restaurant, gabbing, smoking, eating wienerschnitzel, hash-brown potatoes, green salad, and drinking schnapps or bottles of the local wines. They were a happy lot. The restaurant windows were open now, and out came the air, thick with the combination of food, pipe smoke, and the smell of market-day manure. In one window I saw a group of pipe smokers. Some pipes were curved and carved personally, trademarks as such, undeniable proof of ownership. Like cattle brands in Texas. Proud farmers with handlebar mustaches, blowing smoke out of the larger, more elaborate pipes, brought to my mind outlaws back in early Texas blowing smoke off the barrels of their notched-handle pistols. It seemed Texas was on the tip of my mind. I rattled my head.

Some of the farmers spilled out of the restaurant. They each wore faint gray-and-white-striped, one-piece work suits, and huge black rubber boots, gooey with fresh manure. I inhaled deeply, relishing these earthy odors. Janie trotted crisply through the crowd and the farmers saluted her. She had quite a reputation, thanks to Rudy. Otherwise, they were fascinated with such a little dog as they were accustomed to their appfenzels or St. Bernards, dogs who would find Janie an inadequate hors d'oeuvre. I thought of making bets with the farmers, like Pete did with me, "Yes, Mr. Farmer man, I'll put 100 francs on Janie . . . she can beat up your Swiss mountain dog." I needed Pete home so we could start a new scam.

Paralleling a fast moving river, we followed a wet brown trail up the road to a closed ski-lift station at the base of the Wasserngrat, the highest mountain within walking distance.

"Let's do it , Janie," I said, pointing the way. She barked shrilly in reply, swirled in a tight circle, ran across the little wood bridge and up the slope. She turned once to bark at me . . . "Hurry up, hurry up." What a great dog . . . always ready to go, to experience, to live. I think she taught me that. Now that Janie was with me, I had the world by the tail.

The storm had damaged many trees, splitting hundreds of magnificent arolla pines, some sixty to eighty feet high, into pieces all over the mountain; spruce, fir, and larch trees lay scattered like a giant game of Pick-up-Stix. Luckily, the milk cows had been brought down from mountain pastures a week earlier; otherwise the tempest would have been devastating. The air was filled with a solid perfume of fresh-cut lumber mixed with pine mulch. Rain water dripped from branches and soaked the ground, stirring up a multitude of fragrances I knew I would never forget. Several distinct shades of green, from the leaves to the grass, were amplified by crystal drops and puddles.

I hiked slowly but surely up the gentle slope for over an hour. Janie zigzagged all over the place at twice her usual speed, sticking her head into barns, jumping in the fresh water which dripped into big pine troughs at each farm. When we got above the timber line, we crossed into marmot territory. Marmots are the most commonly seen Alpine animals: bushy-tailed, plump little rodents related to the woodchuck family, similar to a beaver in size, living in little groups. The entrance holes of their burrows are scattered all over the slopes, with a labyrinth of tunnels underneath. They scamper playfully in the meadows and grassy areas or sit upright outside their burrows scanning the terrain. Their most fascinating skill is the way they can pitch their high sharp whistles—like ventriloquists—from one place to another, throwing off predators or little dogs like Janie and driving them bug nuts. Marmots were big league now that chickens were off limits.

A fat furry marmot watched us from a rock pile outside his burrow. He had a gray-black head, but his body, mostly his chest, was covered in reddish gold fur, lightened from lazy hours of lying in the sun. We were fifty yards away when he started scolding us roundly, standing up like an annoyed parent with his hands on his hips. Gads, he reminded me of Edwig! Janie ran amok from one hole to another as the impregnable marmot craftily dashed through the tunnels and poked his head up in a new place each time. The entire exhibition reminded me of the Wack-a-Mole game at the rodeo back in Texas. There—I was thinking of Texas again.

After Janie had run the marmot deep into the ground, I set up a picnic on a grassy knoll and enticed her back with a bit of cheese. The marmot stuck his head out of a near hole to tease her, chirruping and clucking, but Janie pretended to be more interested in the cheese. The marmot came farther out of his hole than I thought was wise, but then I knew Janie better than he did. Trembling like a wet cat, she could no longer stand the torment and dashed at him, but he moved lickety-split, his sharp chatter penetrating the air with the rapidity of machine-gun fire, into his hole, safely under the earth again. Dirt flew in the air as Janie dug furiously behind him.

At 8,000 feet, I looked down on the captivating village below and remembered Herman Wouk's description of Switzerland as "picture-book villages; smoothed and polished for centuries, by the people who had lived and died there, to the perfection of a single master painting." Perfect. After seven years in Switzerland, I had come to the conclusion that the Swiss, on the whole, were just as impersonal as that. I had often felt that I was just passing through, never a Swiss at heart, not even a transplanted Swiss, simply because they are an undemonstrative people, as phlegmatically oblivious to strangers as elephants to pin pricks. I had had the occasional date, some sessions, the odd rowdy romp even with a few, but until Janie, I never really had anyone to go home to. Just passing through for seven years made me wonder if I had wasted my time, or missed something back home. Some of my friends were probably already married by now. Did anyone miss me? What had happened to everyone I grew up with? Did I belong anywhere? The majesty and the power of the mountains was making me dizzy with heavy thoughts and philosophy.

Seven years. It was September, and Pete's tour was over in one week. He was due home in the States in ten days, after one stinking year in Vietnam. He was in the home stretch. Safely perched in the mountains, I couldn't help but feel a sheer panic that something would go wrong for him in the last week, the last day, the last hour. I was overwhelmed with the wish to see him, and the fear, the ever-present threat, of not seeing him again. What a strange war, a war with a time tag . . . one-year tours. How could anyone believe in a war when all that mattered was staying alive for 365 days? I thought of Pete, the dashing lieutenant, in starched green fatigues, his earnest face and big brown eyes; his naughty, mischievous look. I tried to think what he would look like now. Would he have grown taller? Would he be more handsome? And most of all, would we still be close? It scared me that his letters had dwindled to two in the last month and had become completely impersonal. From what I had allowed to reach me about the war, the My Lai massacre, Agent Orange, napalm, it was a soured situation. Through Pete's silence, I felt that he was not proud. I had lost him in a way, but he *was* coming home and I was going to New York to find him again.

Mom had rented a little apartment on 57th Street in Manhattan for her work back in the States, and we were all meeting there before she headed out to California to work on *Doctor Dolittle* with Rex Harrison, Anthony Newley, and Samantha Eggar. While I was sorting out what to do and where to go, Mom was sorting out whether she needed to renew the lease on the chalet. She had arranged to farm out Janie with friends of hers in Gstaad who owned a very jaunty, slobbery, brown-and-white St. Bernard named Willy. Janie was full grown now, and Willy, at 100 enormous rambunctious pounds, was ten times her size. I hoped she wouldn't hurt him.

I sat in the pasture memorizing the panorama and inhaling as deeply as I could, filling my lungs to bursting with the clean air, hoping to keep something of Switzerland alive inside me forever. I had no idea what I was going to do next. With a fantastically charmed life behind me, I had no college plans and no desire to teach skiing again, at least in the immediate future. I just needed to see Pete home. Then it would be time for me to grow up and make a real living or go back to school. I hated to leave Janie, who no doubt would continue to live a life of pure pleasure and luxury, one that I had enjoyed living with her and one that she had taught me to handle well, making the most of each day. I would always have that with me.

Retrieving Janie from her archaeological site, I walked slowly down the mountain with her, stepping around cotton grass, orange Alpine poppy, and alpenrose. I had taken it on myself to identify Switzerland's wildflowers, the highlights being edelweiss and blue gentian, high on the Diablerets glacier. I thought of the simple fresh vases of flowers at every restaurant, crimson geraniums and purple petunias in boxes on the balconies throughout the summer, hanging baskets on the lamp posts in the village exploding with pansies, cyclamen, and forget-me-nots. I leaned down, realizing I was really going to be leaving Switzerland, by choice, and sadly picked a wild orchid, slipping it behind my ear. Forlorn, I returned slowly to the chalet.

That night I lay in bed in a warm nest of quilts thinking again about the Swiss. They appeared to live a stress-free life, but they were not the least bit lighthearted. I never felt that they were lucky to have me, but more that I was lucky to have their country for a while. They were not grateful, but they were tolerant. They had such a different way of sticking themselves into the world. Or maybe it was just the opposite. They didn't stick out anywhere. They stayed home. Of course! They stayed home in their beautiful country.

Home! There's a word I hadn't thought about much. To my surprise, I realized that I strongly missed Texas. Maybe I could go back to Texas . . . to the sun, the wide-open spaces, the horses, the cowboys singing sappy country and western songs, the overall good cheer. I reached over and patted Janie who lay next to me on the red-plaid bed cover, wondering if she would like Texas. She was so little, Texas was so big. She would turn Texas upside down.

Closing my eyes, I put Gstaad in her winter clothes, remembering how the snow gently covered the village, muffling it, silencing it; boxes and bars of chocolate, their paper wrappers each a different photograph of a Swiss scene; cheery, chirpy cuckoo clocks; cheese, sixty varieties, each distinguishable. The old warm chalets, the sheer staggering beauty of the mountains, whether stark white or lushy green, and the jet-setters coming from every corner of the world . . . the women dressed in fur hats, coats, scarves, gloves, and tight, brightly-colored ski pants; the men in fur and cashmere . . . all buying the newest Bogner ski gear, hiring private ski guides for noon lessons, that being about the time the jet-setters were getting up, lunching for three hours, skiing only one. In the evenings, more fancy clothes. Out came the Gucci, Pucci, Hermes, Givenchy, big jewels, big hair, eating in four-star restaurants, playing backgammon all night. They flocked to Gstaad to experience sophisticated freedom, simplicity, ease. Thinking of the assorted princes, dukes, earls, movie stars, and authors, and how I didn't fit in there, I thought of the Swiss peasants, asleep at nine in their quarters over their cows, their leather jackets and thick wool clothes, and did not see myself there either. I was not connected to any mountain, any slope, any river, any meadow. Nothing in Switzerland kept me there. Except Janie. I didn't want to think of leaving her. If she could drive, I supposed she would be the only one seeing me off at the station. I felt pretty empty after all those years. No one here to hold on to, no one anywhere else to run to. I felt utterly homeless.

Janie moved under the covers, jerking occasionally as she dreamt no doubt of her aggravating interlude with the marmot who got away. When I was gone, would she miss me?

I fell asleep seeing a white cross on a red flag, the lovely and simple symbol of Switzerland. With no picture of my next stop to comfort me, I could only tell myself how lucky I was to have called Switzerland my home for seven years.

Nine

After the announcement that the Japanese had surrendered and World War II was over, *Life* magazine ran a cover picture of a sailor spontaneously grabbing the first nurse he saw after getting off the ship, bending her over, and kissing her. To me, that was grand! She looked like her knees had buckled. Pete, on the other hand, landed in San Francisco for processing in the dark hours of the night with no one there to greet him. For the boys getting off that plane in late September, and for all the other boys whose tours were over, there were no ticker tape parades, no hero's greeting, no nurses kissing them back, nothing. We never got to give Pete a hug till he got to New York three days later.

In the fall of 1970, Mom, Pete, and I spent a few weeks together in Mom's comfortable two-bedroom apartment, anxiously trying to pull our family back together before we all went our separate ways once again. Our lives had been on hold for a year, and Pete set the stage by telling us he would not talk about what had happened in Vietnam. I did not want to hear about it so I was fine with that. But he didn't want to talk about anything else either. He looked the same, even though at twenty-four, his hair was turning salt and pepper, and he had lost weight; but he seemed bottled up—I felt there was nobody home when I looked directly into his brown eyes. He had started smoking Marlboros, drawing in deep, long breaths, making me wonder if he cared about anything at all. I mentioned I wished he wouldn't smoke so much, he simply shrugged his shoulders. Silence. I had always been proud that Pete was my big brother, but now with him shutting down, I was feeling deep hurt and frustration, and could think of nothing to make it better. I felt closer to him when he was in Vietnam than I was with him in front of me in New York.

Mom, I guess, believed it was just a matter of time before the new shapes of the family puzzle would fall into place, and she stayed busy, leaving for California as planned, then back to Gstaad, swooping up Janie and taking off for Paris, Rome, Athens. Janie was small enough to go under the seat on the airplane and I could well imagine that she was becoming a mini version of Mom. We got postcards with big red lips and Janie's smeared paw prints. I could tell Mom was letting my well-trained sidekick get completely out of control and couldn't even keep her still long enough to sign the cards.

With Pete home safely, in body at least, I felt it was time to sort out my feelings about America, and about being American. I was proud that my brother had served, but only because he had lived. Confronted daily with explicit coverage of the war on every channel, where I had avoided television before I now became addicted. I visually absorbed endless reports on antiwar movements, student groups for democratic societies, long-haired boys burning draft cards, and police brutality. Then, sitting with my mouth open in front of the television, I watched coverage of National Guard troops gunning down thirteen students at an antiwar demonstration in the heartland town of Kent, Ohio, at Kent State College. America was the mess I had feared and I was appalled. I chose emphatically to be against the war. In those days, if you weren't for the war, you were made to feel you didn't love your country. We had assassinated two Kennedys and Martin Luther King, we were sending babies to fight for some country that no longer wanted us there, and we were killing our young on a college campus in our own country.

While I had been longing for some sense of belonging, I had been toying with the idea of going to the University of Colorado on a ski scholarship I had been offered, but I decided against that. With my deep sense of moral outrage towards what I saw as a country coming apart at the seams, I turned my back on America for the second time and accepted a job offer from Martine Fields, a close friend of Mom's, to work at her jewelry store in London. It started in November. When I asked Pete what he thought about my going back to Europe and did he want to come, he shrugged his shoulders. A few days later he told me that he was going back to Texas, as in his mind Texas wasn't all that American, to San Antonio to finish two more years in geology at Trinity University. He and I were to part again, but this time I felt a helpless relief.

One afternoon before we left, Pete asked me to go with him to visit a Brazilian friend of ours, Paul Portinho, who was in the Veterans Administration Hospital in New York. I remembered Paul from Le Rosey where he and Pete were classmates and two of the members of the self-appointed Suicide Six ski team. A truly tall, dark, handsome and wildly sexy boy, Paul had once whooped and hollered in seven odd languages, skied like a gonzo down the slopes in Gstaad, swept me into his arms at the end of a run, kissed me like he was Rhett and I was Scarlett. He took my breath away.

At the end of his tour in Vietnam, Paul had stepped on a land mine and part of his brain had been blown away. When Pete and I walked into his hospital room, he recognized both of us, saying our names, hugging us, which gave the doctors their first ray of hope, as he had hardly recognized anyone else. His head was wrapped in a huge gauzy bandage which covered one eye, and there were several bumpy red and blue scars over his face and hands. As I hugged Paul, Pete motioned to me not to fall apart and kept me from doing just that. Sweet Paul was mindlessly happy, garbling and slurring words like a child, trying to talk as fast. The doctors told us chances were good that Paul would be able to speak normally again in a couple of years, that he was, at this time, starting all over. *See Spot Run* sat on his bedside table. When we left, Paul hugged me again, but this time he started crying and asking us not to leave him. Pete was wonderful, calling him "Buddy" and promising to come back. Paul hugged Pete for a long time and they said nothing. He stopped crying and we left him. It was my turn to cry. I was seeing a whole new side of the world and I did not like it. I was too young, too removed, maybe even too spoiled, to even feel involved. I had done a good job of protecting myself by living in Switzerland. I could hardly wait to flee to London, where I pictured an untroubled world.

Until we parted, Pete remained unmovably and eerily distant. All I could do was bite my fingernails. For once, Babbling Brooke had very little to say. Not sure about anything anymore, I flew to London, alone and lonely. The only familiar theme for a while would be Mom's constant stream of postcards. How strange, I thought, how strange, that Chanel's Really Red lipstick could offer such solace. Janie's smudged prints only made me lonelier.

I moved into a basement flat in Ovington Gardens. It was two blocks from my work at Kenneth Jay Lane Jewelry in Beauchamp Place, four blocks from Harrod's. The flat was small, a bedroom and a living room set up as two with no doors to separate them. A tiny kitchen with a minuscule refrigerator. I decorated slowly and plainly as my paycheck of thirty pounds came every two weeks. I soon had a cozy little home, and I was coping on my own.

My hours at Ken Lane were spent on the second floor, in a small workroom above the shop. Ken Lane was one of the first designers to manufacture "fake jewelry," renowned for bright enameled pieces. I was one of two girls, the other a robust English girl, sweet as honeycomb, named Knoxy. We both filled out wholesale orders for jewelers around the city and were supervised by a very jolly Englishman named Mr. Bacchus, a fitting name for someone whose color was not due solely to the weather. He was a blast to work with. The three of us worked in casual clothes, jeans were fine from nine to five. We checked the enameled pieces for chips or broken clasps, or glued rhinestones of different sizes on dressier pieces. My personal favorite was a huge Maltese cross, enameled in deep navy blue and Coca-Cola red.

I had no television, and reading became my new obsession, starting with Paul Gallico and Daphne du Maurier, falling head over heels in love with Gerald Durrell. I bought a funny little bike called a Chopper for getting around the city. It had a big wheel in the back, a small one up front, to fit in with the newest "wheelie" craze—the front wheel high in the air, like a circus act. I was too mature for wheelies but I do remember one incident as I was flying into a roundabout and out of the corner of my eye saw a gorgeous bloke in a bright red Mini Morris on the other side. I zoomed around at a rapid pace, circling madly left around to the right, considering a wheelie *incroyable*, like a rodeo queen on a big hunk of gorgeous horse, but to my dismay I had lost my bearings and only a traffic policeman was watching me. He found me funny, not alluring. I still, sadly, had no one to show off for.

Having heard dreadful reports about the weather before I came over, I nonetheless loved it, even the wet, raw, cold days, and I loved London. There were exquisite flowers, arranged flowers, different from the flowers in Switzerland where they were wild and free, as opposed to London where they were meticulously and proudly grown. It was like *My Fair Lady*, flowers on every corner, in every mini-grocery shop. I filled my happy little flat with daisies, sweet peas, tulips, and tuberoses. I had slipped into a new fantasy. But the truth was, I missed Janie. I missed kissing her fuzzy little nose and having a reason to get up and go on an adventure. Last I heard, Mom and Janie were in Portofino, photographing Rex Harrison and his wife, Rachel Roberts, for *Look* magazine. And yet, as surprised as Rex Harrison in *My Fair Lady*, I'd grown accustomed to her face.

As bad as things were back in America, England was having its own crisis. The Beatles were falling apart and they knew it, which I thought commendable. It was the beginning of rampant overexposure and drugs; everybody was "in your face;" people started "looking out for number one." How ridiculous, I thought. The world was on the verge of the RE era: replay, redo, rewind, remake, repeat. Other than in Mexico where they had been refrying beans for years, originality was dead. As far as I was concerned, the world around me was shifting, not as Dickens had called his own era, "the age of foolishness . . ." this seemed the age of selfishness. I felt that anxious times were ahead.

I buried myself in books, learning about my world, spending each non-working weekend in the country with friends from Montesano, or alone, taking buses and trains for adventure. In late January, remembering that David Rook and I had birthdays in February, I thought of looking him up to wish him a happy, maybe even getting him to meet me at the Manor House in Moretonhampstead. After all, I had read the only other person capable of putting up with an Aquarian was another Aquarian. But I didn't have his telephone numbers. I remembered to mention it to Mom when she called from a shoot in Russia, and after a long silence that I thought had to do with bad telephone reception, she told me gently that, two months earlier, David had been killed in a car wreck. He was driving, it was late at night. Having spent a year worrying about Pete and anticipating the worst, even expecting it, I buckled at the knees over the loss of David so quickly, so unexpectedly. And something new for me, I wondered who would love his animals and whom they would love in his place. I also wondered if life, even my charmed life, was going to keep getting harder. I was suddenly frightfully lonesome.

Months later, on a clear and promising weekend weather-wise, I rented a mini-car of some sort, half the size of a twin bed, and, calmly, challenging myself to drive a stick shift on the left side of the road, explored Stonehenge. It dates from 3,000 B.C. to 1,000 B.C., and is known as the most mystifying and famous monument of prehistoric Europe. The construction was attributed in earlier centuries to giants, and currently, UFOnauts. I found the structure surprisingly small, and curiously, the huge stones and continuity of the ruins reminded me of the Alamo back in San Antonio. When I had first seen the Alamo, after imagining it to be monumental, I was disappointed to discover it was merely a tiny mission tucked between progressively larger buildings in the middle of downtown San Antonio. At the Alamo, I felt big, whereas at Stonehenge, standing tiny and isolated on a chalk down, I felt small. I decided the Alamo would have looked magnificent standing out alone, free of the overwhelming press of progress. One thing about the Alamo, once inside, there is an undeniable mood that is hard to avoid. A very humbling mood. Reading names on the plaques on the walls, all the men fighting for Texas . . . from Ireland, England, Germany, Kentucky, Oregon, California, and many other states . . . places and names I expected to be native Texas names. Walking around Stonehenge I got the same feeling as I had had at the Alamo the first time I was there: the big, silent rocks or walls, their quiet power, and feeling the secrets.

On the way back to London that afternoon, no longer stripping the gears, I found myself in the ancient town of Andover and stopped for a cup of tea. The town surprised me because it seemed to be a near miss; a mishmash of boroughs, visually forgettable, oddly pushed aside, and appearing destined for no future boom.

At the front door of the Andover Pet Shop, with David's face vivid in my memory, I was nostalgically drawn to a handwritten note in the window. Rather than the Jack Russells of Peter Tavy, this one notified me of six-week-old golden retriever puppies for sale, and there was a map. I cannot explain what came over me as I followed the directions. Ten minutes away, I found the spot: a small, green-and-gold English farm, perfectly trimmed and neat, a silver pond with ducks and geese, and a tidy blue barn. The breeder, a medium-sized man smoking an old pipe, vanilla blend, showed me a litter of eight fuzzy, gold-and-beige puppies, romping and wrestling in the hay of a horse stall. After the excruciating elimination of six, I bought two, at eight pounds each. About $36.00 total, and I was as startled by my impulse as I had been by Mom's.

They rode in the back seat, occasionally popping their heads up to look out, and, not liking the motion, settled next to each other. As I wondered what to name them, tears filled my eyes. I pulled over and stopped the car, got out and opened the back door. The pups looked quizzically at me and I picked one, held his face in my hands, kissed his head and called him David. I ruffled the other one on the head, remembering his was larger and squarer, and named him Dustin. I had met the actor Dustin Hoffman years ago in the South of France, and liked him enough to name a dog after him.

David and Dustin ate kibbles and cottage cheese, mastered house-training in half a day, slept at my feet, and behaved well when I went to work. But within three days, they were sick. The veterinarian, Dr. Grazebrook, called it distemper. It took David three days to die in agony. The disease rotted his brain before I even got to know him. Depending on Dustin's disposition, the vet told me, he would live if I could keep him from giving up. David had given up. Dustin was depressed and weak from the fever, but not nearly as advanced in the disease as David had been. I wondered if my heart actually could break.

Desperate and helpless, I felt like everyone around me was slipping away. That's when it hit me: it did not *have* to be! I was not going to let Dustin die! Knoxy and Mr. Bacchus rallied, covering for me while I stayed home three days to take care of Dustin. I read him Gerald Durrell's *Birds, Beasts, and Relatives*, taught him gin rummy, and almost booked us on a cruise to Alaska to keep him happy. I lost six pounds dancing around the flat and almost landed a singing part in the play *Hair*. He lived. He became attached to me and I was certain he had hung the moon.

By the time Dustin was six months old, he weighed seventy-five pounds. His coat was reddish-blond and thick, with feathers and bloomers all over his bottom. His eyes were the color of my favorite dark Swiss chocolate and he had beautiful white teeth. He was my best and handsomest companion. We went everywhere together. Dogs were allowed in restaurants, and he sat under the table, with friendly waiters bringing him leftovers. Outside shops, he sat and waited for me where he could socialize as so many people stopped to talk to him and scratch his ears or pat his handsome head.

Dustin and I walked six blocks early each morning to Hyde Park, meeting assorted dogs and their owners. We were all kin in spirit, all aware how lucky we were to have access to such a big, beautiful clean park. Dustin loved swimming in the Serpentine, one of two huge ponds inhabited by white swans, mallard ducks, Canada geese, and enormous yellow and white goldfish.

When I was at work, Dustin spent the days sleeping and growing, and each evening at sunset we returned to the park for another hour. We walked the streets of London, and with no formal training, Dustin waited on the curb for me and we crossed the street together. I felt like I was being escorted by a gentleman. I loved his company, his ease, his calm. Not at all like the incendiary relationship with Janie, who was always on the verge of destruction and chaos, yet great fun. Dustin had good manners in greeting people, looking them in the eye, unlike Janie who appeared to have no real need for them and made no bones about it. Both dogs had excellent posture: Dust held himself as erect as a Buckingham Palace guard, and Janie had never once slumped, not even when she was a teenager. Comparing the two, I realized how much I admired each one for being exactly themselves, with no apologies. I hoped one day they would meet. Mom had been back and forth to London a few times in between films, each time bearing pictures of Janie: dancing on the beach in California with Goldie Hawn, walking in Central Park with Michael Caine, playing soccer with Tony Bonner in Madrid, sitting properly for Robert Bolt and Sarah Miles in Porto Santo Stefano, listening to Anthony Newley and Leslie Bricusse compose. When Janie wasn't hobnobbing, she was farmed out in Gstaad with Willy, who, from his pictures, was looking increasingly thinner, with a frown on him you could plow a field with. He would be needing therapy by now. Janie, on the other hand, wore a smile you could see from an airplane.

Responding to good manners and chivalry, Mom loved Dustin and stated that he was "perhaps" good enough for Janie. Ha! Look what had happened to Willy!

After two years of building a simple and comfortable life close around me, enveloped by the warmth of a marvelous dog, and out on the occasional date with different English gentlemen who were not intimidated by my football arm, I was secure and happy but still alone in the love life department. Probably because my heart belonged to Dustin. We were inseparable, we were like one. My friends loved him and always included him in invitations.

All was going along swimmingly when I received a letter from Pete asking me to come to his graduation in June. It felt like I'd been hit upside the head. Texas, where I was raised and shaped, was calling to me. It had to be like the feeling a homing pigeon gets. An instinct. A timing. After almost ten years in Europe, I knew it was finally time. I was going home, Dustin right by my side. For once, the postcard from Mom did not have the usual laconic message. This one, from a health spa in Baden-Baden, read, "Good for you. I'll send Janie. Just don't buy a pickup!"

Ten

In the spring of 1971, Dustin, in the baggage compartment, and I, in tourist, landed in flat, brown, hot San Antonio. Pete met me at the gate and he looked wonderful.

"Hi, Kid," he said. Tan, fit, and right offhand seemed like his old self. It was good to see his face, and it was the first moment on the trip from London that I put aside my dysfunctional worrying about Dustin. I had seen him and let him out during our stopover in New York after the seven-hour trip and he was fine, so I could only hope that the final four-hour leg to San Antonio was a snap for him.

"Hello, big brother," was all I could manage before I was rendered speechless walking into the 95-degree heat with 98-percent humidity. The sun shone like a laser beam, strong and direct, as Pete guided me to his copper-colored Mustang convertible. Blinded, like I had stepped out of a daytime movie into the shock of sudden sunshine, I could hardly block out the glare as I got in the passenger seat. When I sat down on the cooked beige leather, I let out quite a yelp!

In lovely London (now that I was in Texas, I wanted to be back in London) ten hours earlier, it had been 75 degrees with a cool, green breeze. There was no breeze whatsoever in San Antonio. Could this be anything like the aftermath of a nuclear fallout? Dazed and confused, I could show no more enthusiasm for my only brother, my war hero, my reason for being there. He drove me to the other side of the airport, to rows of shiny tin-roofed hangars, warehouses, and piles of freight. I was cooked to about medium-rare by then. Dustin came gingerly out of his big, jail-like kennel, and his fluffy feathers, just like my long, brown bouncy hair, went limp.

"Now, *that's* a good-looking dog," Pete said.

I leaned over Dustin and rubbed his feathery chest. He reached up and licked my chin. He had made it.

Pete liked him enough to place a towel on the seat for him. He drove us fifteen minutes away to a white stucco apartment building in Terrell Hills. During my aphonic lapse, I just followed him up to the second floor into a furnished apartment, through a large living room decorated with heavy furniture in a wagon-wheel motif. A two-seat, brown plaid couch faced a fireplace, which seemed a ridiculous feature, a swaying bookshelf, and a noisy window-unit air conditioner, which, thank heavens, was spitting out a veil of cold air, completed the room. Down a short hallway were two small bedrooms. The kitchen, which had been modern twenty years earlier, was painted throw-up green, and the cabinets throw-up brown. I almost cried. Did our tickets say round trip?

Pete pointed out the redeeming feature: the apartment complex backed up to Fort Sam Houston, one of San Antonio's many military bases, giving us full run of the vast, grassy parade grounds and the woods around Salado Creek. After the luxury of Hyde Park, where I used to brag to dog-walking buddies about the "wide open spaces" of Texas and how I could walk for hours without seeing a soul, I would have been mighty disappointed if Pete hadn't shown me something quickly to keep me from fleeing. I had made many flippant decisions in my life with no thought to the future, and this decision to return to Texas was scaring me so far.

Right away I got a job as a waitress at the River Roost on the San Antonio River which flowed through downtown. The riverwalk, lining the river, is one of the reasons San Antonio is the most visited city in Texas. After ten years' absence, this odd but remembered city had grown but not changed; a big booming hick town, with cowboys walking around wearing hats of maximum gallonage, shiny boots, crisp striped shirts, starched bluejeans with knife-sharp creases down the front, and round tins of chaw in back pockets. My fantasy wide-open spaces sprawled two minutes outside the city limits. Horses, cows, and deer grazed up to their chests in native grasses, and great silver power lines, seemingly going nowhere, stretched across the horizon, preparing for imminent growth.

Within a short time, I got our home decorated with little homey things; flowers, plants, pillows, cookware. I had many of Mom's black-and-white pictures framed and hung; pictures of Mark Lester and the pony, David in the bog, Janie and Goldie Hawn, and a superb picture of Dustin in Hyde Park with his paws crossed around a dandelion. My flower child.

Over home-cooked meals, I discovered that Pete was still not as happy-go-lucky as he had been before Vietnam. It was not awkward like it had been in New York, it was just quiet. We had more verbal exchanges than individual shrugs and silences of old. He chain-smoked Marlboros and read a lot. I cooked, cleaned, and did the laundry. To a stranger, we could have been married. Some knew we were brother and sister, saying we looked so much alike, but I thought he was still the handsomest thing alive, and I did not feel equivalently beautiful. Rather than taking me for granted, however, he was a man smart enough to be grateful. He mentioned once that he wasn't as lonely, and, being bowled over by such a demonstrative admission from him, I felt needed and was going to stay.

To my delight he took a deep liking to Dustin, and vice versa. Since meeting Janie, I had been an advocate for animals bringing out the best in people. With Dustin, Pete relaxed, acting like he didn't have to explain "nothin' to nobody." He would romp around in the grass with Dustin, throw a ball, laughing, rolling Dust over, inventing phony ferocious games. My favorite was Pete stalking from ten feet, lurching towards Dustin, arms up, fingers spread, telling him in a spooky, deep voice he was going to rip his teeth out and tear his ears off. Dustin listened to the idle threats, crouching, wagging his tail calmly, never taking his big, caramel-colored eyes off Pete as he approached. The climax would be Dustin leaping gamely in the air at Pete, who turned his body erectly, gracefully, yelling, "Ole!" Dustin brought out a born-free laugh in Pete, one I had missed in my brother, the blue-sky boy.

Pete was an honor-roll student and graduated with a Bachelor of Arts in Economics and Geology from Trinity University in May 1972, and without delay got a job with an oil and gas company called Petrolero. It was a grand job: spending days searching for oil in the fields all over South Texas. The first time he asked me if he could take Dust along for four days to Cotulla, I almost fainted. I had never been apart from him and was so used to his company, I wasn't sure *I* could handle it. Knowing Dustin would love the great outdoors, and feeling all puffed up and proud that Pete loved my handsome man, I let him go. Talk about moping. I moped around the entire four days with a pitiful look of a roommate left alone for the weekend, working longer hours, making oodles of tip money that I stashed in an old caviar tin on the bookshelf when I came home to an empty house in the late hours. I chewed my nails and paced, lost five pounds, and cut my bangs crookedly. I restlessly awaited Dustin's return. I hadn't heard from Mom in days and wasn't sure exactly when it was that Janie was arriving, but I needed her to hurry. At the rate things were going, I was toying with the idea of getting another dog. Or intensive therapy.

When at last, after 93 hours, 36 minutes, 08 seconds, they returned, I was on several new types of over-the-counter tranquilizers and my left eye twitched each time I said the word "missed." Pete was tanner, his unfailing sunny nature had conceivably been restored permanently, and Dustin wouldn't leave his side. I needed commitment. In more ways than one.

After the tranquilizers wore off and bits of hair I had pulled out grew back, Pete, Dustin, and I took off on a flat, breathless day in August to pick up Janie at the Braniff Airlines freight depot. She waited calmly as I opened the grated door, then bounced out as if she had just arrived from Austin, not another country. Delighting bored employees, she ran around the warehouse. An envelope attached to the pet carrier contained Mom's instructions about raw meat, plenty of sleep, and other nonsense, and inside the carrier, for Janie's traveling comfort, was the red cashmere sweater. Janie, being Mom's dog, knew the value of cashmere. It was neatly folded in a corner.

As she swung past, Pete grabbed her. "She's kinda cute," he said, holding her up. She was three years old, fully grown, and unmistakably an incredible natural athlete. In prime shape, she was built square and strong; the canine version of an American quarter horse.

"You look great, Janie," I said, patting her head. I felt the old twitch in my left eye when I told her I had "missed" her, and she wouldn't even make eye contact with me as she started wiggling insanely in Pete's grip to get down and meet Dustin, who had been sitting like a gentleman, watching her trenchantly. She was importunate in her demand and Pete was no match for her. She launched out of his hands, landing at Dustin's feet, staring directly at his throat. He stood and backed up. She moved forward and held ground right up under him, unblinking in her focus on his jugular. Dustin arched his neck, stood on his tippy toes, and wagged his tail smartly, withstanding the stern scrutiny of the little beast. She popped up at him, he held. Pete and I watched as a silent arrangement was reached; Janie liked him. He was fortunate.

"She reminds me of Mom," Pete said, as we headed to the car.

"Janie's not nearly as much trouble," I answered.

"I'm gonna tell her you said that," he grinned.

"I'm gonna break your face," I snarled, baring my teeth. Another side effect.

We rode home with the top down, the dogs sniffing and stretching into the hot wind. Janie did not seem to wither in the heat the way Dustin and I had on impact the first day. I was on top of the world—a family again—my brother and two keen dogs! Albcit, Pete and Dustin had become a little too Butch Cassidy and Sundance Kid for my liking. The arrival of Miss Janie Russell evened the odds. I didn't know why I would ask for anything more. Being that content never let the thought enter my mind that I could be missing something, that there was more to life. I have always been one to live in the moment and handle life as it landed on me. I was wishlessly happy.

Janie took to Texas in a heartbeat. Squirrels—gray fox squirrels in town, rock squirrels in the country—became her favorite game. Squirrels sat in trees, clucking to her, harassing her, teasing her. No squirrel could get a foot on the ground if Janie was in the area, and when she had chased every one of them out of her reach, she was resourceful, and learned to climb trees, scrambling up mesquite trees that bent to the ground or up trunks of leaning scrub oaks, scaring the squirrels into stupors. Drivers in passing cars slowed, pointing at the little black-and-white dog, ten feet up in a tree, like they were watching a tightrope act. When Pete deduced that we had few fleas because there were no squirrels on the ground dropping them, my neighbors borrowed Janie to get rid of squirrels in their yards. Janie was a useful commodity and seemingly a natural Texan.

I drove my newly bought, slightly used, red Chevy pickup truck to visit Ernie and Winnie Willie, ranching friends living on the Louisiana border, in Orange, Texas, a five-hour drive from San Antonio. Dustin and Janie liked road trips and adventure and I accepted all invitations to see new parts of Texas.

Orange is located in the timberlands of East Texas. Juxtaposed against the rest of the state, the timberlands have the look and feel of another country. For those people who perceive Texas as a land of astounding sky and spare, dry features, the forest region is a dark and brooding surprise. Rain and soil set it dramatically apart; the average rainfall is fifty-six inches per year, as opposed to El Paso to the far west with eight inches. I had heard there were more than 2,500 kinds of wildflowers in Texas and I began my education on Highway 90

East, traveling through ranch country, on the road with small, rusty trucks loaded with firewood and huge trucks carrying cattle. With brand-spanking-new copies of *Roadside Flowers of Texas, Texas Wildflowers,* and *Texas Wild,* I identified tall, white spider lilies, like hundreds of mini-helicopters with six long white tentacles protruding from them, spread across semi-shaded swampy areas, rooted in the mud. The roadside, flanked in crimson clover, looked like a dark red velvet carpet rolling out in front of me. Janie and Dustin rode with their heads out the window, breathing in new smells, interested and curious. Great song on the radio, "Don't it make my brown eyes, don't it make my brown eyes, don't it make my brown eyes blue . . . oo." We were certainly in good voice.

I slowed the truck and turned into the rock driveway of a prosperous looking blue-and-white Victorian ranch house. I hadn't finished greeting Ernie and Winnie before Janie vaulted out of the car, ran at warp speed over to the smaller of two barns and started chasing chickens. When the dust and feathers settled, she stood proudly with a dead chicken dangling from her mouth. The explosive chicken was a forgotten memory.

"That's the durndest sight I've ever seen," said Ernie.

"What about the explosive chicken, Janie?" I threw my hands in the air, looking back at Ernie, sheepishly.

"That's a chicken I've never heard of," Ernie said.

Janie stood triumphantly before us, the big, red bird hanging from her mouth, head limp, feathers wet from the gumming. As I sorted out my feelings and reaction to the newest predicament Janie had put me in, I concluded with a private smile that I couldn't help but admire her. She hid nothing from us, presenting herself haughtily, willing to take full responsibility for her deeds. She was neither embarrassed nor was she sorry. Admirable.

"Oh gads, Ernie," I said, "it's a long story, dead chicken on a stake, boom! . . . she should never have killed another one."

"Well, I know chickens, and that one is dead," said Winnie Willie in a breathless, tinkly voice. Her skin was as smooth as a Georgia peach and as colorful. She wore a long, multicolored cotton blouse over tight jeans, her long black hair wound softly around twice, settling on top of her head and kept in place with a brilliant silver Mexican comb. She smelled of jasmine.

Janie, pleased with herself and her prize, growled at Dustin when he ambled over to sniff the body.

"No, Dustin, don't you ever touch a chicken like that!" I scolded. His tail went between his legs and he looked at me through big, sad eyes. Poor Dust. I should have been more careful knowing he was so sensitive. If I'd told him he was silly looking and his mother dressed him funny, he would have died. Janie, on the other hand, would have bitten my hand for insulting her mother.

"Well, there's our dinner," Winnie said, not the least angry, adding that she had always wanted to know what a Rhode Island Red tasted like. Leave it to Janie . . . she couldn't have killed just a plain old barn chicken.

"I am so embarrassed. Please let me pay for the bird."

"Of course not," Winnie said. Smiling at Janie for permission, she picked up the chicken by its stiff, waxy feet, and added, "Ernie, you and Brookie catch up for a minute while I put this in the smoker. Then we'll go down and see if this little gal can get rid of the varmints eating up my vegetables."

"Oh, Winnie, I'll leave her here with you for a week. There won't be a cat, mouse, squirrel, frog, horse, cow, or friend in sight after that," I said. "I'm really sorry. That looked like an important bird." I squatted down to rub Dustin's chest. He cheered up immediately.

"There are plenty more where that came from. Don't you worry," Ernie said. Always smiling, he reached down to pat Janie. Ernie was my favorite kind of cowboy. His skin weathered to a healthy brown, handsome in a khaki shirt, chew in his mouth, faded bluejeans, a rather thick tummy hanging over a large, silver-and-gold belt buckle that was prettier than any pieces at Ken Lane. In the back, his jeans sagged where cowboys seem to have no butts.

"You're a little terror," he said kindly to Janie.

Janie stood up, spat out a dark red feather, and, gathering her charm about her, put both paws on Ernie's leg. An Academy Award performance. I explained to Ernie that it never occurred to Janie that she couldn't do something she wanted to do. Maybe I needed to start thinking that way myself. I was not surprised when Ernie said, "I'd be obliged if you'd give us a puppy when you breed her." He was cooing at Janie who turned her head over to me and smiled like Farrah Fawcett.

"I'll keep it in mind." Breeding Janie? *There* was a scary thought. What kind of male would it take to handle her?

We had a hot September afternoon, humid and sticky, a withering heat, the first day of dove season. The sun crackled, and fat, full shaving-cream clouds hung breathlessly in a good blue sky. Ernie said we were going hunting and lent me a 20-gauge, side-by-side Browning, a camouflage vest, and a three-pocket game bag that buckled around my waist. Winnie changed into a light-brown shirt, something the doves wouldn't flare off of, and held Ernie's hand as we walked down the dusty caliche road to the tank. Brown-gray mourning doves, fat from seed, grain, and gravel from the roads, flew lazily into a big cement tank, thirsty but unaware the season had opened. Ernie educated Dustin in the fine art of retrieving, a simple task for my clever dog. He was a natural, enjoying himself immensely. Dustin was always a dog to be proud of. Ernie got his limit of ten quickly, what with Dustin's help in finding the birds in thick, thorny shrubs and tall bluestem grass. Janie moved like a ramjet, searching for anything to give her a crusade. She chased one little cottontail into his hole, but lost interest when Dustin stayed with Ernie, not backing her up.

Ernie loved hunting with Dustin, and at sunset Winnie and I followed them around the oil rigs to work the flight path. We were having a lovely time until Dustin jumped in a sludge pit to retrieve a dove. I had a flashback of the bog in Devon and realized this mess was a lot worse. My beautiful English gentleman was encased up to his neck in thick, black oozing tar. An indelible combination of waste byproducts of oil, gas, and used drilling mud, it gathers in settling tanks and fortunately is not hot. Dustin still had the dove, who didn't look much better than he did, in his mouth when we bailed him out.

Ernie was sorrier about Dustin than I was about the chicken. Dustin followed us, dripping globs of black tar into the sand, gathering weeds and grasses to his sticky coat, and by the time we got to the house he looked like something out of the creeping unknown. Winnie and I washed him with Ivory soap and water, getting about nowhere. It was going to take baby oil and lots of time. To my horror, many of his beautiful feathers had been left in the pit. We got him to the point where his coat was merely a stained gray. He may have been a touch embarrassed, but I think overall he was ecstatic about his new accomplishments as a retriever. And since Janie had proven many times that she had no intention of doing anything for anyone else, like getting a bird when she was *asked* to do so, Dustin had found something he could do without letting her go first.

Sitting on the wide screened porch as the sun went down, we ate delicious and expensive smoked chicken, baked potatoes, and fried okra. In the center of the table was a lazy Susan with the typical condiments of isolated ranchers: a gigantic bottle of ketchup, fresh chile petins, extra hot Pace's, and a Louisiana Hot Sauce bottle full of toothpicks. As I caught Ernie sneaking bits of chicken to Janie, I thought of the life the Willies led. Winnie grew vegetables and fruit, preserved jams, smoked and dried meats; Ernie did the ranching and made the money. They lived off the land, and lived as well and graciously as Len and Mariuca, proving to me that it did not matter as much where you were as who you were with.

I was still thinking about this as I drove home in the dark. I looked at my sleeping partners: Dustin, a pitiful sight at the moment but consistently a warm, wonderful and steady companion. And Janie. Janie . . . filling my life with intelligent chaos and interminable entertainment. And now—after today—she would be a renowned chicken killer on two continents!

I fell asleep that night believing that one day my Ernie would come.

Eleven

Mom flew into San Antonio on her broomstick late one after-noon in the fall. Pete and I met her at the gate. As always, she looked elegant. She wore wide, flowing black silk pants, a ribbed gray top, and a fancy beaded necklace. Her pure white hair was pulled back and tied in a black satin bow at the nape of her neck. The requisite Hermes scarf, this one with white peonies, was tied to the strap of a black patent leather purse, matching her pointed-toe shoes. People stared, trying to recognize her.

Seeing Mom again made me wish I had given more thought to my appearance. My jeans were ripped at the knees, before distressed was "in," my shirt tail was out, my tennis shoes untied, and when-oh-when was the last time I had brushed my hair? To make myself better looking, I tucked my shirt in—a minimal effort. Pete was dressed in clean jeans, a white polo shirt, and brown loafers. Clever boy.

"Well, I see that you two are getting along and doing fine," Mom started, as we walked to baggage. We traded a look, believing we were always adorable together and certainly a great joy to be around.

"I have six pieces of luggage, Pete. Here, the tickets," she said, waving them royally in his direction. "And what on earth have you done to your hair, Brookie?"

My hands automatically ran through my hair, trying to tame the unruly mess. The humidity in San Antonio had turned my normally long, thick straight hair to a short kinky bob, like an Afro perm gone wrong. And the color was hard to describe. What with the sun and all . . . it was somewhere approaching brassy orange.

At the carousel, Pete struggled with two of the larger Louis Vuitton bags. He looked at me like maybe I could make an effort and help, but my hands were busy trying to keep my hair down.

"What's the matter with this prehistoric airport? Don't they ever get any quicker or more efficient around here?" Mom asked angrily, snapping her fingers like castanets as if that would produce a manservant.

"Don't worry, Mom, we'll get a caddy any minute now," Pete said, dragging a Gucci hanging bag and two smaller Louis Vuitton cases to the pile at her majesty's feet.

For as long as I could remember, Pete had mixed up his words—so artlessly sometimes that I myself wasn't sure of the correct expression.

But this one I caught. "Yeah, then we can play the back nine," I said.

"Leave me alone," he said, hauling the heaviest bag, weighing about one hundred pounds, onto a cart. I helped by kicking it.

Out of the corner of his mouth, he snarled, "How long did *your* mother say she was staying?"

Pete and I knew it would behoove us to unite when Mom came to town. She, like Janie, was easier to handle if you had back-up.

To scare him, I said, "With six bags, hmmm. She could stay about ten days!"

Paling, he heaved another bag on top of a pile. I ignored his grunt.

As we both started pushing and pulling the cart to the car, Mom followed us regally. If she'd had a whip, she could have passed as Ben Hur.

I was over my hair trauma and helping Pete stuff the last pieces of luggage into the car when Mom announced, "Now we have to go to the freight department because I have brought you a present, Brookie."

She put herself in the passenger seat, turning on the air conditioning full blast. Since Mom had raised us to believe that overhead lighting was "for upstate prisons," Pete, accommodatingly, had the top up on the Mustang. What a shame, I thought. Everyone would have stared at the fancy woman in scarf and sunglasses, driving along in a convertible.

"A present? Neat," I said, lying through my teeth. She had given me pretty odd things before. And this time she hadn't mentioned anything about a present for Pete.

"Maybe she brought you another whoopee cushion," Pete whispered to me behind the protection of the open trunk. "That was a beauty."

"You mean the pillow that unzipped into a raincoat?"

"Yeah, the orange one," he grinned.

"That was blue, dummy. But maybe she just brought me another pair of slippers that stick to the floor," I giggled.

"With any luck, it'll be something that will go with your hair. The orange cushion sure did." I smacked him.

"Hurry up, you two, I don't intend to spend the whole day here," Mom shouted. "It was 70 degrees and lovely in London when I left; what is it here? 180?"

"You hold her down, I'll kick her," I said. We snickered unattractively, still hiding behind the trunk, shrugging our shoulders and bobbing up and down like a pair of courting sparrows. After all our fancy schooling, we were still hicks at heart and we didn't know exactly how to treat our jet-set, sophisticated mother. Pete got behind the wheel. I was stuffed in the back with some of the smaller baggage. I was always in the back seat!

Mom fanned herself as if she had been subjected to a blast furnace, saying, "I don't know why you two choose to live here. It's hot as the hinges of hell."

Somehow that reminded me of my favorite Swiss wine, *La Braise d'Enfer,* the Hinges of Hell, and I pictured the cool green mountains as I looked at the flat, still, parched land. Fall in Gstaad. Ah! The first snow would be coming any day. I missed that season.

"Gosh," Pete said, "it's only 85 today, and the humidity hasn't even kicked in. You're the one who raised us here, and you always acted like it was your bag of tea. What's different?"

"My bag of tea?" Mom exclaimed, laughing. "He's still doing that?" She had turned to speak to me as if Pete were not in the car.

"Come on, Mom, Pete really wants to know what's happened to your bag of tea." I was glad to hear her laugh.

Pete pulled up to Braniff Airlines Freight, a long low warehouse, its tin roof blinding in the sunlight. He gave the attendant the last ticket stub and soon was presented with a pet carrier.

"Wait till you see what I've brought you," Mom said, smugly.

Wrestling impatiently with the latch on the carrier door, she finally yanked it open, and reaching in, brought out—not one—but two Jack Russell puppies! She held them up like trophies at a boxing match.

I was dumbfounded. I couldn't believe my mother would bring me puppies as a present when she had mentioned only about 400 times that I had "gone to the dogs" with Dustin and Janie. Not to mention I felt slightly bamboozled: if I was going to get another dog, *I* wanted to choose it.

Admiring them, Mom said, "I only saw them briefly in London before they were put on the plane. They're from the woman who sold us Janie. She found a male and a female for me." She looked around suddenly, and demanded, "Where *is* my Janie?"

"She and Dustin went hunting cottontails on the parade ground," I told her. "They knew you were coming in . . . they'll be back at the house when we get there."

"Well, I'm going to the men's room," Pete announced.

"Pete, take them with you. I'm sure they have to pee after that long flight," Mom said, putting them down. They sat there, yawning.

"What do you think I'm gonna do, pee in the grass? You take them, Kid, they're *yours,* aren't they?" And he stomped off towards the restroom. I gathered by his tone of voice that he was annoyed with Mom. Maybe she shouldn't have given me two puppies while I was living with him. Or maybe he too wanted a present, after all.

I clucked to the puppies. Their ears shot up, intrigued by the noise, and they trailed me across the hot pavement to a patch of grass. Following the action, Mom told me she'd bought a boy and a girl so I could start breeding Jack Russells in Texas.

I remained silent, recalling that I wanted to breed Janie, yes, but now I had new orders. I watched the puppy with the longer coat squat down, his bandit face showing great relief as he rid himself of about two gallons. He was mostly white with a black patch at the root of his tail, a large, black patch with tan in it over his right eye, a small one over his left, and big pink ears that stood straight up.

"I don't like the way his ears stand up," Mom said.

"I think he's kinda cute," I said, picking him up.

"His ears are not supposed to do that, Brookie. I can't believe that woman sent him with me. I know his ears are meant to flop. Aren't they?"

"I don't know," I said, looking into the biggest pair of brown eyes I had ever seen. He licked my chin. Puppy breath.

"He's all wrong," she continued. "His ears are too big and they stand straight up. Look, they don't stay bent." She picked and pushed at the little fellow like a mother monkey and he began to tremble. "I should have looked at them more closely. I paid good money and look what I got! Wait till I get her on the phone." Mom often used the phone as a deadly weapon.

"What about the female?" Pete asked, coming back just in time to egg Mom on. The female sniffed the wind, looking for action. Unminding of us, she seemed a lot like Janie right off. She had short hair and was white all over except for a sliver of black out of her left eye.

"The female is fine," Mom snapped. "Take me home."

Pete drove to the apartment, laughing and saying, "Looks like we have a jack *rabbit,* not a Jack Russell. Brookie, you could call him Radar. Look at those big ears! He's probably receiving from Russia right now." Pete was being cute, trying to soothe Mom with humor, but he was annoying the crud out of me.

Not that anybody was running a poll for my opinion. I said, "You know, just *maybe* these ears are an asset. Imagine that he could put them to the ground and hear like no other Russell. Like an Indian, listening for stagecoaches. Or like the booby birds! They hear vibrations of fish, don't they?"

Mom turned around and stared at me like I had meowed.

Pete said, "Ah . . . that would be *feel*, Brooke. Booby birds *feel* the vibrations."

"Like you know," my voice escalated as I added, "I'm going to keep him and call him Tarzan! He's *mine*!" The evening sun was shining through Tarzan's huge, erect pink ears as we arrived home.

"I want my money back," Mom barked. "I'm going to get that woman on the phone and tell her what I think. While I'm phoning, you should drown him!"

I knew she was just being silly, in her own way. Hag. Putting the puppies on the grass in the front yard, I turned to Pete and said, "We have that insane Janie and I have always thought we would name a male Tarzan. Get it?" I smiled. "Tarzan and Jane?" I really could have used a little approval.

"Tarzan and Jane," Pete repeated, shaking his head. He heaved the bags out of the trunk and said no more about it as he carried the two largest bags up the steps. Upstairs, I could hear Mom squealing over Janie and Dustin.

"Tarzan? You like that?" I said to the puppy, as he looked at me sweetly. He stayed happily in my arms, unlike Janie, who no more wanted to cuddle than get a brand on her butt. I sat in the grass and put Tarzan down. The female came back from exploring and investigating. "And what shall we name you, little lady?" I said, picking her up and nuzzling her. She struck out like a rattlesnake and bit my nose, leaving two puncture wounds and drawing blood. I pitched her away from me.

"Well, she's quick." I wiped the blood off my nose. "I'll call her Swifty! How about Swifty?" I asked Tarzan.

He went over and pushed the female affectionately. She turned and started chousing after him. Tarzan, clearly a kindhearted and simple pup, thought this was a game and jumped on her, throwing her off balance and knocking her over. She righted herself instantly and lashed out angrily at him, shoving him over on his back. I thought she was just being a poor sport until I saw her sink needle-sharp teeth into his throat and rip at him viciously!

I had never seen a young puppy fight like that, much less male-female. It was an impersonal act, like a hyena with a long-awaited kill. Leaping to my feet, I grabbed her and pulled, but she was locked on his throat. When I tried to get her jaws apart, she liberated Tarzan and bit straight into my thumbnail, clamping down hard. Pain gave way to anger, and I seized her throat with my other hand, trying to cut off her air. She let go of my thumb, wriggled out of my grasp, and trotted off coldly.

"Ouch, ouCH, OUCH!" I screamed, blood still on my nose and now dripping from my thumb. Tarzan was on his back, out of kilter because his back legs were, in fact, too short, and, like a turtle, he was finding it a real endeavor to turn over, much less get up.

I picked him up as the menacing female circled us like a shark, staring back and forth from Tarzan's throat to my bloody hand, stalking us, growling sadistically.

"Help! . . .." I shouted. "Dust? Pete? Janie!"

I felt that Janie could match this spooky animal. Maybe clean her clock, set her straight. If anyone could do it, that would be Janie. The puppy watched me steadily. "Mom?" I yelled. "Here's the one we should drown!"

Tarzan's big eyes looked at me and said, "What are we going to do?"

"First of all," I declared, "we're going to call her Mischief. Then, I'm going to sign us up for a martial arts class. I'm thinking a black belt would come in handy right about now."

Mom finally got Sandra Turner, the breeder in England, on the phone. It wasn't pretty! We were in the days before touch tone, speed

dial, do-it-yourself, and 1971 was still the era of long distance opera-
tors, when callers had to go through an operator to reach their party.
Mom, however, went over, under, around, and *through*, in every
sense of the word, this unlucky operator. And when she got poor Sandra Turner, Pete and I hid behind the heavy furniture while she was
"telling the woman what she thought." In the end, slamming the re-
ceiver into the hook, she knocked the pretty yellow phone right off
the kitchen wall, leaving a mighty ugly wound. As she turned to tell
us how angry she was—like we couldn't tell—the dogs scattered,
heading out the door, stumbling over each other and Pete, as he tried
to get out, too.

Mom stayed crazy for about twenty-four hours, rehanging pictures, sewing curtains, potting plants, and bursting into flames each
time she recalled the "crooked deal," while we tiptoed around the
apartment. But then she flew off somewhere, camera bags bulging.
The dust settled and she resumed her safe epistolary relationship
with us.

Twelve

As we drifted deep into November, Dustin and Janie seemed to be accepting the new members of our fuzzy family. Accepting, in that they hardly acknowledged them. At night, Janie curled up against Dustin's chest as he put his head down over her, keeping her safe and warm. They were best and devoted companions, needing no one else. Oddly enough, I was not jealous. Dustin was still my best friend and Janie made us tick. The instigator . . . she made getting up every day an adventure. What could I possibly do to stay ahead of her? Tarzan was innocent, vulnerable, and kind. He would lie supine, showing off his remarkable speckled belly. He loved being carried around like a baby, turning enormous brown bedroom eyes on me. As he grew into his ears, they got pinker, remaining erect. His white coat was coarse and long, but it changed to baby soft when I shampooed and conditioned it. He was a moonbeam of a dog. Mischief's coat was short and thick, and, unlike the others, she shed all over the place. She had a strong, athletic body and floppy ears, as well as the bona fide speckled belly. But, like Janie, she would not consent to being rolled over on her back. Mischief was independent, cranky, unpredictable, and sure to lose her temper. Yet we had not had a repeat performance of her neurotic behavior on that first day. Mischief was not a happy puppy. She didn't care a hoot about Dustin, Janie, or Tarzan, and even less about Pete or me. She appeared to be consumed with jealousy of the sort that didn't mean she wanted attention—she just didn't want anyone else to get any.

A frippy concoction of four dogs, all different sizes, shapes, and personalities. All in my care. My family was growing and I thought that was nice. Pete was not often home, but when he was, he looked somewhat undecided about the multi-animal nose-count. He continued to take Dustin but knew better than to try and handle Janie. He told me she was more trouble than she wasn't worth. Tarzan and Mischief melded into life nicely and rarely got under foot. It was a good team.

Late in November, the first dry cold front came blasting down from the north, dropping the temperature from 82 to 54 in less than half an hour. In contrast to the föhn in Switzerland, the commanding front was invigorating. Every day the four dogs and I slipped under the chain-link fence to walk on the parade grounds at Fort Sam, with the sky swirling in grays, blues, yellows, and pinks. Trees were changing colors, leaves rushing and floating above us. Janie and Mischief took the lead across the flat, grassy expanse where years earlier, when I was growing up in San Antonio, I rode my horse, Playboy, from the livery stable at Fort Sam Houston. Riding was easy then, and welcomed; with trails and paths, and the parade grounds like a big park, stretches of vivid green between rows of military homes, clean and orderly, going on forever.

At one end of the alley of parade grounds, Brooke Army Hospital, a gigantic red-brick building, ruled over the area. It was known to have the best burn center in America. Even as a child, I was proud to see this great hospital had an "e" at the end of its name—not that we were related in any way—it just made me feel connected to something important. I suppose the same theory goes for people who name their children after biblical figures, or after movie stars—some kind of "root," so to speak. The other end of the grounds stopped at San Antonio's main street, Broadway, where an abandoned Playland Park, containing only a skeleton of a roller coaster and a frozen merry-go-round, ghosted the skyline. The parade grounds themselves stood empty, off limits to horses and riders now, due to progress, I guessed. A sad sight for me as I revived the memory of racing my little, fat black-and-white pony across the grounds, insouciant, chasing big-earred jackrabbits and running like the wind. I smiled sadly, recalling those days clearly. At least for the time, I could walk the parade grounds with the dogs. As in London, there was no leash law, yet.

Dustin and Tarzan hung back with me until the females called them to order with hysterical barking as they put up a quick-swerving jackrabbit. Off they went, Janie in front with her ears flat, running like a cheetah; Mischief a close second, paddling her front feet, scraping the tops of her toenails, a minor handicap that never slowed her down but always left the raw ends bleeding. With his big stride, Dustin soon caught up, passing Mischief, running nose to nose with Janie, knowing, for fear of her wrath, not to pass her; Tarzan, bringing up the rear, bouncing dandily, hardly moving, as though he was going to have to stop and smell the roses. My kind of guy.

After a carefree hour, we would return to the apartment with the subtle scent of white bush, sweet clover, and hackberry trees, their pale purple, fanned-out flowers in bloom, drifting on the air. Hackberry trees yield sugarberries and grow in every yard, in every field, all over the place. They produce a seed that is sought after by birds in the winter, especially after a freeze when the sugar in the seed turns to alcohol and the birds have "happy hour in the sky." Cold fronts have an exhilarating effect for me, too, bringing one of the two season changes in Texas: from hot-as-hell to cooler, or perhaps brutal cold. In Switzerland, I always knew there was going to be a white Christmas. In San Antonio, the question was, will I be turning on the air conditioner on December 25th? But in that November, there was a good cold front, and I felt the first thrill of winter.

Stirred up and looking for a project, I hit on the idea of putting a natural rock garden on the bare slope outside the front door of the house. I needed to get out to the country to gather rocks and flowers, and that made me think of my old schoolmate, Sharon Dorn. We had been at St. Mary's Hall in the third and fourth grades and were best friends growing up in San Antonio. The kind of friend who, after ten years of not seeing each other, acted like not a day had gone by, picking up right where we left off. Sharon always reminded me of a Dallas Cowboys cheerleader—even her long brown hair was perky, and she had a gay, full laugh that caused everyone around her to laugh, too, even if they didn't know why. Pete liked her, and secretly, I wanted him to marry her. We had nicknamed her "Lively." I phoned to see if she would go to her family's ranch in the Hill Country and help me with this new crazy project. She told me she couldn't go at that time but gave me the lock combination and said she would call ahead to warn the foreman. She also said to take all the rocks and cactus and whatever I wanted. Take it all, she begged. Clear the place if you can. I asked if she wanted me to take her two dogs, Wolfgang and Butterfly, but she told me they were going with her to her other ranch in West Texas, and I was, by all means, to take my dogs with me.

The 1,200-acre ranch spread across the Hill Country, in Kendall County near Kendalia, with a mile of the Guadalupe River running along one boundary. I started my study of plants and wildlife through new eyes, suddenly fascinated and enchanted in the old native patch of ground that I had hardly noticed before, even though I'd grown up in it. It was a splendid place to find rocks, flowers, top soil, cacti, and shrubs, as well as being perfect for letting the dogs have a good run. I had with me a canvas duffel bag containing a virtual library of cactus, wildflower, bird, and reptile books.

Normally the dogs rode well in the bed of the pickup, but that day, going to wide open spaces, they rode in the cab with me. I knew full well Janie was likely to jump out if she saw a wild animal, instigating the rest to do the same. During the thirty-five-minute drive to the ranch, the dogs slobbered up the windows, watching everything like a surveillance crew. They waited patiently in the beginning, but all four were verging on hysteria by the time I opened the first of two gates. As I stopped at the second gate in front of the foreman's small adobe house, Janie leaped onto my sideview mirror and started a bloodcurdling war whoop. The other three went nuts trying to get out, charging at me like a pack of demented hyenas. I smacked at them and cussed a whole bunch.

The foreman, a tall cowboy, his face eroded like a Western bronze, came out and, staring at the menagerie, reluctantly opened the gate. No doubt we made a poor impression. It had been nice and quiet out in his space before we got there. But then the dogs became surprisingly still. Maybe they had caught the look in the foreman's eyes. It was the look one expects to see behind a pistol in a dark alley, a quiet, menacing look that gets children and dogs to straighten up and take heed. He condescended to nod at me, and I smiled back, sheepishly telling him I was a friend of Sharon's as I drove by. I liked cowboys. They were clean, they could dance, they sang schmaltzy songs, they had a lot of hardworking skills, they loved their wives, their horses, their dogs. And I truly believed they didn't waste words. Wow! I said to myself. I needed to find me a cowboy! But this fore-man, I had noticed, wore a wedding band. I drove on, watching him fade in the rearview mirror.

Following the limestone road, I stopped at a high point of the ranch and let the dogs out. Janie darted off like an escaped convict and encountered her very first armadillo. She rushed up to the little beast so fast that she crashed into him. Armadillos are mostly deaf and blurry blind. For that reason, the Creator put them in little ar-mored shells for protection. The armadillo apparently hadn't heard, seen, or felt Janie, and continued digging for acorns with his soft, anteater-like nose, seeming to ignore her. Like a bottle-nosed dol-phin, Janie bumped his shell as the other dogs gathered round and barked. Shocked and dismayed, the armadillo suddenly took notice of his audience and bolted, terrified, crashing into trees and rocks in his kamikaze escape. "Oh, ouch," and "Eeh," he seemed to say. He was the most uncoordinated and oddest, prehistoric-looking animal I had ever seen. He found his hole by a keen natural instinct and threw himself into it. All four dogs, scattered to the four winds in the ricocheting path of the little beast, ended up smashing into each other at the entrance to the hole. Janie, barking and digging behind the armadillo, tried unsuccessfully to chew on his hard, nine-banded behind. Eventually, the four gave up and went off to search and destroy somewhere else.

I pulled out from behind the seat my bag of necessary gear that I carried permanently: leather gloves, a hand fork and spade, clippers, and a shovel and rope for getting dogs out of trouble. Putting on the gloves, I gazed around me at the rows of low rolling hills covered in cedar. With dark green, pinelike needles, cedar grows thickly up to twelve feet high, thriving on heat and drought, insuring the sale of many bottles and tablets of allergy medicine.

I made my way through a cedar brake to an open plateau where I collected honeycomb rocks to use as borders for the garden and to circle beds filled with bluebonnets—the state flower—mealy and scarlet sage, pink phlox, purple verbena, fat yellow dandelions, and frail, burgundy-colored winecups. I separated deep-rooted bulbs that developed into my favorite wildflower, the evening-star rain-lily, which has a fragrance to rival a fragile Hawaiian ginger. The delicate six-petal, bright white lily comes out after warm-weather rains, in clumped masses, covering large areas, but only smells wonderful for a moment and does not do well cut. I dug up wild onion to add to a rice recipe for dinner, hoping I wasn't confusing it with crow-poison. I didn't want to kill Pete, just feed him.

I tried to find Philadelphia fleabane, which in the old days farmers dried and crushed into a white, floured composite to stuff into mattresses to kill fleas. I thought I should be doing something clever like that for my brood. If it didn't work to keep the fleas away, fleabane could also be brewed into tea to cure sore throats. Surely the dogs had sore throats from all the barking and squealing they were doing. Last I saw them, they had taken off after a white-tail deer, as common as grass in that country and by no means worried about being caught. Whitetails run like the wind, snorting warnings to each other, flipping their white flag tails back and forth

Following the advice of my cactus book, I took a specimen only when there was more than one in the area. I dug up lace cactus growing in clusters, in all different sizes, reminding me of families, or as I wanted to call them, cactus communes.

Growing apart from each other by several feet, yet obviously a family, were thick hedgehog cacti, their spines slightly hooked at the ends. I cut out the middle-sized one, hoping it wasn't the mother. I took pieces of prickly pear which grows rampant all over Texas, its flowers blooming in the spring and summer in amazing colors: highlighter yellow, pumpkin-orange, or traffic-light red, depending on soil conditions. It's a tall, flat-padded cactus that can be penetrated only by desert rats and rattlesnakes. Neither of which I had any desire to see. Each pad, or joint, is capable of rerooting itself wherever it falls.

Overhead, turkey buzzards dominated the sky with lazy grace, threading the hot air currents through long fingers of their mourning-black feathers, scanning the terrain for the next meal. Redtail hawks soared, balancing effortlessly. Painted buntings, like clowns with their vivid scarlet, yellow, and purple feathers, blue grosbeaks with startling denim-blue feathers, and tiny, rosy-red vermilion flycatchers hovering like miniature helicopters, together filled the sky with as many colors as the NBC peacock.

The dogs came back, dropping at my feet, panting like they had finished a Hill Country marathon, ready for the river. I loaded my specimens and we headed down to the Guadalupe River. In the middle of the road stood a roadrunner with a snake tail dangling out of his mouth. I read in *Texas Wild* that roadrunners would walk around for hours this way, with the snake's head in the stomach being digested. It can't swallow a whole big snake at once, so it feeds it in slowly as room becomes available. Roadrunners kill rattlesnakes by toying with them, spreading their wings to present a big target like a matador with a cape, and when the harassed snake strikes, it harmlessly hits feathers, exhausting itself. Then the bird darts in and out, back and forth, pecking skillfully at the skull until it splits open. I read that the roadrunner had been clocked running a four-minute mile. Now, how did some person happen to clock him running? I wanted that kind of job! I regarded the roadrunner as the stand-up comedian of the world.

At the river, the dogs plopped into the cool, tealy-green water as I watched a rafter of twenty wild turkeys on the other side, startled by our appearance, disappearing into the cypress cover. They are the wisest of the game birds, the most elusive and exciting to hunt as they travel from their river roosts to the fields, out at dawn and back at dusk, moving carefully, instinctively aware of their surroundings, rarely caught in the open.

Walking along the river bed, I remembered that the river could rise over eighty feet in a flood. I looked up at twenty- to thirty-foot cypress trees where debris was clinging. There was a prickly pear cactus thriving at about fifteen feet on one tree.

The river was low now and moving calmly. The combined aromas of cedar, cilantro, goat weed, and mesquite made me want to start a fire and cook something, or at least make a cup of tea. On the banks of the river, I picked woolly ironweed, with its lovely explosion of purple flowers, and sticky clammyweed, which could stick like Velcro and smelled worse than a lumberjack's armpit. I wanted to take cut flowers and grasses home to hang from a beam in the kitchen, to see how well they dried and how well they kept their color, for a new hobby I was trying out with dried-flower arrangements. I gathered an armful of hard, yellow buffalo gourds to put in a bowl for decoration at Thanksgiving.

The dogs had started up again and were running as one hyperactive body, showing no signs of fatigue, while one or another occasionally circled back like a scout to check my whereabouts. On the way up from the river, the pack found another armadillo and ran it helter-skelter into a huge, dead-brush pile. For five minutes they circled the brush, barking and marking, dredging and digging. Dirt flew everywhere. I kept walking. When I reached the truck, I started calling their names over my shoulder, "Tarzan! Dustin! Janie! Mischief!"

I might just as well have been yelling for Robert Redford or Tom Selleck!

Dustin finally came up panting and gasping. Then a little behind him came Tarzan with a pile of dirt caked on his nose. Janie appeared momentarily, but noting that I had not started the engine, took off to chase a fat black-and-brown rock squirrel.

Mischief did not come back. I scanned the horizon, whirling around, listening and calling her name. The rock squirrel chattered in bewilderment as he watched Janie climb his tree. The sun shone on my back and on the trees in front of me, but in the distance, fifty miles away, the sky was navy blue turning to black as a storm worked on the horizon. Standing in the sunlight, I felt all lit up, like Neil Diamond in concert. But I was too worried about Mischief to burst into song. There was not a sign of her. I got the shovel and rope.

"Damn dogs! Always when I'm just about to leave. Janie, get out of that tree and come help me."

I started down the hill. The dogs bounced around in renewed excitement, like we were beginning all over.

"Where did I last see her?" I asked Dustin. He stopped panting and closed his mouth over his tongue, staring at me.

"That's an intelligent look, Dust," I said. He just kept biting his tongue.

With shovel and rope, just as David Rook had told me—mentally thanking him for the advice and thinking of him fondly—I retraced my steps. No Mischief at the brush pile. But I found a mound of fresh dirt piled up, and I called her name. From deep down there was a muffled bark. I looked at my watch. She had probably been in there for fifteen minutes!

Then I remembered David's words, "Digging in can be fatal," and I panicked. She had dug in and cut herself off from the entrance and was down in some maze of tunnels, confused and running out of air. Having not faced any hands-on trauma in my life so far, I felt alone and deficient as I started digging as fast as I could. Mischief heard me and barked again. I dug till my arms were as sore as if I'd been water skiing for twenty minutes straight. It was agonizing, especially since I kept hitting roots and rocks. Frustrated, I tied the rope around a root the size of a man's forearm and using all my strength, winched it back towards a tree. Then I started digging underneath it. Tarzan and Dustin helped dig as best they could, but I think they thought it was a new game. I started crying and feeling like I was never going to get her out of there when all of a sudden I hit her paws and she yelped. God, it was good to see those little battered paws! With my hands, I scraped enough of a hole for her nose, and she proceeded with whining, coughing, and a frenzied hysteria. I tried to use the shovel again, but she wouldn't move her nose out of the way. She hung on to her lifeline.

"Come on, Mischief," I begged her. "Let me dig some more!"

She lay over on her side and frantically started digging sideways. I rested for a moment, watching Dustin sweetly touch noses with her. The squirrel had made a successful escape which left Janie with nothing better to do than sit next to me, questioning my agitated actions with great but unhelpful interest. Tarzan had found a dung beetle and was patting it into the ground, jumping back each time it moved again.

"I suppose my asking you boys for help would be ridiculous," I said. Dustin, in a supporting manner, licked me from my chin to my hairline.

"Oh, thank you so much. Yech!"

Afraid I might cut Mischief with the shovel, I returned to digging with my hands. Dirt was packed under my broken fingernails and my hands were bleeding from several cuts caused by the razor-sharp honeycomb rocks. Just when I thought I had a lost cause, Mischief forced half her body out the hole. So disguised in dirt, she looked like a badger, not my little dog. I grabbed her front legs and pulled. At first nothing, but then with a last frantic yank and a big squeeze, she popped out. What a delivery! Her coat was matted with dirt and spear grass, filled with stickers. There was a pyramid of dried dirt an inch thick on her nose and over her eyes. She dropped at my feet, breathing heavily, tongue protruding. I patted her head and cried out, "Good girl, you made it!" Taking my sweaty blue bandanna from around my neck, I wiped her face and cleaned the corners of her eyes. She licked my cheek, the most demonstrative thing she had ever done.

I leaned back on my hands, lifting my face to the setting sun and watched as the sunset wrapped the Hill Country in shades of purple and gold. The light flattened out behind the cedars and the long shadows of the trees pointed towards the river. Thousands of invisible cicadas buzzing in shrill enthusiasm made the air tremble, replacing our mere whimpers. I was glad to hear them.

"David would have been proud," I said to the dogs, weakly, tired. Things had turned out so well I wished there had been someone to laugh with. I had survived a Jack Russell happening and it had made me feel good. It could have gone either way, what with the night closing in on us and the armadillo hole being so deep. Lucky, lucky us.

As I stood, Dustin jumped in the air and barked. Janie took the opportunity to bite his leg. Tarzan got squished when Dustin fell back down on him. Mischief trotted around in front of me, reared up, and blocked my path.

"Surely you don't want me to carry your filthy little body?" I exclaimed. Her tiny raw paws landed on my leg and she turned her head to the side, begging.

"Okay," I sighed. I picked her up, adding her to the shovel and rope, and walked to the pickup truck in the mellow golden light. I felt like an advertisement for Jack Russell terriers. I could see it now, people calling madly for these peculiar little feists. Maybe it was a sign. My destiny . . . to breed Jack Russell terriers and make money. Even make a living! The copy would read, "Don't go digging around for Jack Russell terriers, call Brooke Thompson at . . . " It was surely time to think about thickening the plot.

Thirteen

I discovered that veterinarians loved me. Dr. Tom Vice, at the Broadway Animal Hospital, and his associate, Dr. Mary Mainster, sent me Christmas cards. They gave me a multiple animal discount for the dogs and treated me like gold. They wanted me to adopt cats, too, saying my life wasn't really complete. After all, the legal limit in San Antonio was five dogs and three cats. I was light.

Shortly after a safe holiday season, I had Dustin in Broadway Animal Hospital to get ear mite medicine for a sick ear. Mary Mainster, convincing me we could handle a nice, homeless kitty, sent a stray cat home with us. It was one of my weak moments . . . which, I believe was noted by my name on the file card, "Will take strays in weak moments." Sadly true. This particular tomcat had the look of a feline capable of starting a two-alarm fire at an orphanage. He was mammoth, with eyes the color of applesauce and about as revealing. He sat in the back seat, growling like a mini-lawnmower the entire seven minutes home. Dustin sat up front with me, occasionally cocking an eye in the back, hoping the cat didn't notice him.

"Wait till Janie sees what we've done," I told him, trying to hang some of the blame on him.

Watching me from the dining room window as I got out of the car, Janie was at the door when I entered with my suspicious burden. The cat positioned himself on a high, built-in dresser in my bedroom. Janie studied him, settled on her haunches at the bottom of the dresser. Dustin became more interested in Janie's behavior than the cat. Tarzan was scared of it and looked like he was about to get whapped with a carpet beater every time he neared the dresser.

Mischief hated the cat, but out of respect for Janie, conceded that it was not her kill.

Janie kept vigil all night, in the dark. It had to be about as exciting as watching a treadmill. She never slept, she never moved, she probably never blinked. She did whine, almost a whistle, marmotlike, a siren forty miles away. Except, perhaps, for the cat who coolly ignored Janie and would not be drawn into the ring, no one else slept either.

In the morning, Pete told me nicely, "Take that friggin' cat back or you bunch find a new place to live!"

And that morning, red-eyed and exhausted, I returned the blasé cat.

Mary and Tom were both disappointed. I told them I would keep the cat if they would take Janie. I went home alone.

My dogs were as enthusiastic about going to the veterinarians' as a boy is enthusiastic about a broom.

"Want to go walkies?" I asked Tarzan, Jane, Dustin, and Mischief one bright morning. All hell broke loose. I opened the truck door quickly and they jumped in at the same time, growling playfully in sheer delight, looking forward to "walkies."

I lied. We were going to the Broadway Animal Hospital for their yearly checkups, but if I'd told them that, they would have been hitchhiking to Hondo. They were my best friends and I didn't like lying to them.

As we drove out, they started some most interesting tumbling acts on the seats and one at a time turned in my lap, except for Dustin, to check me out, lick me, then return to their favorite team sport, bumping and bouncing. I turned up the music and acted natural, singing badly.

By the time we turned the corner and passed the park, they somehow knew we were going to the vet. They had some weird sixth sense about that, and I must say it was pitiful once they grasped it. Dustin and Janie's heads flipped back and forth from the passing park to me. Tarzan, with his most woeful look and high hopes, nudged me to remind me of our original plan. I felt like a traitor.

"Oh, Tar, we'll come back to the park after the vet's. Whoops!" I slapped my hand over my mouth. They shuddered in sync at the word "vet" as it lingered on the air like burnt toast.

I pulled into the parking lot of the Broadway Animal Hospital, stopped, got out, went around and opened the passenger door. The dogs scooted en masse to the other side, squashed together like pioneers circling the wagons.

"Don't be ridiculous," I said, reaching for them. Eight eyes, the size of espresso saucers, pleaded with me.

"How nice to see you," said Dr. Tom Vice over my shoulder. Dr. Vice drove a Mercedes. He was able to drive a Mercedes because of me and my multiple animals. He even came out to meet me in the parking lot. I teased him about that.

Tom's assistant, John, a mild-mannered and deathly timid boy with long sideburns and bright white teeth, came out to help, carrying four colorful leashes. He nodded a hello to me. For many years now John had lived at the Broadway Animal Hospital, in the back, on a cot, and away from the world. He had never gone far afield in his pendulum path between the back of the clinic, the clinic, and back to safety. Tom had given him a home of sorts, and I knew my animals were in good hands with him. Now to convince the dogs they were in good hands with John.

I put my hand on his shoulder to say hello. He smiled at me.

Tom tried to open the door from the driver's side, but Janie had locked it.

"Come on, boys, it's just a checkup," he said.

There were squeals from the interior of the car.

"Oh dear," I said. "I hadn't broken that news to them yet." Tom was such a handsome man, soft-spoken and chivalrous. And he had great humor. "Tom Vice," I said, "would you marry me so I wouldn't have to spend so much money on these useless mutts?"

"Sure, Brooke," Tom replied, smiling shyly, renowned to be

happily married and safe.

John had taken my keys and unlocked the driver's door. Searching under the steering wheel and behind the seats, he muttered, "What mutts?"

It took three of us, but we got leashes on the dogs and dragged their clenched bodies out one by one to take them into the examining room, the first down a long hallway. We passed framed pictures of perfect poodles with bows in their hair and Siamese cats lying on pink satin cushions. I did not envision my dogs on that wall.

Each time Tom worked on one of them, the remaining cowards jammed themselves up in the corner, trembling and moaning like galley slaves until John tugged them over, one at a time, lifting him or her onto the table.

Half an hour later, my darling Tom Vice had made his car payment. There were sore necks, legs, shoulders, and bottoms, and, I thought, even a general morale problem. And that was just from Tom and John. I laughed to myself. They had earned their money.

On the way home, my best friends were docile and grumpy, not jumping all over the seats, not vying for lap position. My attempt at eye contact was greeted with unpleasant surly looks and vain efforts to put me on a guilt trip. I had to point out, "Okay, team, that was fair and square. Not even! There were four of you and only three of us. Don't act so abused."

We stopped at the park.

"Look! I promised you the park, and here we are!" I opened the door and the miserable bunch disembarked like four old biddies getting out of a nursing home van.

"You're all so orderly. I like it!" I told them. They each shot me a nasty look.

When I tried to entice them into a game of hide-and-seek by hiding deep in the woods and behind a tree, they staggered back to the truck and lay down beside it. It was a good thing I had the keys.

We managed to avoid any more doctoring for a while, but when

Janie stopped eating for two days and her gums were pale, we went back to my highly paid vet. We were in the waiting room when Mary Mainster, her long, thin pony tail swishing behind her, walked by and asked me to hold Janie in my lap or wait in the car to clear the room for the animal coming in. Intrigued, I gathered Janie up and hoped she would behave. Mary went out to the parking lot and returned carrying a bobcat. A nice-looking, well-ironed cowboy followed. He wore a buff-colored Stetson and smelled of Old Spice.

It was an adult bobcat, with a soft, spotted coat and tufted ears. He looked straight into my face with eyes as big and brown as Tarzan's. I humbly turned away, hating to see this wild animal in captivity and despising the cowboy for capturing him. The bobcat focused on Janie, and a growl came from deep in his chest, slow and low, scaring Janie so badly she crawled behind me.

"He hasn't been himself," said the owner, whose hands were the size of bear paws.

Speaking to him, Mary asked, "You saved Crockett about a year ago, wasn't it, Sam?"

"That's about right," Sam answered.

"Did he get into any trash on the property, or maybe poison set out for rats or anything like that?" asked Mary, caressing the bobcat and putting her face down close to his. The bobcat stopped growling and turned over in Mary's arms, exposing his stomach to her.

"Did you see that, Janie? That bobcat knows Mary is going to make him feel better, and he's showing her where it hurts," I said, peering behind me to see if my suddenly spineless companion was listening. She was all there, wide-eyed and scared spitless.

"Not that I know of," said Sam. "He's just been throwing up since last night."

"Well there, Crockett, let's see if we can get you more comfortable," Mary said, scratching his chest. "John, come give me a hand."

Expecting to see shy, little John, I was surprised as a great big, barrelchested boy came from the back, a mountain man with a curly dance of blond hair, a Grizzly Adams. His blue eyes skimmed over me as he leaned way down, taking the bobcat from Mary. He reminded me of someone, but I couldn't think who.

Mary spoke to me as Sam followed the new hunk into the examining room.

"Hello there, Brooke and Janie," she said, reaching around me to scratch Janie's ears.

"That's a beautiful animal, Mary," I said, meaning the bobcat, of course.

She punched me on the arm, saying, "That's the cat for Janie. I'll see if Sam will let you take him home for the night." Ducking farther behind me, Janie shook so she made the bench bang against the wall.

"I'm not all that crazy about Sam, Mary. Why does he have to keep that wild animal in captivity?" I whispered.

She told me that Crockett had been found on Sam's property, in a trap, not his, and Sam had caught the trapper and beaten him so badly that the man was still limping. Sam had spent a small fortune to save the cat, and with a useless leg, the one mangled in the trap, the animal could never be released. At the conclusion of the story, I felt foolish. I'd been so quick to judge, so quick to criticize. So wrong. Sam was my new hero.

Fifteen minutes later, I sat up straight and smiled my biggest smile as Sam left, carrying Crockett, who appeared calm. Sam looked around and behind himself when he caught my smile, then went out the door, shaking his head. Maybe I had spinach in my teeth. I had noticed a gold band on his left hand. Oh well, oh well, I would just have to keep looking.

Mary came to me in the waiting room with her tall companion whom she introduced as John Karger, a recent graduate from Texas A&M. I kept staring at John, trying to place him, as he assisted Mary. He hardly acknowledged me but was enthralled with Janie, who licked his tanned nose, behaving like a perfect lady. He spoke once to her, in a deep, libidinous voice, telling her he'd like to have a dog just like her.

Mary gave capricious little Janie a shot to settle her stomach and some huge, white chalk pills to take for three days. On the way out, I grabbed Mary and dragged her to the car with me, asking about Karger. He was going to be at Broadway only for a short while, working as a vet's assistant. His specialty was birds . . . he was a falconer. And it hit me. He reminded me very much of David Rook.

Driving home, I took stock of the kind of men who had liked Janie . . . sweet David Rook, happy Ernie Willie, engaging John Karger. For some time I had made a concerted effort to emulate her: I had energy, I had spirit, I was athletic, I had a mind of my own. The parallel between us that needed changing was the independence. Guys fell in love with Janie on the spot. No one was telling me they wanted a dog just like me. What was it about her that I was missing? Cute ears? A speckled belly? Or was it that she didn't try very hard to be all these things? *She* was a natural. I was so tired of over-thinking, I decided to let my deep thoughts swim ashore and lighten up.

Just after I paid off my previous bill, I took Tarzan in with major halitosis, to have his teeth cleaned. He could have knocked over a camel when he yawned. While waiting to be called in, Tarzan and I tried to teach the clinic bird, Mr. Magoo, a blind parrot, to say "Howdy." Mr. Magoo lived in a cage in the waiting room and talked to the clients. As we worked with Mr. Magoo, an arrogant man came in the door with a big, zipped-up pillow case. He deposited it on the bench across from us and went to the counter to check in. He was wearing baggy, olive green shorts and a T-shirt with triangles cut out of it. Patches of brownish hair were escaping through the holes, a glamorous vision of masculinity, South Texas style. His new tennis shoes, laces untied, were as large as skate boards. He wore a diamond earring and his hair was shaved on the sides. The rest was slicked back on the top with low viscosity crude.

On the bench, the pillow case moved. I squirmed back on my seat. Tarzan's ears went up as he moved into my lap, sticking his nose in the air towards the bag, curious, shaking a little.

Mr. Magoo squawked, "What is it? What is it?"

"A python," the owner turned and said to me, then returned to his scribbling, dismissing me totally.

Tarzan and I stared at each other. I mouthed, "A python?"

Finishing, the man sat down on the bench and unzipped a space at the top of the pillowcase. Sure enough, a python head the size of a fist poked out. It stared at me, then Tarzan. The man returned to the counter to speak to the receptionist as Tarzan and I sat in a breathless stare-off with the snake.

The receptionist asked, "And what do you think is wrong with Sadie, Mr. Torres?"

"Wrong with Sadie, wrong with Sadie," sang Mr. Magoo.

"I'm pretty sure she has a sore throat," Mr. Torres replied, indifferently, in a dull voice. At that point, I decided that Mr. Torres' choice of cologne was not as bad as the asphyxiating amount he used.

I coughed dramatically and pretended to sneeze, saying smartly, "Gads, what kind of spray are you all using around here to kill the bugs? It's pretty strong."

Mr. Torres shot me a pissy look.

The python inched further out of the bag. Tarzan was hypnotized. To him, I whispered, "What's up with you?" I shoved him but he just kept staring at the snake.

Then Sadie slithered completely out of the bag, and her tongue checked out the surroundings with little darty, zippy motions. Her eyes focused on Tarzan as though he were an appetizer. For once in his fear-free life, Tarzan seemed to have stopped breathing. At least I didn't have to smell his breath.

"Mister Torres!" I said. "Hey, Mr. Torres!" He went to the snake on the floor, grabbing her in the middle, and thrust her back in the bag. He glared at me and then, turning back to the receptionist, he said, "She's been breathing through her mouth."

"Keep that snake away from me or you'll be breathing through a broken nose," I said, under my breath, not much liking Mr. Torres, the brute. "Tarzan," I hissed. Like E.T., he was imitating a stuffed animal. "Hello . . .?" I screeched like a ventriloquist. He looked up at me. "Do we want to go home?" He concurred with hopeful, bright eyes.

"Time to go home, time to go home," lilted Mr. Magoo.

At that moment, Tom materialized from the back, escorting an elderly lady who was using her standard poodle as a walker. The lady and the dog wore matching red bows and shuffled along, the poodle moving slowly for her as Tom accompanied them to the car. I wondered which one had had the checkup.

"I'll be right with you, Tarzan," Tom said to us. With that, Tarzan knew he was next and tried to bolt. I clutched him.

Sadie slid out of her bag again and came stealthily across the room. I began suffering from hypertension, and my hair felt like it had set itself on fire. No one paid any attention as I sat there, paralyzed, and the snake wound her warm, thick body around my defenseless leg. Evidently, Mr. Torres was putting on the Ritz for the receptionist.

"Tarzan!" I cried, for what I feared was my last time as I gripped his throat with the same force the snake was applying to my leg. "Get help!" My brain had turned to syrup. Tarzan crawled from my lap to my neck with his hair standing straight up like he'd been caught in an electrical storm.

"Okay, Tarzan, my man, we're ready for you," said the lovely voice of Tom Vice, stepping over the snake, reaching to take him off my shoulder. From Tom's arms, Tarzan looked down on me just like a captain who would never find it beneath him to abandon a sinking ship.

"It's too late for me!" I told Tom, only half facetiously. "Save yourself!" Dimly, I wished I could have seen John Karger one last time.

"Joaquin," Tom said, as calmly as you please, "I think you'd better get Sadie."

Joaquin Torres oozed over unhurriedly, smooth as Dippity Do, and unraveled his snake from my leg.

"Are you always that color?" he asked, a high and mighty smile spread worldwide across his face. I would have reached out and slapped him but my arms weren't working.

Perceiving my discomfort and remembering how valuable I was, Tom stretched out his hand and lifted me up. My legs were like wash rags.

"I didn't think there was an animal on this earth that you don't like," Tom said.

"Yeah, well, I guess we just found one," I snapped, feeling oddly vulnerable.

By the time Tarzan, with his new minty-clean breath, and I left an hour later, I had regained my color and most of my composure.

Mr. Magoo was crooning, "Okay, love you, bye-bye. Ya'll come back now, ya hear? Don't be strangers. Whoopee kye you, kye yeh!" Somehow he reminded me of the way I behaved around Mom: always real talkative when she was about to leave.

With Tom Vice, Mary Mainster, and John Karger, salt-of-the-earth people, as my veterinarians, I often pondered why I didn't want to be one. I thought about the heartwarming, uplifting, and rewarding moments . . . but what about the hard times, the sad times, the blood? I knew I couldn't stand the suffering, the pain, the horrors, and without doubt could see myself getting more wrapped up in wanting to punish the people who had trapped, beaten, or hurt the animals. The less I knew, the better. Just as I had ignored the Vietnam war, I chose again to ignore the reality. I could help my own animals and find homes for as many strays as possible but that *had* to be enough because it was the best I could do. Helping, even on my small private level, I felt responsible and competent. That worked for me.

Fourteen

As memories of my former European life faded with time, I renewed my proud Texas status. The Lone Star State . . . my first home, the place where I really belonged. The place where I could sleep under big and bright stars, deep in the heart of Texas. Nowhere else are there so many land forms and climates: from wet southeastern woodlands to dry southwestern deserts, from the Trans-Pecos mountains in the western part of the state—part of the Rockies—to the waters of the Gulf of Mexico slapping its long, flat shoreline in the south.

In late August, I got a postcard from Mom in the Seychelles, another place I had to look up on the map. She was having a wonderful time, wishing we were there. Pete was in New Mexico, doing field research near Ruidoso, not due back for a week. I wanted to go somewhere, anywhere, to get away from the pounding summer heat in San Antonio. It was brutally hot and humid, which was not unusual but very tiring. The constant attack from mosquitoes, their incessant whine, their beastly buzzing, along with the feeling I was walking in peanut butter every time I hit the humidity, made me get on the phone and once again call my friend Sharon Dorn. I caught her as she was preparing to fly to the family retreat, Glendorn, in Pennsylvania. She told me she wouldn't come back until she'd heard that the first cold front had blown into San Antonio. She offered the dogs and me the family house in Port Aransas.

I joyfully loaded up the truck and drove 150 miles south, through Karnes City, Beeville, and Sinton, arriving in Aransas Pass two and a half hours later. The dogs, spread-eagled all over the seats, clocked the trip perfectly and woke up to the smell of salt water. I drove the last eleven miles across a hot, flat road sprinkled with sand from a hard, hellish wind, to get to the ferry. The bay was opaque green, a little blue, looking like leftover soup. A few bright white boats zipped across the water, leaving a bubbly wake behind them. It was quiet, the heat of the day, not much movement, and there were few other cars out and about. On popular weekends—4th of July, Labor Day, Memorial Day—the wait in the ferry line could be half an hour to an hour of cooking in the hot sun. But this trip, at 4:30 on an off-Monday afternoon, we had the ferry practically to ourselves.

The heat must have taken all the stuffing out of the dogs; they were remarkably controlled as an attendant pointed at me to park in the front right slot on the nine-car ferry. I rolled the windows down and cut the engine, Janie crossed my lap and perched out on the side-view mirror, watching three bottlenosed dolphins darting and leaping in front of the flat ferry, escorting us on the four-minute trip to the dock at Port Aransas. Dustin and Tarzan took up the passenger seat window and since Janie wasn't calling them up for duty, closed their eyes and held their noses high into the hot wind. Mischief collapsed into my lap, resting her cool nose in my hand. It was just too hot for her to get riled.

I drove through the old fishing village of expendable wooden shacks clustered around a few solid structures like the Coast Guard headquarters which sat on massive concrete legs. At one time, Port Aransas was called Tarpon, for the fish which were abundant before they all but vanished from gill netting, shrimp trawling, and hordes of people hanging them on gin poles for showy vacation photos. Theodore Roosevelt once fished for tarpon on Port Aransas. In the late seventies, the Gulf Coast Conservation Association had begun teaching people to release and limit their catch, but the town wouldn't be changing its name back anytime soon.

Turning on Avenue C, I followed Sharon's directions to the enormous wood structure sitting 100 yards back from the beach, looking big enough to be a hotel, not a one-family weekend beach house. It was painted pale lime green with white trim, and built on stilts for protection in hurricanes or times of high water. I parked under the sprawling house in the shade. The dogs took off in every direction. I guess they got a second wind, thinking of surprising napping cats or scaring small children. Ransacking the neighbor's yard, they rushed about madly. Luckily, the only things left of the neighbor's were plastic trash bags.

After surveying the eight bedrooms, I settled in one with twin beds and shell fabric on the curtains and bedspreads. Opening a few windows around the house, I wiped off the rust each time I touched a fixture, and I shuffled and crunched through a ubiquitous layer of sand on the camouflaged beige-and-tan linoleum floor. Along one of the three hallways, I examined a series of family photos. My favorite was a recent photo of the family all together, in Africa, with Dale, the father, Jean, the mother, and all four children, Tucker, Clayton, Sharon, and Johnny, AKA Caboose. I had grown up between Clayton and Sharon and remember envying their strong family bonds. But Dale and Jean were gone now, and the children married and living in other towns. They were still close, but the photo pinched my memory of how unattached I was. I looked out the window and saw Janie in the yard, on full alert, as if she had been parachuted into enemy territory. A good distraction, I went outside to spearhead the move to the beach.

From the back of the house, we walked on a long, warped, wooden ramp, stretching across rolling sand dunes and patches of sea oats to the beach, and turned right, heading south toward Mexico. The Gulf of Mexico is often thought of as a smallish backwater, when actually it is the ocean on a diminished scale, and often a Texan's first look at any sea. Milky and transparent cabbage-head jelly fish, shaped like big mushrooms, and scattered blue and pink balloon-like man-of-war, with their long, stinging tentacles floating on the water behind them, decorated the water's edge, along with plastic milk bottles, soda bottles, baseball caps, and Styrofoam cups. Splotches of melted tar from the occasional disastrous oil spill coated everything, including my bare feet and the dogs' paws. I won't say it was as bad as the sludge pit, but here again Dustin's beautiful fur was dealing with the not-so-romantic side of Texas' abundant natural resources. The dogs tested the water, certainly not liking the salty taste of it, much less the globs of tar which floated on the surface. Preparing for the weekend, I had stocked the trunk with two cans of WD-40, a noteworthy tip Sharon had given me for removal of tar from skin, carpet, hair, or fur. And the family's house if it got that far.

Back at the house, I put water in a the dogs' bowl and stuck it in the long kennel running under the house, and as they lapped up the fresh water, I closed the gate behind them.

"I've got to go to town for groceries, and it's too hot to leave you in the car," I told them.

They were appalled, staring at me as if I had delegated them to a life of misery.

"See ya," I said, hurrying to the car before they had worked out an escape.

At the Family Center, I bought food for a couple of days and stopped at a fresh fish market for shrimp. When I got back to the house thirty minutes later, the dogs were sitting in the same spots I had left them in, not a changed hair, and were surely surly. I let them out and, sulking, they stuck close to me, watching my every move, getting under my feet. There would be no further trickery or desertion.

The kitchen had every pot, pan, and gadget I could wish for in a *first* home, much less a weekend home. What with a Wolf stove, stainless steel counters and sink, and excellent soffit lighting, I wasn't sure I was as good a cook as it was a kitchen. After my dinner of shrimp and baked potato, salad and peach tea, I cheered up the dogs by giving them smoked milk bones, a designer treat I had bought in town. Turning on the outside lights, I led the dogs along the ramp to the beach at sunset. They darted around the sand dunes and galloped along the water's edge, in a good humor once again.

Sitting on a huge piece of driftwood, I watched the orange ball of fire sink into the water, so big and clear I thought I could see the edges burning, and I decided the world looked grand with nothing but beach, sea, and sky. The gleaming reflection reached to me from the horizon, across the water and wet sand, a nonstop trail where the tide had receded, stopping at my feet. When the sun disappeared, the dry air turned cool and we made our way back to the house as it got dark. Lights from the house shone in our eyes like searchlights, illuminating the dunes, making spooky shadows out of tall grasses and sea oats. My imagination ran a little wild as I thought I could see rattlesnakes and sand crabs all over the place on either side of the ramp. Safely back at the house, I cleaned off all our feet with an old towel and WD-40 and went upstairs to an outdoor porch. Sitting on built-in benches along the railing of the porch, we took in the clear night and bright stars. A warm wind picked up, rustling through the grasses, turning a shell mobile into a lovely one-piece orchestra, and a full moon rose on the perfectly flat horizon. I turned in pretty early, putting the dogs on their quilt in my bedroom, shuffling through a new layer of sand on the floor. Tarzan and Jane sneaked into the bed with me as soon as the light went out, and I slept fitfully, scratching at the sand and dreaming, with the help of the full moon, that we were being attacked by sand crabs.

In the morning, we went out early on a six-mile walk to the cutoff at Mustang Island Park. The dogs were having the time of their lives: Dustin in the water chasing mullet; Janie running up and down the shoreline barking at the waves like Canute; and Tarzan and Mischief chasing sandpipers and willetts. The salt water had a miraculous effect on the dogs' coats, softening them and healing their routine cuts and scrapes. By noon, as the sun started to take a death grip on the air, we returned to the house to siesta and stay out of the sun.

By late afternoon, the island lay breathless and heat-exhausted from the end of a long, sweltering season of the sun's unrelenting rays. The sky had faded to a pale powder blue and the water was thick, beige, and about 85 degrees. The dogs could hardly move after their busy morning, so I drove them to Channel View, a private marina, where they could relax on a little beach, chasing speedy sand crabs, swimming without waves crashing on them, and I could perch on a cement wall—a barrier for tides and wakes—facing the channel. Backing off each time a boat's wake crashed into the wall, I watched bottlenosed dolphins glide adroitly on their backs. The males were showing off cotton-candy pink bellies, squeaking and singing as they circled the females and slapped their tails in the water. It was mating time and they were flirting outrageously, but charmingly. The males seemed to be such gentlemen and so willing to make fools of themselves for a mate. Who could ask for anything more?

Near the shore, minnow and needlefish swam along, breaking the surface of the water with little plopping sounds, stupidly alerting bigger fish or birds. Tremendous, cumbersome brown pelicans, on the road back from extinction thanks to the banning of DDT by the Federal Government, and hard work and care by Texas Parks and Wildlife, flew gracefully some thirty feet above the water. Flapping and gliding unhurriedly along, these aerial clowns scouted mullet below. The mullet, in enormous schools, snapping their gaping mouths along the top of the water, were never aware of the pelicans until too late. The pelicans paused in midair, then stopped dead still for a brief moment before folding themselves up like director's chairs and plummeting into the water after their catch. As they smashed into the water headfirst, I could not believe these kamikaze pilots were not knocking themselves senseless. But they soon bobbed up, rattled their heads, then threw them back to swallow, their huge bills and gullets stretching like Spandex to accommodate the wriggling mullet.

At sunset, it turned into rush hour in the channel. Fishermen were returning from fishing for redfish or trout in the flats—the shallower water in the bays—and from offshore where they tried for kingfish and marlin. For an hour I inspected a constant parade of ships gliding through the seventy-three-foot channel: a huge tanker, the *Spyradon*, from Monrovia, loaded with crude oil and refined products, on its way to storage tanks in Corpus Christi; a Navy minesweeper returning to the base at Ingleside; barges; pilot boats; the orange-and-white boats of the Coast Guard; jetty boats; fishing boats—all passing so close I felt I could reach out and touch them.

I turned back from the marine activity to see Tarzan and Mischief playing down on the beach. It looked as if she was gnawing on Tarzan's neck, but I got the feeling something was not quite right. She looked kind of crooked. Sand was flying, but there was no noise, no growling, no barking. Counting my blessings that the dogs had been good so far, I walked over to them, hoping this wasn't going to be a problem, but as always, expecting just that.

"What are you two doing?" I leaned down. Mischief had a tooth stuck in Tar's collar and, during the struggle to get free, had twisted herself around so many times his collar was choking him. I tried simply to unravel them, but couldn't tell which way to go. I got that old panicky feeling as I realized I couldn't get a finger between the collar and Tar's throat. His bulging eyes were begging me to help him. Annoyed that she was stuck, Mischief sat down, exhausted. I stood helplessly, rifling through my mind for some obvious solution, when suddenly Tarzan went limp, and slumped to the sand.

In useless frustration, I popped Mischief on the head. Out of the corner of my eye, I saw a handsome young man walking towards us, observing us with a mixture of curiosity and interest. He reached into a front pocket of his khaki shorts, pulled out a shiny, red Swiss Army knife, and very intelligently cut Tarzan's collar off.

Tarzan lay there in a pitiful heap, barely moving. Angrily, I picked up Mischief and threw her into the swirling channel.

"What was that?" the handsome man asked.

"Shark bait," I replied in a gruff voice. Then I immediately became embarrassed by my action. Tarzan was up and making his way over to me, hacking and gargling. I picked him up and spoke gently to him, "Poor little man. She's a terror, beating up my little guy." He kissed my chin. Dustin and Janie came back from rolling in a dead fish on the beach, and circled us, inspecting the man. He stood calmly, waiting for their approval. They gave it by moving off.

I looked at this man who had just saved Tar's life. He was tall, with a sunburned face topped by an unruly thatch of fair hair the color of dried tobacco leaves. He looked to be about my age, and he was wearing a blue cotton shirt, faded to the color of bluebonnets dried by the sun, and frayed old khaki shorts. His very large and very brown eyes had a private and humorous twinkle in them, and crow's feet lined the fine skin at the corners. A short, hawk's-beak nose curved over a wide, massive jaw. I gathered from the tan line on his neck that he was a fisherman.

"Dick Negley," he nodded.

I stared at him absently. He smiled at me.

"My name is . . .." he tried to help me.

"Oh, of course," I mumbled. "Brooke Thompson." Was that my name? I was dumbstruck for the first time in my life. This was a lucky man. Everything, it seemed, had gone quiet except the shrill keening of the seagulls.

"Poor feller," Dick said, in a rich, deep voice, as he reached out to scratch Tar's ears. "Do your males always fight?"

"She's a female," I said, disgustedly, nodding my head towards Mischief who was out of the water, shaking off like nothing had happened.

"That's really unusual. What kind of dogs are these?"

"Jack Russell terriers."

"Well, I'm intrigued," he said.

Mischief came around in front of him, stood up, and planted her feet on his leg.

"Look, this dog wants to go home with you now," I said.

"Well, little missy, I'd have you in a minute," he said, "but my weimaraner would eat you up."

At that point, such a solution would have been fine by me. I was tired of Mischief being so unpredictable. Dick leaned down to pat her happy head.

"What else do they do?" he asked.

I started to tell him about their antics, but nervously began stumbling over my words, clearing my throat, spitting, and trotting in place. When, for some odd reason, Dick asked whether I was free to have dinner with him, my jaw dropped open, and I froze. In spite of a strangled dog and his would-be killer, two other dogs who smelled like fishmongers, and me, need I say more, the man had asked me to go somewhere. There was something wrong with him.

I must have said yes, or nodded, at least. But I don't remember it.

"Good!" he said, with a dazzling smile. "Then I'll meet you at the Tarpon Inn. Is eight o'clock all right? You know where it is?"

I think I heard myself say something intelligent like, "Gerabab," or was it, "Shleeclick."

In any case, he said, "Okay. Till eight." He turned back towards a grand yellow house on stilts and was gone.

Later, as I showered, I felt as though my ears had caught on fire, and after I dried off, I couldn't stop tripping over the dogs who were strewn throughout the house exhausted. I waited in pseudohysteria for five minutes of eight to roll around so I could race over and meet Dick at the Tarpon Inn.

We ordered catch of the day, red snapper, prepared in a light, lemon-dill sauce. He drank a vermouth called Lillet, with a twist of lemon. I drank club soda for fear of making a gigantic ass of myself if I had wine.

I thought he was so mature and solid and I felt small and goofy except, perhaps, when I was telling him more than he ever wanted to know about Jack Russell terriers. He watched me coolly as I babbled on like a Swiss mountain stream. I devoutly wished I could relax, but with him not interested in talking about himself, I was hellbent on taking up the slack.

Dick wore khaki pants, old beat-up topsiders, and a freshly ironed shirt. I wondered who had ironed the shirt for him. He wasn't a cowboy, he wasn't a veterinarian, but he had an aura about him, a mysterious quality. And he smelled good. I believed at that moment that curiosity was the first emotion leading to passion. My heart was thumping inside me and I could feel the future.

He never spoke a needless word and promised to call.

Back at the house, I let the dogs out into the clear, sea-riddled night. Because of them, I had met a very nice man. Mischief was forgiven. I fell asleep around 3 A.M. with all four dogs on the bed and the faint scent of Eau Sauvage on my unwashed hand.

Fifteen

In the morning, I wished for a phone call from Dick, or a drive-by sighting, but there was never a hint. I had told him I was leaving in the afternoon and not wanting to miss him if he did come by, I walked the dogs to the beach and watched the house like a spy while the dogs rushed around and jumped into the water, coming back and circling me, trying to get me to engage in the venture. By high noon, my hopes were dashed and I took the dogs for a long walk. They were asleep by the time I got on the ferry in the afternoon. Shoot. And I thought this was the start of something big.

On the way home, I wondered, would he ever call? He promised he would. I had no idea. I decided to write him a thank-you note for the dinner, then decided against it. He'd think I was after him. Maybe I'd call him back in San Antonio. He lived in San Antonio! I could surely find a way to bump into him there. Or call him to thank him for dinner. No. Too forward. I was from the old school, Mom's school, "Girls *never* call boys." Was that the very advice that was keeping me so pasteurized?

Back at home, I queerly became struck by intuitive homemaking impulses. I started by attempting to upgrade the dinner menus. As Pete and I ate fresh shrimp in a familiar, light lemon-dill sauce, steamed rice, and vegetables done in the wok, I told him about Dick. He remained silent, working so slowly at his dinner that I thought he was trying to get up the nerve to tell me he was going to have to make a run to Bill Miller's Bar-B-Q for a slab of ribs, dripping in thick, bloody sauce. A real dinner. Finally, he looked up from his plate with an oddly wicked grin and told me he had known Dick at the San Antonio Academy in the fifth and sixth grades.

"You did?" I asked.

I desperately wanted him to continue, but he didn't. I went to the kitchen and started preparing Bananas Foster, so curiously distracted that I almost blew up the place by pouring De Kuyper's banana liqueur into a high flame. I was growing up to be an Edwig!

Before Pete went to read his book, I stressed obsessively that he was to let me know if Dick called. Day or night. Sleet or snow. Anytime.

"He won't call you," he said, somewhat tauntingly. "Nobody would call you with all those smelly dogs." He was such a kidder. He added I should not get my hopes up, that Dick was a "catch," from a good family, a man of property and great wealth. He ended by telling me that I, especially I, a waitress, should not "hitch my wagon to a planet."

Well, there was the challenge. Eat my dust, Cinderella!

I waited by the phone day after day, dreaming of big ranches and four-wheel-drive, all-terrain vehicles, flying around in private airplanes, and best of all, acres and acres for the dogs to roam. And there was also the Mom factor. How proud would *she* be if I caught a Dick Negley in spite of my hair?

But one can stay by the phone, groveling, only so long. Thus, a week or so later, with my shattered ego in my back pocket, on a muggy, airless, steamy morning with showers predicted for the afternoon, I loaded the dogs in the truck to take them for a walk behind the cemetery at Fort Sam Houston. I needed to get out . . . to the sprawling fields and woods around Salado Creek. I stopped at Sharon Dorn's house to pick up her two dogs, Butterfly and Wolfgang, in return for the favor of letting us go to her ranch and the coast house. Sharon again was out of town. I could not fathom how I was going to cupid a romance for Pete and Sharon if she wouldn't stay home. And he sure wasn't making any of the right moves. I was convinced, of course, being an expert on other peoples' romances.

Butterfly was a gigantic, ladylike Great Pyrenees, her long, thick, white hair turning yellow around the edges from the sun. Wolfgang, a dachshund, was long and fat with minute bow legs, enormous protuberant eyes, and long flopping ears. Seeing me with two strange dogs, my four barked wildly, jumping all over in the truck bed, making the simple task of putting down the tailgate a dangerous one as they charged me, slobbering, kissing, howling. Butterfly and Wolfgang watched my village idiots from a distance, straining against their collars to return to the safety of their own territory. As I bravely eased open the tailgate, my dogs fell out in a pitiful heap, then turned to jump back in, not wishing to miss a trip, the first one turning, blocking the others from getting in, like they were playing last-one-in-is-a-rotten-egg.

"Load up," I instructed Wolfgang and Butterfly. They sat stone still, looking at a wall of gaping, panting mouths. "Get back, you useless mutts," I said, slapping gently at the faces of my brood as if they were the Marx brothers. Butterfly risked it and jumped in at the same time that I heaved little Wolf up, his small ratty tail tucked under him all the way up to his neck, the misery of his situation heralded clearly by his big, bulging brown eyes.

I turned up the music as we drove and sang at the top of my lungs . . . "You fill up my senses, like a night in the forest, like the mountains in springtime, like a walk in the rain . . .." The dogs listened through the little back window and shuddered, hoping this wasn't one of the long road trips. I passed Fort Sam Houston National Cemetery, parked the truck down a dirt road by the dump, and got out. When I came around to the tailgate, the dogs sat quivering like a suppressed volcano. When the gate opened they shot out and ran every which way. Unlike flocks of birds that appear to have one constant leader who keeps the rest in formation, my dogs had no idea who was in charge or where they were going. They only knew that each one wanted to get there first. It was like watching a bunch of kids play tag when they had forgotten to name someone "it." Janie finally headed off on a path and the others funneled behind her.

I started down the path, brushing off some of the dog hair from my upper body and legs as I went. Within moments, in the distance I heard the dogs yelping. Then it died away, then there was a pause, and they started to bark in chorus. Evenly spaced barks meant they had found something interesting, but I wasn't worried: on their own turf, the creatures around Fort Sam—squirrels, rabbits, whitetail deer—could outdo the dogs. And they would just give my bunch a bloodpumping run.

A jackrabbit the size of a lawnmower ran straight at me. I stopped, heartbeat and all, as he went around me and veered off towards the cemetery, running steady like he was on a flight plan. I heard the dogs coming my way, Janie whooping up a storm, hot on his trail. Within seconds all six sped by me.

"Janie, STOP! Tarzan! NO! Dustin, COME BACK HERE!" Who am I kidding, I thought. "Butterfly? Wolfgang?" They had joined the pack. I tried, "Clint Eastwood!" Just *once* I wished someone would come when I called. I ran after them, screaming like a bad parent with no authority, but they were far, far ahead. In horror, I watched the rabbit run right through the gate of the low, stone wall around the cemetery, the dogs tapering behind him. I had to go after them. Underneath an army green tent, about twenty people in mourning clothes watched a casket sink into the ground. When I heard a blast of gunshots, I ran faster. The guns fired a second time, I pulled up, then a third. "Oh, thank heavens," I said to the scenery, fifty feet from the site of the service, "it's a twenty-one-gun salute."

The reports didn't faze the jackrabbit which sped frantically away from the dogs near the burial scene, and raced over the hill towards the golf course. All six dogs spread out, heading right at the funeral. I could only stare in anguish at what we were doing to this ceremony.

One young, tall woman, standing ruler straight at the side of the coffin, a black veil hiding her features, reached out with black-gloved hands to accept the flag, folded into a triangle, from a soldier in dress greens. The dogs hit, tearing through so fast that the funeral party hardly had time to react. For a brief moment, it looked like bowling; a few people fell out of the setup, then went back in place, and I heard a few bursts of laughter. The young girl flicked a look my way and then looked back at the disappearing coffin. Could it be her husband? I wondered. Father? Brother?

The animals were gone, the exhibition over, and one lone man in red, white, and blue dress uniform played a crystal clear taps, slow, haunting. I bowed my head, finding my heart in my throat and my eyes involuntarily filled with tears as I stood there a respectful distance from the graveside.

Shortly after taps and a final silent pause, I looked up to see the young girl walking in my direction carrying her flag. I wanted to bolt, let the dogs fend for themselves, but I couldn't take my eyes off her approach. Her black spike heels hampered her progress across the ungroomed terrain and she picked herself up ever so slightly to walk gracefully on her toes. Lifting her free arm, she wiped tears from under the veil with a lacy, white handkerchief.

I had been holding my breath, knowing I was, yet again, in one of those awkward predicaments where I had to explain my doggy life and apologize sincerely.

But she said, "Thank you," raising the veil. Her large, clean blue eyes held mine. Her perfume smelled like sweet peas.

I deliberated for a moment, but caught in the cross fire of relief and sorrow, I could think of absolutely nothing to say.

"My father would have loved that," she reassured me.

"Really?" I said.

"My father loved dogs," she told me.

One by one, the dogs came back panting. She leaned down with them, patting each happy head as they gathered around her, and let them lick her face. She began to cry again, her tears no longer hidden by her veil.

Feeling some kind of gesture was called for, but not sure what it would be, I chose to stand speechless.

"Well, good-bye," she said, straightening.

Tears filled my eyes as I said, "I'm so sorry."

Continuing to cry, she put a hand on my arm, nodded a response, then turned and walked back to her father's grave.

In a moment, I stooped and said, "Well, boys, you did a good thing. It wasn't exactly what I asked you to do, but it turned out okay this time." All six wagged, unerring in the proper gesture. Sometimes I wished I had a tail instead of a mouth. The dogs fell in beside me as we walked in order into the woods at Salado Creek for water. It had rained three inches earlier in the week, turning the burned and dry land into dazzling landscapes of scarlet muskflowers, smelly and sticky when picked; Texas nightshade, little egg-white and yellow flowers shaped like columbine; leggy, orange flameflowers; and scarlet spiderling. They were bursting into bloom like it was spring. I stepped around a low-spreading, green leafy plant covering the terrain in matty clumps. It was called redbud. Its tiny, bright red buds bloom into pale yellow flowers, perfectly two-toned, appearing to be two different flowers growing out of the same plant.

Salado Creek ran clear and the dogs drank and cooled off. The entire area along the creek bed was trimmed as always like a Christmas tree, with trash from flash floods—the famous flash floods of Texas. You go to bed one night with the sky clear, and when you wake up in the morning you can find your car washed into another block. With each storm, more trash collects, strewn up to twenty feet high in the trees and impossible to clean up. I thought of the parks in Europe and the impeccable way they are kept, wondering why trash was not offensive in the States. I thought of New York, garbage on the streets, garbage strikes, and here, garbage everywhere. How sad, I thought, how sad. I turned back to the truck, contemplating how I would start by filling a plastic bag each time I came for a walk.

"All dogs on deck," I commanded, putting the tailgate down. They jumped up, but engrossed in the logistics of my trash crusade, I didn't pay close attention as to whether all six were in. As I drove off I felt the truck bump over something. Not recalling anything on the smooth dirt road like a piece of wood or a hole, I looked in my side mirror. My first thought was that I had run over the jackrabbit and I felt terrible. I was still moving when I saw, in my mirror, Mischief's little white body flop down in the dust, ten feet behind the truck. I had run over my own dog!

I put the truck in park and started to get out. Then I sat, frozen, thinking that if I didn't make the next move, the accident really hadn't happened. But I had to go to her. I got out of the truck, looked in the bed at the team, hoping I would see her little face amongst the others, but she wasn't there. The other five stared at me, questioning me, oblivious, were we going on another walk?

Tarzan, Jane, Dustin, Wolfgang, and Butterfly watched me, like an audience waiting for the curtain to go up. Caressing Dustin's soft muzzle, staring into his warm eyes, I began to feel the first explosive moment of tragedy. I held onto him as long as I could, then walked behind the truck.

Mischief lay on her side, convulsing, dying. I slumped to the ground, crossing my legs, and, trying not to cause her any more pain, drew her gently into my lap. I picked up her front feet, one in each hand, and looked at her little battered toenails. How peculiar that her strange gait caused the middle toenails to become exposed after scraping them on cement or rocks. How strange it never slowed her down. It popped involuntarily into my mind that Mischief was like Black Gold, the horse who broke his leg in a race, yet finished on three, only to be put down afterwards. He had heart. Like Mischief. How sweet were the excruciating sucking noises she always made as she cleaned her paws while lying down, licking the raw, bleeding ends endlessly. Her head rolled limply over my leg. I ran my hand along her side, touching her still, warm body. I remembered some of the battles she'd fought to prove how tough she was . . . and thought of her great love and pushy control of Tarzan. I begged her to stay, but I knew even my beloved Tom Vice couldn't do anything this time. Mischief—her little raw paws, her spirit, her independence. I looked around to see if the young girl was still at her father's graveside. I hoped not because I didn't want to upset her more. And yet I hoped so because I badly needed someone to help me.

I sat rocking Mischief until well after the life went out of her, then placed her on the seat beside me in the cab of the truck. The other dogs had no earthly idea what had happened, but they had picked up something in my behavior that stilled them. They rode quietly, without movement, in the back. I turned off the radio quickly so I wouldn't hear a song that would always remind me of this heartsick moment. I drove home with my hand resting gently on Mischief's lifeless body.

Sixteen

Pete was not home when we got there. I couldn't think if he was in town or not. I was in the grip of shock when I buried Mischief in the back yard. I couldn't believe I had lost one. My other three came one by one to sniff her little body then gathered somberly at the other side of the yard, very disturbed and insecure about my mood. I put rocks on the mound and planted some mint. Mischief had been only three years old.

Life was starting to play out like a Larry McMurtry book, moving along like a cattle drive, uncomplicated, obvious, set in basic happiness and picturesque surroundings, and then BANG! the real stuff, the tragedy, the sorrow inserted itself into the routine. I was realizing that life, after all, was not just one long ski slope, or meeting the next movie star, or moving to the next country. For quite some time I felt horribly responsible and guilty, and kept going over what I could have done to avoid that horrid moment when I ran over Mischief. It had happened so fast, in such an ordinary way, on such a normal day. It seemed to me that tragedy should have to be announced . . . by appointment only, even set up—like Pete in Vietnam. It wouldn't have been such a shock if Pete had been killed because it seemed inevitable. Compared to the multitudes of people who had to cope with every kind of tragedy and misery, my tragedy was nothing. But it was *mine*.

Pete was somber about it when he came home. Startled that I had done it and very sorry for me. One day, he put an unusual flint rock he had found in the oil fields on her grave. Watching Pete place the rock, I got the feeling he was not new to death. Would I ever understand his pain? I had my own pain now and didn't want to share anyone else's.

At twenty-four, I learned a new lesson. Life goes on. I had up till now never wanted life to stop, take part of it over, take part of it back. My grief remained around, close at hand, like an untradeable secret marble tucked away in a kid's pocket to bring out and show, or not. Sorrow hung around me like David Rook's old beautiful black cloak. I only felt better when I imagined Mischief up in doggy heaven with Dustin's brother, David. It was a time in my life when the one sadness seemed to call other sadnesses up. I hardly knew how lucky I was to have had so few.

Then one day Janie's behavior turned suspect to me and distracting to Tarzan. She began by rubbing up against the furniture and batting her eyelashes at Tarzan. He stared at her with his mouth open and a big question mark hanging over his head. As her blatant clues bounced off him, her next step was to slither shamelessly around the gentle-but-dim-witted-mate of her choice. He, in turn, shyly at first, not used to any sort of affection from her, did what any normal male would do. I was all for the union and recited an on-the-spot fabrication of the marriage vows. When I fell asleep that night, I dreamed of black-and-white puppies all over the place. Maybe as many as 101. And I dreamed of a light at the end of my sad tunnel.

Right about the time Janie's tummy rounded out, giving her the shape of a football, Dick Negley called! I knew the minute I picked up the phone it was he, even though there was a moment's silence as he possibly reconsidered.

Months had gone by since I had met him. Jeez . . . what took him so long? I had damned near washed that man right out of my hair. There was no excuse, no apology, no mention of my, I thought "perky," thank-you note. I had never got up the nerve to make a play for him like a sleazy girl would do. Those girls were probably happily married now. HA! I showed them. Dick was real short of being demonstrative on the phone which made me consider that I'd done so much growing up in these last months that maybe I was too mature for him now. But I was intrigued that he was calling. Dear God, he had an invitation! The invitation was to bring Mom and Pete, and the dogs, of course, to his mother's ranch, Swanlake, outside Tivoli, Texas, the first weekend in December. Somewhat out of sync, I told him about Mischief and that prompted a second silence on his end, which made me question in my mind if I should tell him who I was talking about or if he was profoundly sad about Mischief.

Back on track, I accepted for me and Pete, knowing I could bully him into going, but told Dick I would have to check with Mom and I'd let him know. I played it cool talking to him, and asked for his phone number like it wasn't highlighted with a heart in my phone book. Now it was my turn to call him. I promised I would.

In near hysteria, I phoned Mom as soon as I hung up with Dick, and she chose to go with us, even though it meant missing a nice, high-powered weekend in Washington, missing the Kennedy Center Honors Program, and a chance to rap with President Ford. La di da, I told her. She had already met him anyway. She merrily claimed she wanted to see if the Texas Tivoli looked anything like the charming town in Italy. Not believing she was that naive, but wanting to take her to impress Dick Negley, I flat-out lied and told her it probably did, but we'd just have to go there to find out if it was true. I was thrilled the whole family was going. I could hide behind them.

I waited three days to call Dick. "Oh, yeah, Dick?" I said, suavely. His silence made him suaver. Did he remember me? Talking to Dick made me think having all four of my wisdom teeth out at the same time would be a cinch. The appointment was made. Till December, I told him, happy knowing I wouldn't be waiting by the phone anymore. I was *on* to Dick Negley.

Mom blew in on a blue norther the day before we were to leave for Swanlake. She rehung all the pictures in our apartment, gave Janie a bubble bath, and told me how sorry she was about Mischief. She had brought a rock from Marrakesh to put on her grave, which surprised me as I didn't think she was listening when I told her about my rock ritual. Each time I walked the three dogs, I picked up any rock that caught my eye and placed it on Mischief's grave. It was quite a beautiful plot now, with rocks and native grasses and flowers. Mischief would have been proud.

Pete drove his Mustang, I navigated. Mom chose the back seat, tucked in cashmere shawls, propped up against fat, satin pillows leaning against a locked door, with the three dogs curled around her feet. We pulled into a rusty, two-pump gas station in Tivoli at four o'clock on a gray, soggy and cold Friday, after a three-hour drive southeast from San Antonio. Mom was quickly disillusioned when the filthy attendant in a filthier blue-gray jumpsuit called the town "Tie-VOLL-ah." His cheek was crammed solid with chewing tobacco, some escaping in a thick juice trickling down his chin and oozing onto his brown-stained collar.

Hoping to get ahead of Mom, I said, "And to think you could have been with President Ford."

She said nothing.

The man cleaned grasshoppers and black horseflies off the windshield, leaving trails of bug juice or something that he had excreted. Tarzan and Jane, sitting together like they were on a double date, monitored his moves silently.

"Did he give you the willies?" I asked Pete as we pulled out.

"No more than you do," Pete answered, with an evil grin.

"He had a lovely smile," Mom said.

He had a lovely smile? Brown and juicy . . . yuk. I decided she had not even looked up from the *New Yorker.* Thank heavens. Glowering at the dreary day we were driving through and watching the roadside, I saw a scarlet muskflower and was surprised anything would bloom in this weather.

"Whoa, what's that one?" I spoke up. "Pete, stop, I've never seen that purple one. It's not a thistle."

"Kid, no one cares what their names are," he said, not braking.

"Stop! I want to see that one close up. Please . . ."

Pete sped up. "You'll never know and I won't have to hear a lecture on the wildflowers of Little Italy."

"Mom! Make him stop!"

"Now, dears, let's be civil," Mom said, snapping open the *New York Times.* "Are we there yet?"

"That's what annoying children say," Pete said.

"Look, an oil rig!" I attempted.

"Nice try. What did you think, I fell off a lemon truck?"

"It's a watermelon truck, or even a turnip truck, you ninny. You're the lemon. I hate him Mom, why did you have to have two children?"

"Well, Brookie, he's your *older* brother, which means you wouldn't be here if I had only had one child," Mom said. Pete smiled smugly at me.

"Look, here's the turn off." He slowed the car and turned off the road, throwing my handwritten directions on the dashboard. As the car *brrrumped* across the cattleguard, the dogs woke up, stretched, and yawned. "Ten more miles on this road and we're there," Pete declared.

We rode in silence, absorbing the scenery. Along one side of the unpaved road, cypresses grew on the Guadalupe River in assorted sizes and shapes, some as tall as fifty feet, making it look like the Manhattan skyline. On the other side was a vast, wet flatland. The fields were spread out like a chessboard, some only the size of a small room, bounded by wide, shallow, muddy canals of brackish water. The canals, or *resacas* as they are known in Texas, were fringed with canebrakes and clumps of tall, skinny green reeds. Red-winged blackbirds clutched the reeds and swayed gracefully in the wind.

"It isn't very pretty, is it?" Mom said.

"It sure isn't a very pretty day," Pete replied.

"Wow, there's a lot of stuff I've never seen before out there," I said.

"This looks like Vietnam," Pete said. "See this road we're on?

It's made of shells and raised to keep us out of the water. Looks like rice paddies out there," Pete swept a hand in front of me.

"Really?" was what I could come up with. Mom and I, both astounded to hear Pete mention anything about Vietnam, were at a loss as to what to say. I had a good feeling that memories of Vietnam were starting to fade for Pete. I could hope for it, anyway.

"Looks like the set of *Run Wild, Run Free* to me," I said.

The forecast was about the same, the dormant grasses, the lack of color. The wind moved a veil of wet clouds across tabletop-flat terrain, which was the only difference. In my mind I clearly recalled the rolling hills of the moors. My memories were undoubtedly kinder than Pete's.

"Oh, my god, you're right," Mom said, sitting up to take a good look. "It's too depressing for words," she added, lying back down across the seat with piles of newspapers, magazines, and dogs. I could tell she wished she were in Washington.

Pete said, "Friends tell me this is the best duck-and-goose hunting ranch in South Texas."

Mom started to whine, "I don't think Dick's very nice, asking us to this place. Pete, are you sure you followed the directions?"

"Want to let her out?" Pete whispered to me.

"I heard that," Mom snapped. "Fine, let me out."

"Well, we're just not gonna do that, Mommy dearest," Pete said. I did not appreciate the "we" part of it. He continued, "We hear alligators eat people in this part of the country."

"We do?" I was none too thrilled to hear that information.

"Oh, shut up," Mom growled.

"Let's take her back to the gas station and leave her with that cutie and his nice smile," I giggled. Mom hit me in the back of the head with a copy of the *New Yorker.*

"Ow," I objected.

"Dick Negley had better be awfully attractive to have a place in this nasty part of the world," she said. "And to think I could have been at the White House."

"Here comes the broken record," Pete mumbled.

"I can't believe you thought it was going to look like Italy," I dared to add.

"Well, who knows? Sometimes little towns can be quite charming. I hate to think what Refugio looks like, or however you pronounce it!" (Mom pronounced it Rae-foo-heo—understandably she would not have guessed the correct, Ruh-fury-o.) Mom's red, black, blue, and white silk scarf had slipped off her head and was circling her neck like a John Wayne bandanna. She threw a hand out in frustration.

"Ducks!" I yelled. Pete lurched forward over the steering wheel.

"Why?" Pete said, looking fearfully back at Mom.

"No, you dufus. Look! The whole sky is filled with ducks," I said, pointing at the blackening sky.

Low rain clouds scudded past like big ships sailing out of the harbor and millions of fast-moving ducks wove in and out, swooping, gliding, landing in different pools or strips of water, skimming along the top until they came to a stop like jets on an aircraft carrier.

Dustin, since the afternoon with Ernie Willie and the doves, had shown a great interest in retrieving. If ever I said "birdies" to him, he would look up in the sky or the trees. He sat up in the back seat, his attention riveted to the activity outside, so many birds he hardly had to turn his head to see them. Tarzan jumped up front and crawled onto my lap, looking out of my closed window. Janie popped over from the back and started jumping on Pete, hoping he would catch on and open the window so she could get out and stand on the side mirror. But he didn't cooperate. Ten miles on, we came to a wrought-iron gate. Pete stopped the car. A wood plaque with "Swanlake" burned in block writing flapped in the wind.

"Get the gate, Mom," Pete said. "Watch for water moccasins."

"Both of you are making me crazy." She popped me again with the magazine.

"Why don't you ever hit Pete?" I protested.

"I can't reach him," she replied, gaily.

"I'm opening the windows," Pete snarled. "Your dogs' yucky breath could gag a hippo."

"Don't be ugly about my boys," I said, hopping out of the car. I unhooked the chain and spread the gate open, bowing gracefully as Pete drove through. The shell road was the only dry spot. The land was mud and water, stagnant and noisome, smelling like mold and stinkbugs. I felt light, fluttery bumps all over my exposed face and neck, like pieces of confetti bombarding me from all sides. Glancing up into the solid gray background, I saw a cloud of black bugs hovering over my head and started feeling the first stinging mosquito bites as I pushed the gate closed and dashed back to what I thought was the safety of the car.

"Jesus H. Christ!" Mom swore, swatting and bashing at hordes of insects that swarmed in through the open door. "What's going on here? Who opened the windows?"

"Put 'em up!" Pete yelled.

"Don't say that!" I screamed, wildly. "Put 'em up" was a cue that alerted the dogs—a dead giveaway. Immediately they lunged forward and sat with their noses pressed against the windows, searching for their quarry.

Several hundred buzzing bugs were caught in my hair and as I slapped at them, I could feel the bites on my scalp.

"There are millions of them!" Pete cried out, squirming and slapping at himself, jetting the car forward, apparently hoping to leave them behind.

"Take me to the nearest airport! I can't bear this!" Mom wailed.

I smacked hard at my arm and killed three enormous, blood-riddled bugs. The dogs thought I was mad at them and slouched down in their seats, looking like weak-minded children.

Pete kept the car fishtailing along the shell road until we came to a pale green wood house sitting on a man-made rise. A white fence surrounded the boundless grounds and dead brown winter grass. Pete steered through the last gate—fortunately already open—sped up the hill, and killed the engine in front of a screen door.

"I'm not about to get out," Mom shouted.

"Christ, we can't just sit in the car, we'll get eaten alive in here!" Pete argued. Mom and I kept batting and slapping.

My neck had a dozen welts and I made like a contortionist trying to get at the thirty-odd bites on my back.

"We *have* to get out," I said. "Dick will think we're weird if we wait for him to meet us like he's a doorman."

"I don't care," Mom sniveled.

"Okay," Pete said, "here's the plan. On three, we all get out and rush to the door."

The dogs stared at our hands on the door handles, preparing for the charge.

"Three!" Pete roared, and opened his door. Janie let out a nightsplitting woof, and, in spite of her extra weight, propelled off his lap and hit the road. Dustin and Tarzan, jumping from the back to the only open door, trampled Mom, scattering her newspapers and magazines, her pillows and blankets. They were off like thoroughbreds out of a starting gate and racing to the four winds.

"Ayyyy . . . Let me out of here!" Mom cried. Desperate, she shoved open her door and fell out of the car, still trying to hold onto her possessions. She lay there on the ground, disgusted, in a full-blown rage.

Having hoped my family would give Dick a first impression of class and style, I was none too happy about arriving like the Flying Wallendas. I sat in the car, annoyed even with the dogs, and watched as the screen door swung open at that adverse moment and Dick, who didn't appear to be in any hurry, came out to greet us. Looking like an ad for Abercrombie and Fitch, he wore a black turtleneck, a light brown sweater with leather patches at the elbows, thick caramel-colored corduroys, and heavy, muddy leather boots. He carried a steaming mug in one hand and held the other out to help Mom up off the ground.

"Welcome to Swanlake," he said, smoothly. "I'm Dick Negley."

At this point, I expected Mom to bite his head off, so I closed my eyes and dropped my head in misery. But I looked up to see Mom rising with Dick's help like a debutante and her escort, smiling at him, saying "Why . . . thank you."

"Hi, Pete, it's been a while," Dick said, watching him hop around like a kangaroo on a Pogo stick. "We need to get in the house before the mosquitoes get us."

He peered into the car. "Where are the dogs?" he asked, as he began ushering Mom and Pete calmly into the house. Nobody answered him and the door slammed behind them.

"Hello?" I said.

The mosquitoes were eating me alive while I got out of the car, slammed the door, and in an angry move for having been abandoned, almost ripped the screen door off its hinges.

I burst into the house, crashing into Pete, Mom, and Dick, who had stopped in the "mud room," which was no bigger than the trunk of a Cadillac Seville. Somehow, the dogs rushed in right behind me to join in the fun, and started leaping about, crashing into us, yelping excitedly. Ten chubby pairs of army-green rubber waders hung by their suspenders on the wall. We were packed in like subway commuters in New York at rush hour.

"There you are!" Mom announced merrily. "What in the world were you waiting for?"

"Maybe for Pete to say one and two!" I snapped.

Dick surveyed me as though he found me only marginally interesting and explained to us like a tourist guide, "You need to cover yourself in Off! whenever you go out the door." He pointed to a row of a dozen cans, blue white, and orange, on a bench near the door. So much for thinking my Charlie perfume would have an effect.

"Let's go have a drink," Dick said as he picked up Janie, who had found her way through the crowd to greet him.

"What should I do with the dogs?" I asked Dick.

"We'll get them some water and they'll be fine here in the mud room for the night," he said. Just when I thought he was going to take Janie with him, he put her down, turning to open a second door.

Oh, the shock of it! Those dogs were used to sleeping on my warm bed. I would have to check out the sleeping arrangements and sneak them in later.

"Okay, boys, you can handle this. I'll come get you later." I patted their heads. "Don't eat the waders." They looked at me like I had committed them to a mental institution.

I followed the humans and we entered a perfectly neat and orderly hunting-camp living room. The fire crackled and threw a light on sturdy wood furniture, couches, and wide armchairs all covered in a duck-printed fabric. Two small stuffed ducks, one green-winged teal and one blue-winged teal, were standing on pieces of wood perched on the mantel. Over it hung a beautiful black-and-white stuffed snow goose in flight. Prints of ducks and geese flying in different multicolored skyscapes with no fewer than two hunters in each scene, either shooting the birds or crouching down waiting for them to come into range (a collection, I guessed) hung on the dark wood paneling. My eye fell on a dry, white jawbone with sharp teeth, resting on the coffee table.

"Alligator," Dick said, following my stare.

"That's one big mother of an alligator," Pete said.

"He was ten feet long and shot right out back here when our foreman was cleaning ducks one day. That gator came out of the river and scared Joe Ray right out of his waders." Dick appeared to be tickled by the story, as he smiled wickedly.

"He was in the river outside this house?" I asked.

"That's the Guadalupe. They come bigger than this one in that river. We might see one tomorrow."

"How lovely," Mom fibbed, as Dick poured her a glass of Blue Nun. Being charming, she acted like it was a wine she craved. "Dinner smells wonderful. What are we having?" she asked.

Dick introduced the cook, Lalo, a big-headed, short-bodied Mexican man, ruddy-skinned, deep black pools for eyes, and a smile to light up the night. His teeth were so white I thought he had found a way to bleach them in Clorox. Shiny black hair topped him off, so thick it was hard to believe he could get a comb through it.

Dick spoke to Lalo in Spanish, telling him we were ready, and seated us, pulling Mom's chair out. I was glad he had nice manners. For Mom. I seated myself.

Over duck breast stuffed with jalapeño peppers and wrapped in bacon, wild rice, green salad with a buttermilk dressing, and cornbread, Mom fell under Dick's spell. I could hear the admonition I'd get later, "You should try to do more with your hair, and put on some makeup. He's very attractive. Boys like that don't grow on trees."

"I'll show you your rooms," Dick announced as he rose from the table. "We go to bed early around here and get up earlier."

"What time is early?" Mom asked, as Dick pulled her chair out, and I struggled to push mine.

"To see the real beauty of the place, as a Texas hunting buddy of mine says, 0-dark-thirty."

"Which is . . .?" Mom smiled charmingly.

"4:30," Dick replied.

Mom paused skillfully, then lied blatantly, "Well, that's just fine." She was so cheery I figured she planned to escape during the night.

Lalo had brought our bags in from the car and put them in the hallway. With no further ado, Dick bade us good night and went to his room. When he turned, I smiled and waved at him from my doorway. He looked a little confused, giving me no response before he ducked into his room.

Since the dogs were quiet, I didn't try to sneak them in with me. It was so drearily cold, I went to bed in my jeans, T-shirt, and socks, not wanting to lose any heat by changing. I slept in an iron bed with rain rattling on the windows, the vision of millions of mosquitoes clinging to the screens and screaming for blood, alligators lurking in the river, and the tortured faces of my poor dogs stuck in the mud room. But the scariest vision was of my mother and the look of frustration on her face as she closed the door to her room next to me, saying goodnight. Moments later, it sounded like she was beating the rugs, but I knew she was massacring masochistic mosquitoes. I clearly heard the words "Ritz Carlton" more than once.

Seventeen

At 4:30 A.M. it sounded like a helicopter landed on the lawn, and the dogs broke into hysterical barking. I jumped out of bed, grabbed my robe, and rushed down the hall. Opening the inside door, with the light from the living room behind me, I saw a man standing in the mud room, stiff as a guardsman, in big, floppy waders, a camouflage jacket, and a red-and-black Massey-Ferguson baseball cap. He was surrounded by my dogs who were growling at him, waiting for my command to rip him to shreds.

"What the hell's going on here?" Dick said, coming up behind me. He wore the same clothes from the night before and I thought he must have slept in his, also. He was holding a copy of *Shooter's Bible* in one hand and a mug of coffee in the other.

"Oh, Joe Ray! Come on in and get some coffee. Brooke, this is Joe Ray Custer, our foreman." That was the first time I can remember Dick uttering my name.

"My pleasure, Joe Ray. Brooke Thompson," I said, shaking his dry, cracked hand. "Sorry about the dogs." The dogs were sorrier. They weren't allowed to kill him, so they eased off.

"Ma'am," he said, removing his cap and twirling it in his hand as if it were an important occupation. He made a pitiful noise and walked a step forward as I screamed like a banshee at the dogs who were blocking his path. He nodded thankfully, squinting through a pair of glasses so thick it looked like his eyeballs were encased in the lenses. He chewed Juicy Fruit, which I somehow smelled even though he was pickled in Off!. He squeezed his rubbery body by me and followed Dick into the house.

155

"Relax, you dingdongs," I ordered. Then touching each dog's muzzle, I let them out. It had stopped raining and they rushed into the dark cold air. I took a step outside, where it was heavy and smelled like wet towels steeped in sulfur. Within seconds, mosquitoes covered my body. I jumped back in, deserting the dogs, but it wasn't like they would come if I called. I closed the door and joined the men in the living room by a snappy fire. Lalo, wide-awake and smiling, placed coffee, tea, fresh juice, and sweet rolls on a thick, round W. R. Dallas dining table with a lazy Susan built in the middle. I got a cup of tea and ruby-red grapefruit juice for starters. Lalo came back carrying a platter piled high with scrambled eggs, bacon, and sausage, reminding me of the early morning breakfast in Devon, and Charlotte, the chambermaid. The smell of bacon on the cold morning was enough to have me overeating right away, but Lalo had fried the English muffins in the bacon grease and they were so crispy and delicious I ate three of them piled high with cream cheese and cactus jelly. Thank heavens Dick read through breakfast, unaware that I was packing away a cattleman's share. On that meal alone, I could have hibernated through the winter.

Unlike me, Mom had already impressed Dick, and she chose to sleep in. Pete, sleepy-headed, with hair sticking out like a madman's and early morning, puffy eyes, grunted his introduction to Joe Ray, then ate breakfast and drank hot coffee silently.

I hurried to change into a brown turtleneck, cable-knit sweater, jeans, and thick socks. When I came out, Pete stood and stretched, flapping his arms like he was trying to wind himself up and told us he was going to change and be out in a minute. I could hear Joe Ray outside talking to the dogs. Dick was in the mud room and motioned for me to try on waders he held out. Size 8 fit, rubber feet and legs, all the way up to my chest, and held up by stretchy suspenders. The thought pinched me hard of David and the day on the moors and I was mentally transported to that day. But I came back to see Dick in his waders, handing me an oilcloth, flannel-lined rain jacket. With all the layers on, I felt like a child on a cold day, stuffed forever in a ski outfit—with no way to go to the bathroom. I watched Dick take a can of Off!, spray his rubber-clad body, his neck and ears, and finally, close his eyes and spray the Off! straight into his face. I followed his lead and thought I'd killed myself.

Pete entered the mud room and said, "I'm glad to see you two believe in safe sex." He laughed and slapped Dick on the back, then leaned over to squeegee himself into his waders.

I could hear my jaw pop in my ears as my mouth dropped open.

Dick seemed to have no idea whether to laugh or not.

Suddenly a noise cut sharply into the muggy dark morning, making it impossible to talk—a major distraction. It sounded like a tractor. We bumped and waddled our way outside like Willy Wonka's Oompa Loompas. Joe Ray had driven around and directed us the short distance to a stepladder at the back of an ungainly and odd-looking machine with a cab on top. Pete and I climbed as best we could to our seats as I envisioned kicking him in the head for his slightly embarrassing remark. Dick and Joe Ray threw Tarzan and Dustin up to us one at a time, then Dick climbed up with fat Janie, placing her on the bench next to him. Joe Ray wriggled to the front and climbed up to and settled in what looked like a tractor seat.

"What is this?" I yelled to Dick.

"A marsh buggy," he yelled back.

Joe Ray flipped on the lights and put it in gear. An exhaust pipe on the side had a flap that bounced open each time Joe Ray changed gears, spurting out little puffs of black smoke. I imagined we looked like a science-fiction movie, rattling along breaking the sound barrier, headlights illuminating the misty marsh. We were escorted, at first, by a cloud of mosquitoes, but they were left behind as we clipped along the shell road at twenty miles per hour. However, when Joe Ray slowed down to turn onto a mud flat, we attracted a new swarm. Thankfully, Dick was right about the Off!. The mosquitoes swirled around us, but none landed.

We puttered across the marsh as the sun came up behind thick layers of cloud, illuminating a blue sky above, but leaving us in a gray, dismal light. Riding along in this odd machine as though we were on some secret mission, I glanced at Pete, curious if this reminded him of Vietnam. If I had ever had to describe what I imagined Vietnam looked like, it would have been Swanlake.

Joe Ray drove off the shell road onto grassland where the buggy left a trampled track of grass, mud, and water as we darted and maneuvered around pools and tanks, putting up an astounding number of ducks who took off and flew away quickly, quacking back and forth, their wings swishing and flapping.

Dustin sat perked up on the bench seat, ears up, ready for whatever life offered him. Janie had moved into Dick's lap, witnessing the activity with great enthusiasm. Tarzan cuddled in my lap shivering, finally nuzzling his way into my warm jacket. A lover, not a fighter. The machine's noise, which splintered the air, prevented any conversation. I leaned over the side and watched the tires make three-dimensional grooves in the thick gray, salty-smelling mud under the enormous tires as we slopped across shallow pools and mud flats. The water level of the pools and bays was consistent with the land levels.

"Watch this," Dick said, motioning in case we didn't hear. Joe Ray slowed, downshifted, and stopped at the edge of a large body of water. The machine bucked a little, then tilted straight in. Not having any idea how deep it was and feeling we were going to sink like a stone, I stood up. The buggy settled like a buoy, floating, then moved slowly along as the tires churned and paddled to the next strip of land. It was like traveling in an amphibious Tonka toy.

"This thing is amazing," Pete bellowed, discovering it was quieter moving on water, and he could be heard.

"It's made by Rolligon. Joe Ray found it," Dick shouted. "He looks after 3,000 acres and 300 head of cattle. It's made his job getting to the cattle feeders a lot easier."

"The tires are incredible," Pete said, looking over the side.

"There's two and a half pounds of pressure per square inch. That's why we float," Dick told us.

"I'd hate to get squished under one of them," I said at the top of my lungs.

"It wouldn't hurt," Dick said.

"You've got to be kidding."

"It wouldn't even hurt the dogs if we ran over them. It's bottomless mud," Dick explained, "but thick, so you don't sink."

"Let's throw Tarzan under and see," Pete teased, always the agitator.

"No," Dick said, adding, "I was thinking of using him as a goose decoy."

"A goose decoy?" I yelped.

"That's right," Dick said, talking to Tarzan, who left my jacket and stretched over to Dick. "We'll just tie you out here by one of the blinds and the geese will fly in to you." Holding him up, he added, "He's the same size as a decoy, and he's white."

Tarzan did not like being held up so high. I reached for him, not knowing Dick well enough to know if he was kidding or not, and said, "It isn't going to happen."

"Well, we're getting tired of using diapers."

"You use diapers as goose decoys?" I asked. Dick nodded.

As the sun rose above the clouds, the sky streaked gold and yellow and it turned into a beautiful, sharp clear day. Joe Ray crossed the water and stopped on land, cutting the engine. The silence was excruciating. We looked across San Antonio Bay. Shallow bays and inlets stretched for miles around us with hundreds of horizontal acres under the sky. Salt water from the Gulf of Mexico mingled with fresh water from the Guadalupe River, the bays consisting of both, depending on the wind and tide. The only break in the horizon came from towering cypresses growing along the Guadalupe. Their long, downwind branches reached inland as if they were streamers blown in the wind; their Gulf-side branches, burned by salty spray and stunted, were sculpted into strange and dramatic forms.

Squinting into the sunlight, I was flabbergasted to see big, gawky exotic pink birds flying in a flock.

"Are those flamingos?" I asked.

"Roseate spoonbills," Joe Ray said, then spat. A man of few words.

"They're so pink!" I exclaimed.

"Those uns 'r' eatin' more shrimp." Spit.

"Let's put the dogs down and see what they stir up," Dick said.

We disembarked with a lubbery kind of grace and helped each dog down, except Janie, who jumped the seven feet to the soft mud, made a soft landing, and tore off like a potbellied pig smelling an Oreo cookie. Pregnancy was not an inconvenience to her.

"What about alligators?" I asked.

"The dogs won't hurt them," Dick replied. Being around Pete maybe gave him the idea of being a standup comic. He caught my glare and finished by saying, "They're not out here on the flats, just back in the river." He started laughing in the direction of Joe Ray.

"That's right," Pete said to Joe Ray. "You almost got eaten by one, didn't you?"

Joe Ray nodded. "They're endangered now," he said, quietly. "You don't see 'em much any more." He passed his hand over his brow, as though even now he could hardly bear to recall the encounter.

As the sun came up full and pudgy with energy, a bland wind blew across the marsh, not strong enough to blow the mosquitoes away but enough to keep them at bay. I hardly noticed them as we spent the morning checking feeders and blinds, and several wood bridges, built for the Rolligon to get to islands farther across the water. Dick, speaking to me at last, taught me to identify canvasbacks, redheads, cinnamon teal, buffleheads, and mottled ducks. Big, fat tan-and-black Canada geese and black-and-white snow geese, huge compared to the ducks, honked and flapped and shook their feathers. This was a bird paradise, a bird watcher's haven.

We sat in the sun on board benches in a roofless wood blind, camouflaged by dead fan palms and local grasses, and watched the dogs run around, noses to the ground, packed in mud like some nifty beauty treatment. A pair of snow geese spiraled down from high above, decoying toward Tarzan's similar white body and black trim, just like Dick said, landing ten feet from him. Tar was half their size and screamed when he saw them, then tore into brave barks, bringing Janie and Dustin to the sound of the hunt. Startled, honking fiercely, these geese jumped up with wings flush to their bodies for initial lift off, snapped open four feet of wing span like a flamenco dancer's fan, and with strong, swooping flushes began their ascent. The dogs ran around wildly underneath, Tarzan barking "Come back here!" now that he had back-up.

At 11:30, we waddled back into the house where Mom was waiting with a smile. Pete and I were immediately suspicious. She must have made some long-distance phone calls to New York and Europe, grasping for glamour.

"It's beautiful here, you're right," she said to Dick.

"Glad you like it," he replied, extracting himself from his waders. "We'll clean up and eat lunch at about 12:30, if that suits you."

"That would be lovely," Mom said. "You all look so cute in your waders."

Yep. She had probably reached Suzy Knickerbocker.

After a lunch of fresh flounder that Joe Ray caught in the bay the night before, baked potatoes covered in guacamole and cheese, salad, and strawberry cheesecake, this time we waddled for a different reason. I went out to check on the dogs. They were conked out in the sun and never heard me. I left them and went to my room, as the others had, to have a nap and let the food settle.

As I lay in my bed, running my hand along the creases in the wood wall, I thought about what an odd creature Dick was; so distant, so private, so mysterious. I was not getting any signal of any kind from him, but I did feel that he was judging me somehow. I fell asleep thinking he was quite an enigma, and more exasperating than anything I'd ever encountered. He seemed a challenge. I hadn't really thought through how much I liked him, I was just sure I wanted *him* to like me.

At 3:30, Joe Ray reappeared noisily in the Rolligon, chewing his Juicy Fruit. I watched him out the window as he jumped down from his seat and walked unselfconsciously to the house. Without the waders, I could see his wish-boned legs and a large, silver belt buckle, an engraved trophy. He had been a champion rodeo rider. I envisioned him high up in the air, clinging to the back of a snorting, bucking, insane Brahma bull, more comfortable in that scenario than in the presence of humans.

The sun was shimmering like a watercolor in the haze when we embarked on the buggy and went to fish in the canal. Mom came this time, decked out in the local rubbery fashion of waders, accessorized with the Hermes silk scarf, green, white, and brown—a bit, bridle, and saddle motif—tied sassily at her throat. And her trademark Tiffany gold-loop earrings.

Marsh hawks patrolled low on long wings over the grass flats and we disturbed killdeer, who took to flight, their plaintive and insistent cry making me feel we were to make sure we felt bad for them.

We took off our jackets and sat in the warm afternoon sun on one of the wood bridges we had checked in the morning. Ugly, two-foot-long silvery fish called alligator gar, with long thin snouts, swirled around in the muddy water, breaking the surface and flapping their tails in fright. With no idea where they would come up next, Pete shot at them with a .22 rifle, as if it was a carnival game. It caused total pandemonium with the dogs.

Mom pointed down the canal and asked, "What's that animal?"

"Uh, oh," Joe Ray muttered. "Trouble."

"What is it?" I asked. We all got up to look at the beast along the canal.

Dick picked up his rifle and loaded it. "It's a coypu," he said. "He'll hurt your dogs."

Mom said, "It looks like a beaver."

Before the dogs reacted, I grabbed Dustin's collar, Pete picked up Janie, and Tarzan chose Mom to escort him as we walked down to inspect the creature, who was not at all afraid of us. He stood upright on the bank, and I thought he was a beaver, with little paws like one. He had long, dark chocolate-brown, coarse fur and a hairless rat tail. The most startling feature was bright orange, chisel-like teeth, long and thick, curved like Chinese fingernails.

"They're rodents from Brazil." Dick kept an eye on him and spoke to us.

The dogs were tired but interested, and sniffed at him, arching their backs and straining at their collars.

"Those teeth are really nasty," I said.

"And destructive," Dick went on. He went slowly up to the coypu, holding the rifle barrel down in front of it. It clamped its bizarre teeth around the barrel with a clink, grabbing it with its paws. Dick said, "The animal is called a coypu, but the fur is nutria. They reproduce like rabbits and eat up the cane which the ducks come for. We don't like them much."

The coypu lost interest in the rifle and turned away from Dick. I got the feeling Dick was going to shoot him, and I hoped for my future feelings that he wouldn't shoot him in the back.

There was no shot. Janie, however, went ballistic. Pete was struggling with her as if she was a large, live salmon and getting too annoyed with the ear-piercing war whoop, he threw her in the canal. Instantly, the water was swirling, and I thought she was being attacked by piranhas.

"Pete!" I screamed.

The coypu took his leave, sliding into the canal and swimming away, moving through the water with otter-like grace, little ears twitching in his ratty head. Janie was safely swimming to the shore and Joe Ray sidled over to help her out.

I slapped Pete.

"What did I do?" he asked. "Your dogs are psychotic!"

"Pete," Mom scolded, "you didn't have to try to kill her."

"Geez," he grumbled, "you'd have to be Francis the Sissy to love this family."

Joe Ray got down to pull Janie out of the canal. She thanked him by shaking off on him and charging down the bank after the coypu with the others following.

"I like that little dog," Joe Ray said. For him, it was a speech.

I was so thrilled, I said, "Would you want a puppy?"

"I'd be much obliged," he said quickly. If he could handle a Brahma bull, he could possibly handle one of Janie's puppies.

"If all goes well, you can have a puppy in February," I said to Joe Ray. He nodded a thank you, I guess, and I added, "I'll let you know." My plan was to stay connected somehow to Dick, and I was blatantly trolling with Janie.

We headed back to the house in the Rolligon at sunset, as the temperature dropped quickly. The sky turned the color of violets and a snow-white full moon lifting over the bay created a hundred miniature reflections in the water, like marshmallows. Ducks and geese clouded the sky, five o'clock rush hour, every one of them getting back home to their nests. What a rare moment. So simple, yet so hard to come by.

The dogs were so tired it was an effort for them to sneak into my room. They lay on their blanket I had brought from the car and hardly lifted their heads when I kissed their fuzzy little dirty faces. I took a hot shower, washing my hair in the sulfuric water, thinking I would never get clean, or at least never smell clean again, what with the Off! and the sulfur. I combed out my hair, splashed myself with Charlie, dressed in a plush beige turtleneck and maroon cashmere sweater V-neck, loose jeans, and comfortable Bass driving shoes, and got out to the fireplace to dry my hair. Dick was reading *Motor Trend* and drinking a Lillet. He asked if he could get me a drink and I told him I could, thanks anyway. As I dried my hair, I decided not to get stupid and babble, or try some newfangled inane way of making him talk. He continued reading, and for the first time I started to realize that he was genuinely shy. Lalo came in the room with a plate of hot bean-and-cheese nachos with chunks of jalapeño peppers on the side. Dick ate four jalapeños to each nacho and I thought he would catch on fire.

"I'm about to blow the top of my head off," he joked, pulling out a red bandanna and wiping his brow.

"I can't believe you can eat that many," I commiserated.

He smiled the nicest smile, but did not know what to say and I did not torture him. Instead, I bravely had one jalapeño on my nacho.

Coming in the room with Pete, Mom said, "Something smells delicious."

"May I get you a Lillet, Nancy?" Dick asked.

"You may," she smiled at him.

Over drinks, we discussed the day and the scenery, the coypu and the dogs, and Joe Ray. Dick told us he had, in fact, been a very successful rodeo cowboy. He had made a good enough living on bucking horses, "landing on his ass," to buy a house in Port Lavaca and raise a family. He had been the foreman for eight years and was one of the most honest people Dick had ever known. As Dick told the story, he spoke smoothly, looking at the floor or at his drink, never into anyone's eyes.

The smells from the kitchen were making my mouth water. I upgraded to a glass of wine during a dinner of fried quail, garlic mashed potatoes, jailhouse biscuits, and ruby-red grapefruit and banana salad. It was a lovely and relaxed evening with my family and Dick.

We all turned in, exhausted, at ten o'clock. I urged the dogs out before we went to bed, and along with the barrage of mosquitoes, I found Dick, looking at the stars. Actually, I smelled him first. Off! was not as captivating as the Eau Sauvage that I remembered from our first night out in Port Aransas. We sat on the bench outside the living room window, with the light shining over us and into the endless night. Dick scratched Janie's ears, which was comfortable for him, and described duck and goose hunting to Dustin . . . the multitudes of birds to be retrieved by one good dog. Dustin and Janie listened to their bedtime story while Tarzan sat in my lap. But shortly the moment was lost to the bombardment of mosquitoes. They won the battle and as we started into the house, Dick asked if he could keep Janie in with him. Of course, I told him, and the boys went in with me. It was a good night.

We left on Sunday morning, a day as gray as tired laundry. Dick stood back when he said good-bye to me, like he was afraid I would touch him. He had no qualms about kissing Janie on the head, patting Tarzan and Dustin like men, and shaking Pete's hand. As Mom hugged him, I witnessed him embrace her and keep his distance at the same time. I drove and Pete handled the gates, Mom set up her nest in the back with the dogs.

"I think Dick likes you," Pete said to me as we drove along.

I was struck dumb.

"I think he likes her a lot," Mom marveled.

Dumber!

"That's because he doesn't know her," Pete said.

"Well, she's not *that* bad," Mom admitted.

"I bet he asks her to another ranch soon," Pete continued, highly unlike him to participate in frippery.

"He has more ranches?" Mom sounded delighted. She and Dustin sat up to hear more.

"Yeah, a big one in West Texas."

"He'll ask her. I think he's quite wild about her," Mom smiled. I almost drove the car into the Guadalupe.

While my family, like a jury, examined my case, I grabbed my pocketknife, stopped the car, jumped out, and cut a tall purple thistle. "Ah, ha! An eryngo! I knew it," I exclaimed, getting back in and stuffing the thorny plant in Pete's face.

"Let me guess: we're gonna have a written exam when we get home on the flowers and ducks of the Texas wetlands," Pete moaned.

"You know, she's actually very good at that . . . she knows all the names of the flowers everywhere," Mom said, adding, "I'm impressed."

"Who cares?" Pete argued.

I decided to ignore my brother's smart retort as I tried to unscramble my thoughts about Dick Negley. If Mom and Pete thought he liked me, did he? How would I have ever known? What did I do right, if anything, and could I keep that up? It all seemed awfully vague to me. Maybe Pete and Mom were just joking. How mean! No! They weren't joking. Ha! I could have jumped over the moon. My head was spinning and I hadn't had any jalapeños. Maybe I could hitch my wagon to this planet after all. That would certainly show Pete, he of little faith. Contradicting thoughts flew around inside my head like changing channels on a television set.

When the flashing lights materialized in my rearview mirror just north of Tivoli, I slowed from 80 and pulled over.

"Whoops, I must have been speeding," I said, pretending foolishly that I didn't know.

"You THINK you were speeding?" Pete whooped.

"Mom! Make Pete behave or I'll get a ticket!"

"Brookie, you were going about 100, I think you're going to get a ticket no matter what Pete does," Mom said.

"No, really," I blurted, "I'm good at getting out of tickets." Probably not something I should have been admitting to my mother.

Dressed in a crispy starched uniform, down to shiny, thick black boots, a towering highway patrol officer suavely approached my window. He lowered his Ray Bans on the dark day to reveal a staggering set of bright blue eyes. His hair matched his boots.

"Oh, dear. Officer, was I speeding?" I smiled as if I was having my passport photo taken.

He sneered at me, "Well, Ma'am, 85 miles per hour in a 55-zone usually's considered speeding."

"85! Wow. I didn't think this car could go that fast," I said, in phony amazement.

"Thank you, Officer. I've been begging her to slow down," Pete leaned around me to say.

"Pete!" I could have killed him.

"Oh, hush up, both of you," Mom snapped. She then rolled her window down and turned her jet-set pose that Pete and I had grown used to, onto the officer. "It's all my fault, Officer," she addressed him respectfully, batting her eyelashes, "I've been begging my daughter to hurry and get me out of this insect-infested quagmire. You see, I'm from New York, and I need to get home . . . to the great indoors, a smoky room at the Carlyle, with Bobby Short playing the piano, and dancing with Rex . . .." she paused.

Pete and I knew full well the officer was going to have to ask, "Rex who?" Confusion curdled his face as he was lured into the presentation.

"Harrison, silly," Mom stated, flipping a hand at him, then checking her hair in the rearview mirror.

"Her close and dear friend," I said through my teeth.

"Well, at least this time she didn't say Malcolm or Aga," Pete said sotto voce.

"It's THE Aga, dummy," I started.

As Pete and I fell into the "shut-up-no-you-shut-up-make-me" part of the conversation, Mom, feeling the hackles of the family rising, said, "Excuse me, Officer, but we're in a big hurry."

The officer stood with his mouth open, not a flattering look for him, and I caught in his face that he didn't see anything funny or appealing about us. Here we were, in the middle of Redneck, Texas, with Mom in the back seat swaddled in cashmere and silk, gold-loop earrings and every gray hair in place, surrounded by literate newspapers and fashion magazines and dogs in fancy leather collars. Surely the officer had seen just such a dog and pony show before.

"You aren't from these parts, are you?" the officer asked. Now we were getting somewhere.

"No, sir, we're from San Antonio," I said. "And Dick Negley likes me!" It wouldn't stay off the tip of my tongue, and there, I had spoken the ecstatic thought out loud. "I mean, we've been visiting the Negley place, Swanlake."

The mention of the Negley name did it. The officer mumbled something but didn't give me a ticket. "Slow down," he said, and motioned me back on the road and out of his county.

As I pulled away, I said, "Told you I could get out of the ticket."

"Ha!" Pete barked.

Remembering Pete's remark, I slapped him, saying, "Not that you were any big help."

"Don't start!" Mom commanded from the back. "Get me out of here, NOW!"

I floored the car, fishtailed through Tivoli and headed up the highway. I was on a roll. Now what was I supposed to do about Dick?

Eighteen

After our weekend at Swanlake, which Mom referred to as Pungent Seepage, she decided that Dick was "good material." That put the pressure on me; did I want him myself or did I want him to please my mother? I always wanted to please my mother, but, truth be known, I thought Dick was quite attractive. However, in the early seventies, the old-fashioned times, a woman was supposed to play hard to get. Not having the foggiest idea how to pursue someone inasmuch as, until now, I had not met the man I wanted to pursue, I waited for Dick to call me. I wrote another "perky" thank you note and waited. He didn't call. I thought he would. Surely I must have passed some initiation test, like not complaining about being eaten alive by mosquitoes, or getting up at 0-dark-thirty and smiling, or, if nothing else, because I owned Janie. Two weeks floated by and there was no word. I knew he had been tending to family business, but I didn't know where, how big his family was, or how long it would take. What had I done wrong? At midnight on New Year's Eve, I held my glass of milk high and resolved to give up on him.

Mom was, as she put it, tucked safely back in New York, in a rented apartment on 57th and 3rd surrounded by interesting and intelligent friends. I had a hunch her small talk was not of hunting in the South Texas swamps. In between traveling and writing for *Town & Country* magazine, she had started writing her first book, about "the beautiful people on their beautiful yachts." From Dina Merrill and *Sea Cloud,* to Aristotle Onassis and the *Christina*, Queen Elizabeth and the *Britannia,* to William Levitt and *La Belle Simone*, Mom was gallivanting around with these people in all parts of the world.

Postcards were coming in from all over the place. Pete was working around Ruidoso, New Mexico, in the oil fields, a geologist looking for oil. Dustin was with him. Tarzan, Janie, and I were taking it easy in midwinter, keeping the fire going in that fireplace I found to be such a peculiar feature when I first came back to Texas in 100-degree weather.

My instincts told me Janie was in trouble at seven in the evening. She started digging in Pete's closet and throwing herself sideways on his shoes, but changed to my closet where she started panting and whining, licking my hand, kicking her feet out, and contracting. After two hours of helpless wondering, I called Mary Mainster at home. She told me to wrap Janie in a towel and meet her at the clinic right away, nothing to worry about, just that she needed to help Janie get on with the labor.

I wrapped Janie's pain-riddled body in a pretty, soft towel and put her in a cardboard box, with Tarzan supervising through big brown altruistic eyes and following us to the truck as I placed Janie in the passenger seat. He flushed with relief as I escorted him back into the house, telling him to stay home and guard. Closing the door, I jumped in the truck, fastened my seat belt, and looked down at Janie. There was a tiny, wet, black-and-white puppy wiggling wildly in the box with her! Befuddled, I carried them back inside and called Mary Mainster. She explained that sometimes you had to scare the mother into labor by taking her away from her security. Swell, I thought, feeling like a mother. She said the rest of the labor would be a cinch, to put her back where she had chosen to have her puppies and bring her in the next day for a checkup.

Back in the closet, Janie settled down securely, whining at me if I tried to leave her, and gave birth to two more black, tan, and white wigglies with pink feet and lips. Number four came out and appeared to be just white with a milk-chocolate-brown head. She was the last. Mary was right, each birth was easier, coming fifteen minutes apart, in tiny wet sacks, popping out of Janie as she pushed and contracted instinctively. Two boys, two girls. Each healthy, fat, and squeaky.

Janie ate each placenta like a good little mother, just as Mary had told me she would do, revolting me completely.

The first day of the puppies' lives was god-awful, in that Mary, with John Karger assisting enthusiastically, docked the puppies' tails, leaving half-inch nubs with one tiny stitch in each. I never heard such pitiful cries and thought what a cruel procedure for an animal just to abide by some trend. Janie whimpered and grumbled so that Mary asked me to take her out and wait in the car. Fine by me. This was one of those reasons I was not to become a veterinarian.

By the time Pete and Dustin returned, Janie had become a nervous mother, growling at Tarzan and Dustin if they came near her babies, never leaving her basket, and trembling and fretting about leaving them to go outside for short intervals. She would rush outdoors to have a quick pee and rush back to the door, waiting impatiently for me to let her back in, growling accusingly at Tar and Dust as she passed them, nowhere near her pups. The boys were so sensitive, her behavior just about crushed them. With their ringleader on maternity leave, they had no idea what to do, and sighing deeply and sleeping soundly became routine for a while.

They didn't have to wait long. Janie separated from her pups like they were a bad business deal as soon as their eyes opened and they were on solid food. No longer embracing motherhood, she called to Dustin and Tarzan, and they went on with cruising the parade grounds, getting back to a more entertaining and desultory life.

I spent many joyous hours feeding the pups Gerber's Rice cereal and milk, clipping their little tiny toenails, rolling in the grass with all four ripping at my hair and clothes, digging tiny holes all over the yard, showing true Jack Russell form.

Pete, home less and less, finally sat me down and, far from pleased about living with seven dogs, implored me to trim the herd. When the pups were six weeks old, John Karger became the proud owner of the older female. He named her Harmony. Checking with Ernie and Winnie Willie in Orange and Joe Ray at Swanlake, the response was the same, they were "not quite ready" for such a handful. But I had other takers, people who didn't know any better—Steve and Susie Beever from Pearsall picked one of the males whom they named Checkers and the other male went to Herb and Joan Kelleher, whom they named Moose. To keep from falling apart while giving the pups away, I tagged the smaller female mine, and, with fleeting memories of Dick, named her Lillet.

Dustin, Tarzan, Jane, and Lillet . . . four again, like when I had Mischief. Any time I thought of Mischief, my heart would go still, and I would stop for a moment to hang my head and wipe away tears that automatically popped into my eyes. I kept sentry duty over Lillet, nervously aware that tragedy had its own timetable, and spent the rest of the Texas winter—not a long one, not a particularly cold one—watching Lillet grow, and reading by a hot, fast-burning cedar fire.

I was in my early twenties and carefree, responding to life as it came along, not steering any particular course but holding steady, when Dick called the second time, six months after we first met. Again with no illustration or regard for the time-lapse, he asked me, Mom, Pete, and the dogs to his ranch on the Pecos River out in West Texas near a town called Langtry. I accepted, fascinated that he had called. I mentioned Janie's puppies and that Joe Ray hadn't taken one, hoping to get a conversation out of him. He told me he knew. That's all. I got directions and told him whoever I could get in the car would be there on Friday, the second weekend in March.

From New York, Mom said she was too old to go that far in the wilderness and also she didn't think she could handle the altitude. I found that a novel excuse since the highest peaks in West Texas may have been 3,600 feet, and she had operated very well skiing with the Aga Khan in St. Moritz at 6,000 feet. But I didn't push it, still relieved she had survived Swanlake.

I can't say Pete wanted to go that much, having just come home from a field survey in Mexico, but I made him. Finding Dick Negley a curious fellow who was not leading me on in any way, I wanted Pete around to talk to in case Dick never spoke to me. Besides, I didn't want to go alone and make a fool of myself. I could be with Pete and do that.

In the afternoon of a cool day in March, Pete, the four dogs and I traveled west on Highway 90, out of bursting city and its ugly billboards and private fences, through miles of rolling hills, via Castroville, the jerky capital of Texas, and Hondo, "This is God's country, don't drive through it like hell." The land opened up after Uvalde, flattened and dried, no more traffic lights, and the fences disappeared. We came into a saucer-shaped valley and the town of Brackettville, where a perfect replica of the Alamo, built years before for the John Wayne film, stood alone. In the middle of nowhere, it looked the way I would have preferred it, the way I imagined it. For Texans, the Alamo is a source of great pride, and the only thing missing at this tourist attraction was the plaque on the real Alamo's front door: "Walk softly friends, for here heroes died to blaze the trail for other men."

The dogs rode tranquilly, as if they knew we were on a long drive, settling in our laps, watching Texas, their Texas, go boldly by. We made it to the wide-open spaces where the blacktop looked like it was going nowhere, where I felt I could walk across the land endlessly and never see another living soul, where Mother Nature had taken a hand to the landscape and come up with images that were as pretty as the Alps, as pretty as the endless hills of Devon. She trimmed the highway with bouquets of mountain pinks, she packed the trees with lavender-smelling mountain laurel blooms, she filled the land with cattle, horses, deer, and antelope, and the sky with buzzards, eagles, and hawks. There was so much space, I felt I owned some, all the way up to the sky. I imagined Mom in a fancy four-star hotel somewhere in Europe, always traveling and visiting, always on the go, and feeling at home like that. I looked around me at the complete isolation, nothing but wide open space and sky. This is what I called home.

The sun had warmed the day to 80 degrees and by the last light in the evening, the colors were sharp, the air refreshing. As the sun hung over the horizon, we pulled into Del Rio and got rooms for the night at the Amistad Lodge, breaking up the six-hour drive.

Pete went straight to his room, grumbling a little about being forced to hang around a bunch of smelly dogs and me. Right, I mused, like he had a better life somewhere else or smelled good himself.

Calling the dogs, I followed a dirt path out a back gate of the ugly green, two-floored hotel leading to Lake Amistad, dodging through a prickly landscape of cholla, ocotillo, and claret cup cactus. I picked sticky antelope horns and snow-on-the-mountain while Dustin and Tarzan scampered off after Janie. Lillet, new at this and still so little, trotted out in front of me, darting bravely in spurts, only to return to me, the self-appointed bodyguard.

For such a barren and isolated part of the state, I was astonished to see the enormous size of Lake Amistad. Reading a notice on a chicken-wire gate blocking an entrance to the shore, I found out that the lake covered 67,000 acres, was a joint effort of the United States and Mexico to impound the waters of the Rio Grande below its confluence with the Devils River, and it hosted sportsmen from both countries. Several clean white motorboats zoomed here and yon on the lake and fishermen sat at the bows of little bass boats, with one booted foot gently steering a pint-sized motor that propelled their boats along the shoreline as they cast and cast and cast.

Before I had gone 100 yards, I could hear the dogs off towards the shore, barking and scrapping with something.

"Now what? Dad-gummit! You dogs make me nuts," I said, kicking dirt in their direction.

Moments later, Tarzan and Dustin sidled up to me looking embarrassed. Dustin hit the ground and started rubbing his face in the sand and dirt, sneezing like he had spear grass in his nose. Tarzan threw himself down in the same ritual. Their eyes were watering and they staggered drunkenly when they stood.

"Oh," was all I could get out before I slammed my hand up to cover my nose. "Skunk! You idiots have found a skunk!" I roared, looking around. "Where's that jerky Janie?"

As she walked out from behind a bush in slow motion, I could practically see the fumes rising from her coat. Her eyes were closed into slits and she was listing to the left.

Fine, I thought, fine! *Ça commence*. It begins!

Going back to the hotel with my smelly brood, I angrily ordered them into the car and drove to town with the windows open, breathing through open mouth. Lillet was the only dog allowed to sit in my lap as she had not been sprayed.

Ask anyone in Texas what to do about skunk spray and the common answer will be tomato juice. I left the dogs in the van and popped into the Piggly Wiggly, bought six large-size cans of Heinz tomato juice, threw them in the seat, and snarled at my stinky companions.

"Just where do you think you're sleeping tonight?" I asked, as I drove into the parking lot of the Amistad Lodge. "Certainly not in the room which I got HERE because they take dogs." They cowered in the back seat. I continued the verbal abuse, "The radio said it's going to be a cool 87 degrees tonight, so you can't stay in the car. Not that I would let you anyway. Have you ever really considered me?" I parked the car and got out as they listened. I waved my hands at the smell and they dispersed.

"Get back here!" I hollered. And they did. They knew I was mad!

I doused the three of them, one by one, with the juice. Janie spit at me, Tarzan sulked, and Dustin lost resemblance of my English gentleman. I've never seen such a gory day.

"There we go. You're all juiced up," I said, tickled for a brief moment, but still annoyed. While I was trying to figure out where to bed their juicy bodies down, the dogs, showing some initiative, with Lillet in tow, ran across the parking lot and jumped into the swimming pool.

"Hey, what are you doing?" I cried, rushing after them. I slid through the pool gate and halted when I saw them paddling along. A petite, gray-haired lady, navigating with a bright blue kickboard, caught sight of all three dogs and their trails of fiery red tomato juice. I guess she thought they were bleeding. She started shrieking.

The dogs swam around long enough to dissolve the juice, scrambled out and shook off. They glared at the noisy old biddy who had ruined their evening dip.

I looked up to the sky for a big idea, then remembered that Del Rio was a border town and that they ate dogs in Mexico. Maybe I would haul their putrid bodies over the border to Ciudad Acuña. It was a thought, but it passed.

The tiny lady shot remarkably quickly out of the pool and dashed towards me, wrapping a towel around her fit yet saggy frame.

"You all had me frightened out of my wits," she said, blithely, holding her nose. The odor had in no way faded in its short contact with the tomato juice, and was even more pungent with the wet fur.

I told her they were looking for homes. She declined, saying she had cats and a parrot. I told her I would trade. She thought I was so funny.

Pete wanted to get a Greyhound bus home in the morning, but I stole his wallet and wouldn't give it back to him.

The skunk smell stayed with us even though we drove top speed with all the windows open, Pete letting me know how much he hoped the dogs would fly out. He was in a messy mood.

"Can't you ever go anywhere and act normal?" he grumbled.

"No," I answered gaily, determined not to let him rile me.

We stopped a couple of hours down the road in Langtry, which a billboard claimed was "A prime attraction on the Pecos Trail, a must-stop to experience the feel of old and remote West Texas.

Population, 30." We were equally intrigued reading a Ranch Realty sign exclaiming that for a mere $750,000.00 . . . the town of Langtry was for sale.

Pete parked the car in the shade of an old broken-down oak tree that looked like it hadn't seen water for decades, the only one for miles, and walked off with his foul humor to have a cigarette while the dogs circled the deserted town.

I sauntered into Langtry Goods and Groceries, with creaky swinging doors announcing my arrival. As my eyes became accustomed to the dark room, I saw a pair of faded blue-jeanned legs with dusty boots resting on a shabby table. Daylight slipped through a window behind the figure and I moved across the floor to get a better look. A man stared coolly at me through dark black eyes. He had a bandit mustache and black, black hair. Something glistened in his hands that made me check for the nearest exit.

"Hello?"

"*Buenos días*," he tipped his shiny knife to me.

"Do you have Coca-Cola?"

"*Si, Señorita, pero no hay hielo.*" He rocked back but did not get up. He may have been the swarthiest man I had ever seen, undoubtedly related to Pancho Villa.

"No ice?" I giggled, nervously. He pointed to several cases of coke, stacked in a corner on the dirt floor, covered in dust. I could see a hint of red and white. Shaking my head, I said, "*Adios*," and curtsied my way back outside. Not a soul in sight. Seeing neither Pete nor the dogs, I could only hope he wasn't throwing them off a cliff. I stepped down the crooked wooden stairs and crossed the street.

The only other building was empty, standing alone, and had a sign over the door: "Opera House Town Hall and Seat of Justice." A wagon wheel leaned up against the crumbling adobe and a rusty horseshoe hung over the door, ends up, holding the luck. The wood door and window frames were painted the same faded green as the prickly pear growing up around the porch. The old building ticked and creaked in the heat.

I climbed the dried-up stairs and looked through the window, cupping my hands to lessen the glare. Three chairs were turned over and a few things were about to fall off the wall or were hanging sideways. The door was open and I went in. It seemed like there had been a barroom brawl years ago and no one ever cleaned up. I found an ancient newspaper on a dusty table and read a short article about Langtry. It said the building was a combination billiard hall, saloon, and courtroom of Judge Roy Bean—the self-appointed "Law West of the Pecos"—a drinking man who once told the governor to mind his own business in Austin and leave the law west of the Pecos to Judge Roy Bean. The article went on to say that Bean named his establishment "The Jersey Lily," for Lillie Langtry, an English actress he was infatuated with, but whom he never met. The old judge had been dead a few months when Miss Langtry finally got around to visiting "her" town. Wow! How romantic was that, that she had a whole town, or at least Langtry, named after her?

Putting the paper down, I went back outside and read the wood plaques on the building:

ROY BEAN'S OPERA HOUSE
BUILT BY ROY BEAN IN 1900 FOR LILY LANGTRY TO PERFORM IN:
ARTICLES OF INTEREST INCLUDE:
2 HEADED CALF
6 LEGGED LAMB
A MUMMIFIED INDIAN BABY OF PREHISTORIC TIME
ROY BEAN'S PHONOGRAPH
OTHER RELICS OF INTEREST

Other relics of interest? Personally, a 2-headed calf and a mummified Indian baby would have been interesting enough for me.

I slumped carefully in a crickety old chair sitting on the porch by the hitching post and imagined I was Judge Roy Bean, who, on this very spot, drunk and rowdy, condemned dirty, smelly, guilty, sometimes not-so-guilty men, to be hanged or dragged through the cactus and then the streets for all to see. I looked out at my vast holdings. The Pecos River cut through the land in a deep, grand canyon. The panorama was staggering and I could see forever. I visualized banditos and mustangs on the Mexico side, unruly and wildly free. Buzzards and hawks flew breathlessly ballet-like, high above me, waiting for a careless rodent or reptile to provide a meal.

"Did you see the guy in the grocery store?" Pete startled me.

"He wasn't so tough," I said, pretending to spit tobacco.

"What do you think you're doing?"

"I'm Judge Roy Bean and be careful, sonny, or I'll have you hanged."

"You and whose army?" Pete was about as much fun as a dead turtle.

Just as I was about to accuse him of impertinence and high treason, all four dogs materialized.

"There are the boys now," I told Pete. They were not bleeding or throwing up and there were no foreign objects stuck in them. "Dustin, you tie up this impudent whippersnapper. Janie, you take him to the hanging tree . . ."

"You wouldn't have to hang me. The smell of these dumb dogs could kill an Arab."

While I tried to catch the meaning of his saucy remark, the gang dropped on the porch, panting.

"Water. You need water," I said, focusing.

"That guy's gonna come out here and cut these dogs' throats for smelling up his town," Pete said, surely humorless. But I knew in my heart he was having more fun with me and the dogs than he ever had in Vietnam, so I put up with him.

"Right, and he smelled of Irish Spring," I rolled my r's. Pete smiled at me, finally.

There was a sun-faded green hose wound up and attached to an outlet on the side of the building. My heart stopped flat when I reached for it and saw the last wriggles of a red, black, and yellow snake, escaping under the house. What was it? "Black and yellow, kill a fellow . . . no, no, red and yellow, kill a fellow, red and black, sit on it, Jack." Well, hell, he was gone by the time I figured out that dumb phrase. When my heart got going again, I turned the rusty handle and the hose jerked and spit, red gunk came out for a second, then clear, icy-cold water. A thick patch of dark green mint grew under the faucet, reminding me how nice a glass of iced tea would be. I cupped my hands and the dogs drank like camels.

"Only three quarters of a million, men! Wanna move to Langtry?" They continued drinking. I tasted the water. It was as good as the water I had drunk out of the pure streams in Switzerland.

"We have about an hour and a half to go," Pete said. "Let's hit the trail."

"Roy Rogers used to say that," I recalled.

"Roy Rogers used to sing 'Happy trails to you,' " Pete corrected me.

"Okay. Was it the Lone Ranger who said, 'Head 'em up, move 'em out?' "

"That would be Gil Favor," Pete said, "from 'Rawhide'." He pursed his lips at me. As we bickered down the dusty main street, the swarthy bandit came out of the grocery store, looking at us steadily through fearless, cold eyes.

"He heard you flappin' your jaw and he's lookin' to cut your tongue out," Pete said.

"He can't scare me. Remember, I'm Judge Roy Bean!"

"Well, I'm Pete Thompson, and I'm going to the truck and leaving this lousy piece of real estate." He started walking and nodded to Pancho Villa as he passed.

"I wouldn't turn my back on him if I were you," I said, not moving my lips, backing through town under Pancho's gaze. He stared at my little dogs like he was thinking about using them in his family's chili recipe.

"Wish he'd been there yesterday in Del Rio. It would have been happy trails to your dogs no matter who said it."

When we reached the truck, the dogs jumped in and sat like mere four-legged lambs. As we pulled away and the dust made a tiny room around us, I said, "Those were the days! Glamorous and romantic days; when the legends were about the good guys and heroes, the bad guys were shot or hung, but never front-page news; when the punishment fit the crime; when we were not at the mercy of lousy, money-hungry lawyers who introduced frivolous lawsuits; where people took responsibility for their behavior . . ."

"Hey," Pete interrupted, "Who put the nickel in?"

"I'd have hung 'em all!" I cried, shaking a mighty finger.

"Get a grip," Pete quipped.

"Well, shucks, I didn't get to see the 6-legged lamb."

"We'll come back," Pete said, smiling evil and patting my leg. "After all, tomorrow is another day."

"Oh, yeah, yeah. Who said that? Was THAT Judge Roy Bean? NO! That was . . . oh, you know . . ."

"Forget it. I'm not doin' that again. You know who said it, now leave me alone or I'll tell Dick what an idiot you are."

"You haven't told him already? Wow, you're slipping." I stopped joking.

"Well, it could be too late. I think this whole thing with you has hit him like a dolt of lightning," Pete said sincerely.

"Oh, please. A *dolt* of lightning? Lightning has BOLTS, Pete." Switching to the subject I preferred to be on, I questioned him, "Do you think Dick could be a dolt? I mean, like be so dolty as to like me?"

Pete shut up immediately. He was uncomfortable talking to me about affairs of the heart. Just when I needed his help.

"You know, if he likes me so much, why does he only call every three months?" I tried that tack to get him going.

Nothing.

We drove for two hours through dry land on either side, miles and miles without seeing a house or a car. The dogs slept peacefully through it. By the time the sun was well up in the sky and had gathered some heat, we arrived at the gate. The hair-raising drive from the gate down to his camp on the Pecos River was on a road through a canyon, down precipices, over boulders, and into an arroyo. And Pete drove it like a man. I held Tarzan so tight his eyes almost popped out. But I liked the roughness of it all. No one would be building condominiums out here for another hundred years.

Dick's camp sat in the river bottom, the only sign of man anywhere. An enormous green tent was staked into place with flaps open and smoke rose from a fire on the other side of the tent. Red and blue Igloo coolers surrounded the site, lanterns hung from tent poles, and four empty folding chairs looked like they were waiting for bridge players to start a game.

Dick Negley stood in the doorway, watching us come to a dusty halt.

Nineteen

Pete and I opened the car doors and the dogs jumped out. They hit the camp, marking and barking, with us behind, flapping into camp like a pair of critics, squabbling at each other, "did-not-did-too."

Since Dick said nothing and didn't look as though he was going to, I decided to crack the ice myself.

"Nice to see you, Dick," I said, looking into his cool, sherry-colored eyes. "The drive in almost killed me."

"I'll try harder next time," Pete grumbled. "You know, " he said to Dick while shaking his hand, "I'm a big boy, but I can *not* figure out how to say 'No' to her." He stabbed his thumb in my direction. "I really don't need this aggravation, and these damn, smelly stupid dogs!"

"Wow, it's beautiful here!" I said, and abruptly fell silent as I became aware of the surroundings. Then Dick looked at me.

"This family always seems to make some kind of grand entrance," he spoke, sleekly.

This was the second time I had unfolded into Dick's life, and I was fully aware how much frantic energy I had compared to him. He was so darn placid and genteel I wanted to poke him with a cattle prod. My only retort was a "harumph."

"She's as nutty as a pancake," Pete said, acting like he wasn't part of the immediate family.

I tried to downgrade my impetuosity, but my mouth just babbled, "Look at those cliffs! Look at those birds! They look like golden eagles. Are they?"

"Yes, they are. You have good eyes," Dick said.

I beamed.

Janie, after racing around, came back and reared up on Dick's leg, thanking him for the invitation. She liked him. I couldn't hear what he said to her, but she grinned at him. He then picked up Lillet and held her high above his head.

"You must be Janie's daughter. If you're half the dog she is, I like you already." He brought her down and kissed her on the top of her head. She licked the tip of his sunburned nose.

"Her name is Lillet," I told him. I detected a sparkle in his eyes and felt childishly obvious.

Putting Lillet down, he said, "Y'all are kind of a smelly group. Where'd you find the skunk?"

"Lake Amistad," I said, and bit my tongue, an attempt to keep it brief, hoping for an air of mystery. That would be novel.

"Why don't we take you boys for a walk," Dick said to Janie, who looked up at him like he was a God. "I always love to see what you scare up."

"This is going to be better than being in the Natural History Museum," I said, trying for sophistication as well as mystery.

The spring was proving to be a particularly rich one and the sun had drawn a special bounty of flowers and grasses. We walked across the arroyo and away from the sandy river bottom to the base of the mountainside. Even though it was still a bit early for the real show, Big Bend bluebonnets, Indian paintbrush, sand verbena, showy white primrose, coreopsis, and Mexican hat bloomed sporadically as far as the eye could see.

"You certainly know a lot about the flowers. What are you, a botanist?" Dick asked. I hadn't realized it, but I'd been naming the flowers out loud since I was so used to no one caring, for instance, Pete. I turned brick red and pretended it was the steep climb, fanned myself, and looked off at the Pecos River.

"Oh," I said, still fanning. "I've picked up names here and there."

"Right," Pete said, as we started climbing again. "She's been dying for someone to notice how many stupid flowers she knows."

Ignoring Pete, I spoke to Dick, "A *botanist* you say? All this time I've been thinking how economical it would be for me to be a veterinarian, but botany, eh? That's another idea. Let's see, if I were a veterinarian . . ."

Pete saying, "We don't call her Babbling Brooke for nothing," shut me up instantly.

Finding my conversation disposable, Dick said, "Your dogs don't look too happy."

At the time, I was bent over, pulling a nasty piece of cactus off my bluejeans at the ankle. It was a cholla I hadn't seen before, low-lying and spread out like octopus legs, medium green, with translucent spines that were different lengths, and very flexible. I looked up to find the dogs dressed from head to toe in the same detachable cactus parts, waiting in place for me to solve their newest dilemma.

Five to six pieces were stuck in each dog. Dick began to pull some off Tar and Janie, I worked on Dustin, and Pete broke down, showing his good side, and took care of Lillet. We used sticks to flick the cactus off the dogs making them wince and whimper, but they stood still. When we were finished, hundreds of little, hot puncture wounds stung our hands and I could imagine the pain in the dogs' paws and sides.

"I didn't know it was so inhospitable for dogs," Dick said, almost apologetically. "I've been looking for a name for this place. How about Awful Acres?"

"Awful Acres," I repeated, laughing, but not really finding it funny.

Once the dogs were cactus-free, they wouldn't move.

"Look at this," Pete said. As he took a step and brushed his boot against the cholla, a piece broke off, popped in the air, like it was fired at him by the plant it came from, and landed in the middle of his thigh, sticking there.

"Oh, my heavens," I said. "It jumps!"

"It's nickname is actually 'jumping cactus'," Dick said, nodding.

"Hey, we could be botanists together!" I flirted. He was coolly oblivious, reminding me that I had promised myself to try to be mature, even uninterested around him. My over-attempting was annoying me.

As often as we could, we found clear trails and coaxed the dogs into following. Dick told us the trails were used by deer, elk, bobcats, raccoons, opossums, smugglers, and ranch hands, and we followed it up the side to the ridge. The dogs brought up the rear, bumping into each other, thinking they wanted to get ahead, but too smart to tackle the jumping cactus.

We reached the top and saw a herd of pronghorn antelope, the fastest mammal in North America. At home on the high plains where they can see forever, they galloped away as fast as the wind with raised heads and flashes of white rump. The dogs had no desire to chase them, but we picked up the three Russells so they could get a better look. Dustin watched with them, and all four started whining in frustration. Janie reached a good pitch in Dick's arms, and he seemed tickled with her. Through Dick's binoculars we saw large mule deer on the hills around us, and down below, seeing us, a herd of ill-tempered javelinas snorted and huffed off across the river bottom. We saw the Pecos River as it wound its way through the valley, looking as big as the Mississippi, and as brown. Few boundaries mark the terrain as emphatically as the Pecos. The depth of the canyon cuts its way through sheer walls rising directly from the river, and century plants along the sharp cliffs look like lonely troops guarding the border of a whole new country on the other side. The sheer isolation filled me with wonder. The air was sweet, the sky unbelievably clean, the silence prehistoric, all making my life seem brief and small.

When the sun was straight up, we went back to camp. The dogs were relieved to be on the sandy river bed and gleefully chased a suicidal armadillo into his hole.

"I was beginning to think your dogs weren't having any fun," Dick said, smiling.

"I tell you, if I ever wanted to keep them under control, I would just need to build a fence out of that nasty jumping cactus."

"You'll never keep them under control," Pete said. "And truthfully, that's the fun of it. The bunch of you always seem to be creating some sort of fiesta."

"Watch it, big brother, you almost sound complimentary," I said, pleased as punch.

As if on cue, the dogs came back all at once, panting and wagging. We sat and had cokes, with hielo; Dick even had ice out in the middle of nowhere. We told him a lively version of the Langtry story, and he seemed to be listening.

Dick explained the setup in his camp, which was that there wasn't one, and Pete got our bags out of the car. I stashed my duffel under an army cot next to a sleeping bag and tried to figure out what the toilet looked like. I wasn't going to ask Dick, so I established my own territory away from the camp. By the time I got back, Pete was asleep on his side on one cot and Dick was reading *Gun Digest* on another, with Janie asleep next to him. I nodded and he kind of waved, then smiled. I lay down and pulled a light Mexican blanket over me and found this the perfect moment for some quiet time. Looking for Lillet, I saw that she was pressed up against Pete's back. Dustin and Tarzan got onto my cot and as soon as I shuffled everyone around accordingly, I fell asleep, thinking how odd it was that a man could hold me entirely without ever having held out a finger to touch me.

In the late afternoon, the three of us took the four dogs to the river for a swim. The Pecos was smelly with minerals and mud, but the dogs found it refreshing. Lillet paddled around daintily, keeping Pete in her sights. He was watching after her so sweetly, it reminded me of how he used to take care of me. Again, dogs were bringing out the best in people. Dick was laughing at Janie as she would try to fetch rocks he threw into the shallow part of the river. Dunking her head all the way, she would pick up the first thing she could find and pulled up some extraordinary rocks and pieces of wood. I threw a piece of wood out in the middle of the slow-moving water, and Dustin retrieved it proudly, snorting as he swam back ashore.

As we headed back to camp, the three of us, the four dogs, I felt that we certainly could have been the Magnificent Seven.

At dusk, the air turned cold and damp and I thought I could smell tamarisk trees. Dick asked us to start a fire while he organized the cooking. Pointing to a tarp, he told us not to take the dried wood from there, it was for emergencies, like rain. With great help from the dogs, we collected wood and grass scattered around nearby. The dugout fireplace had a flat rock bottom with larger rocks circling it. We got the fire going just as the sunlight faded. Putting on our jackets, we sat in the folding chairs and watched the sun stage a multicolored light show in the willows and cottonwoods along the river and on the cliffs across. The fire crackled and popped and my taste buds were on tiptoe as Dick threw a small grill on the fire and cooked doves wrapped in bacon, corn in aluminum foil, and, on the coals, honey biscuits in a pan.

As we ate off tin plates with camp-style unmatched cutlery, I noticed the number of pots and pans Dick had. Summing up the amount of food in the four Igloos, I asked Dick, "Have you left home for good?"

"I'll stay as long as I can," he said, and no more. I got the impression that he could be a modern day Jeremiah Johnson, living off the land, away from civilization, by choice. Mr. Mystery.

After dinner, I cleaned the dishes in a tub of water and Pete dried. We sat around the fire and watched a blue moon lift over the horizon, coating us in a delicate light and astounding us with the thought that a man had actually walked up there. Aware of our comfortable and efficient setup, we discussed how incredible the gap was between Igloos and lanterns, spacesuits and moonwalks.

We turned in around ten. In a corner, Dick had hung two blankets for a changing room, thank heavens. I had been somewhat

189

worried how I was supposed to get into my little red flannel pajamas if I'd had to change in front of the guys. Pete didn't care, of course, but these close quarters with Dick were way more advanced than he and I were.

After we were tucked into sleeping bags with the dogs sandbagging us, our moon was replaced with thunderclouds and lightning, rumbling and cracking through the valley. Rain came in heavy drops, swirling and flushing, and tearing at the tent. Dick had camped well away from the river, warned of flash floods that could cause it to rise up to twelve feet in a storm like this. In the dark, reassuring us we were not going to be swimming any time too soon and that the tent would hold, Dick proceeded to tell some of the dumbest and unfunny jokes I had ever heard. And I was comfortable telling him how bad they were, which made him laugh harder. It was a night on earth when everything seemed to be absolutely perfect.

Dawn was chilly and misted with dew. Dick was up first, stoking a fire with wood he used from under the tarp. The smell of boiling coffee was mixed with the pungent, spicy smell of creosote bushes. The bushes suggested a dryness even though they were actually releasing water into the air. Nature seemed to be cleansed and nourished. Another spotless day, cold down in the riverbed, the air so pure it startled me when I drew it in. Pete emerged just as the rising sun shone on our happy, pale faces. The dogs stretched and rolled in the warm sand, lounging peacefully. Pete and Dick were bewhiskered and scruffy, and fortunately I couldn't see myself.

After bacon and eggs and orange juice, we set off to explore a new kingdom. The dogs this time were perfectly well-behaved and sure-footed on the deer path. Tarzan, Jane, and Dustin dashed ahead to explore a few times, looking like recruits picking their way through a mine field.

We stirred up an enormous mule deer and Pete and Dick spent an incredible amount of time discussing whether he had twelve or fourteen points. I was just glad he was keeping them on his head, and no one was going to be hanging them over a mantel. Dick shot a porcupine, which was the way of the west, since porcupines are notorious for massacring much-needed shade trees, such as pines and wild laurels. He had an audience with the dogs, tutoring them in the dangers of tangling with the porcupines. Instinctively, they stayed back and listened attentively, apparently realizing it was a very important matter. Not far from where I watched, a horned lizard, also known as the horny toad, sat in the sun by an ant pile, occasionally zapping a juicy ant.

Back in camp, Dick showed us his favorite new gadget: a hand-held, battery-operated shower. The hose ran into a big plastic container of water that he filled every morning from the Pecos River and set out in the sun. Having not washed my hair since the previous morning, I'd been feeling like a temptation to no man, and to my delight, the boys let me go first, hooking the machine up to the car battery. Again, Dick had made a curtain of blankets for privacy. That warm shower of muddy Pecos River water made me feel like I was a brand new person. And I was thinking the more time I spent with Dick made me feel that way, too.

The second night, by the firelight, over Dick's venison backstrap and my French fries—our first joint cooking effort—it felt strangely natural to be cooking with him. The conversations were unstudied, the interaction was forthright. Maybe we had not solved any universal problems, but we had not added any either. Dick was a quiet man, a laconic man, and I was very comfortable around him. And now he was looking into my eyes. I was wholeheartedly and dumbfoundedly happy.

The seven of us had an easier night. No wild storms, but a fat moon and stars shining so brilliantly in the navy blue sky that I thought we could read by them. When we got into our sleeping bags, Janie chose to sidle up to Dick again, Tarzan and Dustin came with me, and Lillet pressed against Pete. It was almost unbelievable. I was with my best friends in the grandest place I had ever been. It was the second night in a row I was enchanted by the great outdoors and the man who seemed to be able to show us the best of it.

A raccoon woke us up at dawn, checking out the provisions, pulling a trash can over and rattling the contents to see what appealed to him. We held the dogs and watched him through the flap as he got away with a couple of dove carcasses and an apple. He knew we were watching him, shooting us a casual glance as though he was permitted to steal, in exchange for allowing us in his territory. The dogs were oddly calm watching him. I could only think it was Dick's influence on them.

At high noon, Pete and I packed up and got ready to leave Dick in his element. I couldn't believe it when my mouth opened and I asked if he wanted to keep Janie and Dustin until he came home. Back in the dark areas of my brain, I saw it as my having control of our next encounter. He smiled and picked up Janie, who was, as always, sitting smartly at his feet, looking up adoringly. Dust watched Dick as if he were waiting for the decision, too. After a weighty pause, Dick declined. I imagined he was not ready for the commitment and responsibility, but then he told us he was going to be stalking animals and dogs couldn't do that with him. I found that to be a very diplomatic and acceptable excuse. I think he would have let me hug him good-bye this time, but Janie in his arms came between us and made it difficult. We both looked clumsy—I in trying to thank him, and he in trying to act comfortable. Then he stepped back with a peculiar smile. I wondered if when he came back to civilization, would he call and ask me anywhere without my dogs or my family. If he did, would I know what to say to him?

"Well, Kid, he's a goner," Pete said after I closed the last gate and we pulled onto the pavement.

"What exactly do you mean by that?" I asked.

"That means I think he'll be asking you to more than a ranch next time," he said seriously.

"More . . .." I said, winding my hand to keep him going.

"I mean he likes you, poor fool that he is."

"I don't know how you can think that," I protested.

"You just scare him," Pete winked at me. "He likes you. I mean it. I felt like a third foot around you two."

"Are you sure . . . you really think he likes me?" A third foot? I wrinkled my brow. Pete was starting to get uncomfortable, but I wanted to keep the conversation alive. "He's too quiet, too unresponsive . . . ." Then I added flippantly, "I like my men loud and bold."

"What men?"

Disregarding the question, I said, "He'll probably stay out in the wilderness forever. I'll never hear from him again."

"You like him, too," Pete stated.

I was shocked to hear it out loud, so I lightly added, "It don't make no never mind. He'll wait his standard three months to call, and by then, Robert Redford may have answered my letters."

"Earth to space cadet . . . you'll hear from him, and it won't be to invite you to some other ranch."

"What are you trying to tell me?"

"Mostly that you're thick, Kid, thick in the head if you don't know how he feels about you. I'm a guy, I know." I listened to Pete, becoming enchanted, but when he saw the schmaltzy look on my face, he finished with, "And I'm not saying another word."

That was fine by me. I needed time to absorb the information anyway. Six hours of driving gave me the time to take stock. Twenty-five years old, still heading—as Ida Mae, a splendid black woman who worked for us used to say—where life "flang" me. My closest relationships were with four dogs, a dear, oddball brother, and an elusive mother. Dustin, my best friend, hairy and warm, intelligent and mannerly; Janie, independent and wild, our catalyst, sparkling widespread enthusiasm, a living ramjet of entertainment; Tarzan, the best natured and most devoted of all, the sweetest of souls; Lillet, so far not following in any footsteps, beginning her own legend. Four dogs. Baggage in some people's eyes. Not Dick's eyes. If I wasn't sure how he felt about *me*, I surely knew he loved the dogs. Maybe we were alike in that way . . . finding it easiest to operate around silent partners. Maybe we would be a good pair, cooking and hiking, fishing and reading, fistfuls of dogs all around to liven things up. Life was looking like it could get a lot bigger. It was time to roll the dice and see what numbers came up.

Twenty

By the roll of the dice, Pete, slim and perfectly tailored, with more salt than pepper in his hair, speaking five languages, got a job in California as assistant to Milan Panic, president of his own rapidly expanding, worldwide company, ICN Pharmaceuticals. Pete packed up his Mustang convertible and moved out to the coast, leaving me with the four dogs and all by myself, holding the dice. I was startled that my brother had a life and I did not want him to leave us. Mom was off on an assignment for *European Travel and Life* and with the postcards she had sent over the years, to keep busy and distracted I wallpapered a bathroom. The dogs were in good order, in that they expected so little, but gave me the foundation I dearly needed.

And the big news was that Dick was in my life.

One lovely evening in May, I cooked a superb dinner of broiled catfish, potatoes with Swiss cheese, and brussels sprouts with garlic salt and lemon, while Dick read *Guns and Ammo* in the living room, with three dogs sleeping at his feet, Janie in his lap. After dinner, he asked if I would cut his hair. What a brave soul, I thought, and unusual. Men were usually so fussy about perfect haircuts. Not Dick Negley. He did seem awfully nervous when I sat him down, pulled out a sharp pair of scissors, wrapped a towel around his neck, and breathed on him.

"Do you think you want to get married some day?" he said.

I gave him the short answer, "Yeah, I think so. Marriage is kinda scary," I began, cutting the long mess of hair hanging in his face. "But I think if two people love each other and know what they're getting into, it can be done. They have to establish right off who is supposed to do what, and that they will always communicate, keep the door open, so to speak. And never, *ever* go to bed mad at each other." That was the sum of all my years of experience. I didn't know squat.

He was silent while I finished the hair around his ears, then said, "I meant to me."

Trying to remember the original question, I caught on, and leaned down in front of him, moved the hair out of his face, and intelligently inquired, "Hunh?"

So, on Pete's birthday, July 14, I married Dick. He brought into the marriage four ranches and a sporting goods store, Toepperwein's, in San Antonio. I brought four dogs. What a lucky guy!

Mom was thrilled, seeing the marriage as a coalition of roots and property. She couldn't have been happier for the dogs. Pete's behavior, on the other hand, was confusing. I knew he liked Dick, but when he returned to San Antonio for two weeks, he became reticent, like right after Vietnam, making me think he and I were always expecting the other to be there for one another solely, even if he had moved away. Then I thought he was just going to be missing my cooking and company, all the chaos, and the dog hair. He gave me a long, deep, heartbreaking look the day Dick and I left for our honeymoon in Cabo San Lucas, in Mexico. It was probably because I left him with the dogs, but I was worried. The dogs gave me the same look. No one was used to me doing anything other than taking care of them.

Dick brought two bags on the honeymoon, one large, sturdy one, and a smaller camouflage duffel bag. I had one of Mom's Louis Vuitton bags, filled with beautiful, feminine things she made me take. It was like playing a role and I was genuinely feeling like a contessa, envisioning Dick dressed handsomely in white linen pants and a blue blazer, a la Tony Curtis in *Some Like It Hot*, dancing barefoot in the warm sand during moonlit nights. My inane bubble burst when Dick goofily asked me to try to lift his larger bag. Supposing that I could—still a jock extraordinaire in spite of my pistillate guise—I was somewhat baffled when I could not even budge the thing. Gads, Dick was worse than Mom! But his lofty amusement about the bag really annoyed me when he proudly opened it and revealed back issues of *Shooter's Bible* and *Gun Digest!* Hundreds of them, that he had not had the time to read while courting me! In the duffel bag were some rolled-up khaki pants and a few wrinkled shirts. Hey, I liked to read as much as the next guy, but on our honeymoon?

It was then I discovered to my horror that Dick had married me and was taking me to Mexico, not for a honeymoon but for a fishing trip. So help me God, but each morning at Cabo San Lucas, Dick's huge, loud alarm clock went off, and we started out in the dark to spend all day under the broiling sun, on open rolling seas, forced to catch dinner. It's a good thing I didn't have to row the boat. Perfectly miserable, I was sure that I should have stayed home with the dogs and Pete.

When we finally got home and I was back in the loving arms of my dogs, I called Mom and told her I wanted to have the marriage annulled. She laughed and told me in her leisurely, assuring voice that it was too late, there'd been a clean amputation. She reminded me of one of her favorite lines, "the happiest people alive are married men and single women." Gee, thanks, I told her, that would have been more helpful *before* I got into this mess. Pete fled to Colorado, happy we were home safely, but not prepared to handle my filthy disposition.

Dick's life didn't change. He was always up at 0-dark-thirty, drinking coffee and reading some stupid magazine or other about reloading shells, changing engines in cars, sighting-in rifles, repatterning shotguns. Not having any idea what my role was, or should be, I bought a rocking chair and rocked away endless months, murderously watching Dick as he continued his regime, and in doing so, tuning out life around him. Yikes, I hadn't realized how spoiled I was and how much attention I thought I was due in a marriage. Taking care of the dogs had been a cinch, and besides, they gave so much of themselves back. They needed me, they worshipped the ground I walked on. Well, maybe not Janie. But this man! An independent man, a man of effortless composure, who knew less than I did about living with another human being. To put it mildly, we were not a smart couple. When I had rocked two grooves into the wood floor of our new three-bedroom home in Terrell Hills, San Antonio, it dawned on me that I had some growing up to do.

We started our marriage in a time when "Big Minh" surrendered Saigon and our troops started coming home; when the Watergate scandal transcended all other concerns, and Nixon resigned evasively; when Wallace Stegner, Eudora Welty, and Michael Scharra were winning Pulitzer Prizes for fiction, and Academy Awards for best picture were going to *The Godfather*, *The Sting*, and *The Godfather II*. It was a time when Young, Mattingly, Duke, Cernan, Evans, and Schmitt were landing on the moon and hardly anyone could name two of them; when Emily H. Warner became employed by Frontier Airlines, the first female pilot of a major U.S. airline; a time when a nation became addicted to plastic credit cards. But for Dick and me, it was a time of learning about the real stuff in life. Up till now, my teachers had been Barry Manilow, Kenny Rogers, and Lionel Ritchie. Hey, I believed all the words they sang, from "Somewhere in the night, we will know," to, "Through the years, I'll never let you down, I'll always be around," and my personal favorite, "I'm truly, truly in love with you, girl." And I hung it up on Jack Jones and "I'm irresponsibly mad for you."

Right. Well, that's not how it was. Dick was irresponsible, yes, but not in the way I wanted. And he, on the other hand, must have been listening to George Strait singing, "It ain't cool to be crazy about you, it ain't suave or debonair, to show how much I care." Not to mention that we had married older than a lot of our friends and with so much free secondhand advice from them, their turmoils, their fears, we unconsciously armed ourselves against one another. That's when the dogs came to our rescue. We learned more from them than one another or anyone else out there, as the dogs' only weapons were kindness, unconditional love, and a great feel for life. The one and only thing Dick and I had in common in our early years was that we could rely on the dogs to believe in us, and we could love them. And eventually, that trust and love spilled over into our own two hearts for each other.

As summer showers watered a very dormant land, Dick and I, with Tarzan, Jane, Dustin, and Lillet, none of whom minded his reading, headed out 90 West in our newly purchased, banana-yellow Dodge van with a sliding door. We looked more like road menders than newlyweds. On our way to Spicewood, Dick's mother, Carolyn Negley's 10,000-acre ranch between Marathon and Alpine, we passed the turnoff for Langtry and space came to an end and the void began. It was a land of remoteness, solitude, and such special magic.

As we drove into the frontier town of Sanderson at dusk, the eastern sky behind us counterpointed a brilliant western sunset with soft pinks and blues, yellows and golds. Neon signs lining both sides of the street zapped and crackled as they lit up, going almost unnoticed in the expiring daylight, trying to compete with mother nature, too grand an opponent. The neon night seemed to me to be alluding to a wilder, more glamorous life somewhere else. Thoughts of my chalet mates in Montesano popped into my mind; Swiss, French, English girls, who wanted to hear tales of the wild, wild, west. And I told them well because I was proud of this part of Texas. They would have flipped to see this Texas. As far as I knew, there was no place on earth as wild as the land we were driving through. I imagined the old days of Sanderson: a town frequented by outlaws and gunmen, cattle rustlers and bandits, where the infamous Judge Roy Bean maintained his saloon for a short time. Back then we would have traveled on horseback from sunup to sundown and not been able to make it one fourth as far. Looking around at this simple, quiet open land and thinking of my past, I realized how many important memories had been derived from my travels.

Dick pulled up at the Yucca Cafe, next to the Western Restern Hotel. We let the dogs out and they immediately dashed at a tethered billy goat. Janie, the perpetual ring leader, backed off when the goat, bleating and stomping, put his head down and charged her for a butt. The dogs pretended they had more important things to do than mess with a handicapped goat and went off down a back street for surprise attacks on smaller game.

Rounding up the pack, we put them back in the van and entered a world of memorabilia in the old, warm cafe. A handful of old-timers scarcely glanced at us as they went on with their conversations, no doubt talking about the days gone by, of hanging out with the local yokels like Bat Masterson, of campfires and cattle drives, of the lost gold mine somewhere near, yet never found. A picture of John F. Kennedy hung over an old wooden counter, and on horse-shoe hooks hung a black-and-white braided horsehair rope, a dusty collection of baseball caps, lariats, bullwhips, and cracked-leather bridles. A stuffed rattlesnake in a striking pose sat on the glass counter, giving my heart a start, and then to throw me off completely, on the wall by itself there was a Swiss cuckoo clock. I giggled to myself thinking of a Montesano reunion in Sanderson. How the girls would laugh.

The clock cuckooed seven times as Dick ate a bowl of "fire eatin' chili" without flinching, washing it down with a Dos Equis beer. He sweated freely, looking at me through wet, silly eyes, wiping his runny nose on a red bandanna napkin. I made him get up and dance with me, embarrassing the hell out of him, when a strange song called "Big Balls In Cowtown" played on a psychedelic juke-box. We got into titters of laughter and found that we were the main event for every other person in the cafe. Not one of them cracked a smile which put us into grander giggles. I must admit, however, that "The best chicken-fried steak anywheres" was exactly that. And I be-lieve I still have some of it left on my hips today.

The dogs avoided us and our breath, getting into the back seats for the last sixty miles. Driving in the dark through such isolation, we agreed that we would not have been the slightest bit surprised if we had come upon a UFO convention.

Ten miles west of Marathon, with the help of the headlights I lined up the four numbers Dick gave me on a Yale lock and pushed open a rattly old gate. Glittering away in the night, stars packed the sky, reminding me of those I had last seen camping out with Dick at Awful Acres on the Pecos. Low mountains, black and silent, surrounded me, silhouetted against the stars. With no other light, I began to get an odd, spooky feeling, so far away, of me being small and insignificant. I jumped back in the van.

Dick smiled at me and said, "You're going to love it here."

That was a compliment. I returned the smile. As he drove on a rock road, he told me the names of each critter whose eyes lit up in our headlights; from mule deer to coyote, javelina to the nocturnal ring-tailed cat, changing my feeling that we were all alone.

I opened the final gate and, as it was very late, we drove quietly past the foreman's silent house, past red barns and corrals, three more miles along a winding road and up a hill to a dark ranch house. We got out and I held on to Dick as he shuffled towards a big door. I asked him if there was something wrong with his legs and he told me he was just making sure there were no snakes by the door. I wanted to go home already. Inside, Dick flipped a wall of light switches on and we unloaded duffel bags, Igloo ice boxes, and groceries. The house was ten years old, white stucco, with brown-painted wood beams and roof, nestled into the base of the mountainside. A D'Hanis-tiled porch surrounded it, and in front, facing the dark valley, steps descended to a rectangular swimming pool. The dogs ran off into the dark, returning pretty quickly to see if we were going out or not. Patting their happy heads, Dick told them they would have to wait till morning, then assembled them in the living room as he sat on the couch and recounted a fairy tale of the humongous twenty-two-point mule deer who lived in the dark mountains somewhere close by, very close by, he said. Sitting on trembling haunches, wagging tails at the more exciting intervals, transfixed by Dick's enthusiasm and body language, the dogs were lapping his story up. He paused, and looking at each captivated face one by one, he continued, "the big bad deer . . . who ate little dogs." He jumped at them and they squealed with delight, running in all directions away from him, crashing into the furniture and bashing into the glass windows. It was going to be a fun trip.

In the morning, standing on the patio with the sun warming me, I turned in a big circle, taking in the view and relishing the sight of open land and endless mountains. I imagined what Mom would think of it. It was too rugged for her, too far away from four-star restaurants, movie theaters, and limousines, but just right for me. She had raised me in a fancy lifestyle, some could even say a shallow one, spoiled and privileged, and here I was in West Texas, married to a man who had been born to that lifestyle. At one time Mom would probably have liked to see me married to British royalty or a Greek shipping tycoon, all of whom she had introduced me to. Yet, as of late, she had graciously accepted the style I chose, and she allowed me for the first time to be a hick at heart. She loved Dick dearly and promised not to run our lives. Just when I needed a little help!

I turned to watch Tarzan, Jane, and Lillet inspecting the hillside behind the house, ultra pleased to find that jumping cactus did not exist in this new land. Dustin plunged into the cool blue pool, finding his own haven. Dick stretched and yawned his way outside, looking up at the dogs, carrying his copy of *Field and Stream.* A few barn swallows, their stunning purple highlights radiating in the sun, swept over our heads, darting and winging efficiently around the pool and house.

Dick perched on a low wall around the pool as the dogs returned and gathered at his feet, rubbing against his legs, waiting for a pat. Dustin's feathery tail wagged biggest as he hoped for Dick to tell another story or read out loud from the magazine.

Loading the dogs in the van, we drove down to say hello to the foreman, a short, jolly Mexican man with bright, sparkly eyes and full-moon white teeth and a face like a walnut from long hours in the hot, dry weather. Dick and Efren conversed in Spanish as his wife, Maria, a big, shy woman, bent from years of multiple births, stood in the doorway of the little ranch house, holding a small brown bundle in her fat, bare arms. Around the dusty yard, ten assorted sizes and shapes of children in mass motion, laughing and chortling, chased baby goats, colts, calves, and chickens, as their mother watched over them like a lifeguard. Other than the vacant, mournful look on Maria's face, the scene reminded me of the one in Peter Tavy, Janie's birthplace in Devon.

For ten years as foreman of Spicewood, Efren had watched over 200 head of cattle, a small herd of goats, and thirty horses. Spicewood was a working ranch. For so many acres, I thought there would be more stock, but Dick told me it was all the land could provide for. Rugged and barren West Texas, the least changed and least occupied part of the state, with its scanty rainfall of ten inches or less a year, left nature itself obdurate. Of all the stock, Angora goats survived the inhospitable land best, producing great supplies of valuable mohair.

We walked to the barns and corrals to look at ten gingerbread-colored palominos with white socks and blond manes and tails, a showy, handsome strain of horse built up at Spicewood from stock of Texas' famous King Ranch. Another ten small, droop-faced, oddly-shaped dull-brown Mexican ponies, some swaybacked, stood like mutts with the grander horses. I listened as Efren talked to Dick about the indigenous bunch, by far the better mount for rocky mountain conditions and sandy terrain in the valley. Good for them, I thought, always for the underdog.

In the afternoon, as a handful of isolated storms gallivanted through the valley, Dick and I took the dogs for a walk below the house. With Janie in the lead, they scattered into the sandy arroyo cutting through the flats. Dick packed a holstered .44 Magnum, telling me it was the wise thing to do as we were putting ourselves out in rough country with snakes, tarantulas, porcupines, even mountain lions. I stuck close to him. He pointed out hundreds of little mirrors of water reflecting from limestone rocks across the mountainsides around us and told me that's why these were named the Glass Mountains.

Blue quail, interrupted from an evening meal of red berries furnished by tasajillo cactus, alerted each other, chirping and darting around the bushes, running lickety-split away. Some flew in short spurts, but running was a far more natural maneuver for them. We examined the tracks from where the quail landed to the place where, with a spring that pushed back the sand, they took off. Dick identified dozens of tracks stitched in the sand weaving in and out of each other like patterns in a crocheted blanket. In wanting to learn everything about this wild land, I got to know more about Dick. Less pedantic than I, he proudly and patiently taught me. He was a man of infinite knowledge, a sage, aspiring to be a Renaissance man he told me in a rare, intimate moment when he spoke of himself. He was good company and I could learn something from him.

Red-tailed hawks, Harris hawks, and buzzards ruled the sky, soaring, lazy and unthreatened, combing the land for juicy cottontail rabbits. We scared a family of mule deer out of the arroyo and the dogs chased them across the flats, trying to mimic their powerful, four-point bounces. The deers' notably big ears reminded me of their namesake. Dick told me mule deer could jump seven-foot fences in two strides and broad jump twenty feet, thirty feet downhill. I told him Janie could do that.

In small basins, the water pooled after the storms, and at sunset, moisture in the atmosphere combined with the last rays of sun created a phenomenon called red rain, like great curtains 100 feet across and 100 feet high. Standing there on a majestic ranch with Dick and my best friends—well, they were somewhere nearby—and the remarkable wildlife, witnessing red rain and mountains turning pale pink in the final light, I felt the wonder. I wished I had a sketch pad and watercolors but it would have been too hard to capture the combination of physical and emotional beauty. Dick was showing me one paradise after another where his quiet demeanor blended perfectly with the outdoors. The fact that our trips included the dogs was better yet. Dick and I and the four dogs had lucked into a perfect slot in life.

Back at the house, we fed the dogs and made BLTs for dinner. Afterwards, by the fire, Dick read stories to the dogs about new, improved Gokey snake boots and foolproof turkey calls. They listened for a time but then sighed and fell asleep. We were twenty-four hours into the weekend and none of the dogs needed medical care. Things were going well.

Twenty-One

We started out in the morning when it was still cool. I grabbed my backpack filled with books on wildflowers, birds, reptiles, trees, and shrubs, and the necessary equipment for a Jack Russell owner, i.e., the gloves, shovel, compass, and rope. Dick carried his pistol and binoculars.

Before letting the dogs get away, I attached a bell to Janie's collar, much to her dismay and my delight, hoping to keep tabs on her this way. She glared at me but zoomed off with the others. Aside from the normal scampering and growling noises, all we heard was the little bell jangling around Janie's neck.

This outing I was on a mission to find one of two cacti I had read about: the Ariocarpus Fissuratus and the Epithelantha Bokei. The mission was to either find them or learn how to pronounce them.

Heading up the side of a rocky mountain, Dick taught me first to steer clear of a nasty plant called lechuguilla. It covered the ground in thick clumps, making passage painful with its stiff, erect needle-tipped leaves poking into my calves and leaving hot, stinging wounds. Tequila can be made from the fermented sap, but that didn't make me any happier with it. Tarzan came back to check on me and I could see that his sides were punctured from the lechuguilla, but he ran back to join the pack, too excited to fuss.

Up the hill, Janie's bell was ringing like Santa Claus was coming to town. The sun was up and sitting on a cloudless, bright blue sky, warming us quickly as we moved slowly uphill. I focused on the ground, studying, searching, as I listened to Dick tell me we were in fault-block mountains, meaning deep escarpment on one side turning into gentle slopes on the other. Leaving me to fend for myself and proving that he wasn't that interested in botany after all, he headed over to the top of another hill. I figured he was looking for the dogs since they were more carefree.

I sat on a big round rock and pulled out *Wildflowers of the Davis Mountains and the Marathon Basin, Texas* to look up plants I'd never seen before. The land was dry, like it had absorbed and stored all the moisture from last night's rain. Juniper trees clung to rocky outcroppings all around me. Blue grama and catclaw were the most abundant grasses. Creosote bushes occupied thousands of acres. They were once used medicinally by the Indians and were said to have survived overgrazing because of their terrible taste. The bush is known as the oldest living organism. Mohr's shinnery oak, maguey trees, and soap-tree yuccas, like advancing infantry with funny spiky helmets, subsisted in a land that could only be described as hostile. I saw a tree with limbs the color that cream turns when poured over blackberries, and ran my hand along its smooth bark, actually sensuous bark, that peeled off in thin sheets. Madrone, the book showed me, had the nickname Naked Indian. With its purple-pink shiny green leaves, red berries, and delicate white blossoms, it seemed to have escaped from some lovely enchanted forest.

A thrashing and yelping noise made me look up the hill but I couldn't see the pack. I did hear the bell and smiled thinking how mad Janie probably was that she couldn't sneak up on any innocent animals. I started moving uphill again.

Clumps of strawberry cactus grew in huge, granite rocks, with their roots tunneling deep into soil-rich crevices, putting out bright lipstick-red blooms to feed insects, hummingbirds and bats. After blooming, the cactus produces a red, succulent fruit, tasting surprisingly like strawberries. Walking-stick cholla forms immense, impenetrable, spiny canes, but puts out a cluster of beautiful pink flowers. Ocotillo with long, slender, crooked, thorny wands, grows up to twenty feet, and blooms a showy red flower. Most people think ocotillo is a cactus because it is the same dull green, but I had read that it bears leaves, as no cactus does. All around me bees were busy pollinating and relishing the bounties of the land.

Lillet came trotting up, stopped, and stared at me.

"What's up?" I scratched her chocolate head.

Her caramel eyes gave me no information. I got up, put my book in the backpack and started up the hill again. She followed me closely. I watched her step back when she jumped on something prickly. Looking down I saw a cactus known as a horse crippler, with its lethal thick, curving thorns. Next to it, bright pink flowers bloomed from a flat rocklike plant.

"Yee haw! Look at this, Lillet! Whoopee! It's an Ariocarpus Fissuratus." Lillet was thrilled for me. I pulled my backpack off and took out the hand shovel and fork, knelt down and evaluated the specimen. It was four inches wide and according to my book, the carrot-like root started right below the surface and coned its way deep into the ground.

"Look, Lillet," I touched the plant for her to see it. It had triangular parts and felt like Play Doh. "Isn't it beautiful?" Lillet looked real hard and put a little white paw on my arm. Like Tarzan, she aimed to please. "Thank you so much, little girl. You found it for me." I picked her up and kissed her cheek.

Digging it up wasn't going to be a picnic in the limestone and the hard, chalk-like caliche. I put on my gloves and set to work and fifteen minutes later I had done no more than make a small dent in the earth and create a big blister on my palm. I sat back and thought about going to the house for a sharper instrument or a front-end lifter. Dick was nowhere in sight to help.

Out of nowhere, Dustin appeared and licked me in the face.

"Urp, Dust. Go away. Can't you see what I've found here? Go bite a bunny." I shoved him affectionately.

Next Tarzan came up quietly and sat. He stared at me.

I looked at my Ariocarpus. I looked at Tarzan and Dustin staring at me. "Okay, guys, where is she?"

They both looked up the hill. I heard the bell. Good sign. But

Dustin's tail was down and Tarzan's eyes were as big as saucers. Something was wrong. That's when I realized they smelled. Raunchy, like game. I jumped to my feet, threw all my gear in the backpack and sprinted up the hill to find Janie. I yelled Dick's name a couple of times but imagined he was in hand-to-hand combat with a mule deer buck about now.

I had covered fifty yards when the bell rang behind me.

"Stop playing games with me, Janie! Where the hell are you?"

The bell tinkled ahead again. I stopped and waited. Janie walked out from behind a cedar and stood directly in front of me. I stepped towards her. Her eyes revealed nothing. I patted her head. No wounds there. I looked under her. Blood was dripping from her chest onto the rocks. I picked her up and almost passed out. Her whole chest was open, with a gash about six inches long. She looked like a disemboweled horse in a bull ring and smelled gamey, like the others. I heard a shuffling up the mountain and saw a herd of disgruntled javelinas crossing over the ridge with an ill-tempered mother butting her two babies. I saw Dick on a near horizon, heading back. He knew instinctively something had gone wrong.

"Janie, what have you done?" The blood ran down my hands onto my pants. "It's Sunday, Janie, it's Sunday. Where am I going to find a vet?" I moaned. "Stop bleeding, please." I started shaking.

Sensing the emergency, the three other dogs scrambled down the hill with me. Passing my abandoned Ariocarpus, I realized I had not marked it. It didn't matter.

It took ten minutes to get back to the house. Dick caught up and winced seeing the blood. I grabbed a towel, wrapped Janie in it, and loaded all the dogs into the van. Janie didn't seem to be in pain or uncomfortable, more like she was inconvenienced.

Dust flew drabbly behind us as we tore across the ranch. At Efren's house, Dick told him quickly what happened and he opened the gate for us. We went across the five miles of ranch road in record time and hit the highway, driving 90 MPH for sixteen miles into

Alpine. Dick wasn't sure where the veterinarian's was, but he assured me we would find it easily as the town was so small.

I couldn't imagine how much longer it would be before Janie ran out of blood. In the initial shock of seeing it spurting out of her, my brain must have slipped out of gear because I expected her guts to fall out if I didn't press her chest closed. But when I calmed down and took a closer look, I discovered that she had a rib cage. I had forgotten about the rib cage. What luck! The slice only went to the rib cage. Feeling minor relief that her guts weren't going to fall out, I decided to verbally abuse the dogs, "What a fine mess we're in now, Janie. You should be ashamed! I can't take you guys anywhere!" Dustin and Tarzan were trying to nap in the back seat and saw no reason for this outburst, but they hung their heads low because of the tone in my voice. Lillet was book-ended between them and accepted the punishment, as she was a full-fledged member of the pack now. Janie, on the other hand, looked like I should be thrilled she hadn't lost her bell.

It was Sunday, high noon, and anyone who lived in Alpine, Texas, was not living there that day. We drove up the wide, empty main street looking down side streets, creeping along. At last, a wooden sign pointed to Alpine Animal Hospital to the right, down a back dirt road. Dick turned so hard, Dustin fell off the seat and yelped. The tires raced in the gravel, spitting bits of rock and dirt like machine-gun fire.

Pulling up in front of the hospital, Dick parked at an angle, got out, and came to open the door for me. I carefully carried Janie and the bloody, dripping towel to the entrance. Dustin, Tarzan, and Lillet knew to stay in the van.

Peering through the screen door, I heard a woman's voice and saw a tall woman in a blue clinic coat with her back to us, leaning against a door frame. Thank heavens! I never expected to be so lucky on a Sunday. It was a cheery voice and I was desperate to hand her the problem. Dick banged on the screen. The woman turned to see us through the screen, realized there was an emergency, and said, "I gotta go," into the telephone. She quickly hung up and pushed open the door.

"Help," I sobbed.

"What have we here?" she asked, taking Janie and walking back into the little house with us following her. She put Janie on a spotless white enamel table.

"Javelina," Dick told her.

She let the towel drop. "Oh dear," she said, leaning down to see Janie's wound and gently turning her on her side with strong tan hands. Her shiny black hair was swept up in an igloo shape and she wore a turquoise ring on the middle finger of her left hand. "This is quite a goring," she reported, "but she'll be fine."

Collapsing into a red-vinyl chair, I felt relieved and suddenly exhausted at the same time.

"I'm Dick Negley. This is Janie," Dick said, moving in to look at the wound, patting Janie reassuringly.

"I'm Jan Smith," she said, keeping one hand on Janie, shaking Dick's with the other. She nodded at me when I told her my name. "Sandy, come help me," she yelled.

A young, mousy girl with an unfortunately large nose came into the room, wiping her hands on a paper towel with ducks printed on it. She stopped abruptly when she saw the blood and said, "Oh my!"

Jan, I noticed, holding Janie, worked swiftly, efficiently, telling Sandy what she needed in a deep, woolly voice. Her calm reassured me as I sat numbly in my chair, watching Dick show great interest in the procedure.

"What kind of dog is Janie?" she asked as she filled a syringe with a pale yellow liquid. I closed my eyes as she shaved a little spot on Janie's forearm, wiped it clean with hydrogen peroxide, and stuck the needle in a vein. Sandy held Janie's head to prevent her from biting Jan.

"Jack Russell terrier," Dick answered.

Jan held on to Janie, checked her gums, watching closely. As

Janie slumped, she said, "It'll take us about forty-five minutes to stitch her up. Do you want to come get her later?"

"It takes that long to get back to the ranch," he said, and turned to me. "Do you want to get some lunch, then come back for her?"

"Sure," I said, glad someone else was in charge this time.

As Dick filled out the paperwork for his new dependent, I went to the car and told the others Janie was going to make it. They were relieved, I could tell. They got out of the van, inspected the area, peed quickly and jumped back in, fearing they might have to go into the veterinarian's.

We were back within half an hour and sat in the little drafty waiting room. No other animals were brought in for emergencies on the quiet afternoon. Dick, who never left home without a magazine, always prepared, a man capable of reading at stop lights, was reading a back issue of *Shooter's Bible*. I learned from a copy of *Redbook* that it was questionable whether or not Beryl Markham wrote *West With the Night*. I remembered enjoying the book, along with envying Beryl Markham and Karen Blixen for their solo adventures, women of the winds, brave, individual women. I wanted to believe she wrote it, remembering my favorite line, "Life is life, and fun is fun, but it's all so quiet when the goldfish die." Smiling at the silliness of how noisy a goldfish could be, I looked up as Jan walked over and handed me Janie, wrapped in a corset of gauze bandage, head up and staring out of a drugged stupor. Jan's blue clinic gown was painted with dried blood. She informed us that she had sewn fourteen stitches on Janie's inside layer of muscle and eighteen on the skin to close her up.

"Thank you for saving her," I said, deeply grateful.

"She's quite a little dog. Did she hurt the javelina?" Jan asked.

"Hurt the javelina?" I hadn't thought of that. "I don't think so."

"Were there any babies in the herd?"

"I saw two," Dick said.

"That's where Janie went wrong," Jan began. "Normally, javelinas are harmless little beasts and good for the land, eating prickly pear and all, but a mother javelina would take on a grizzly bear to protect her babies."

Jan, good-natured Jan, spoke so surely, so intelligently, reminding me that veterinarians were God's miracle workers. Jan was another impressive woman, like Karen and Beryl. Would I ever have a farm in Africa, fly across the Atlantic, save a dog's life?

"Well, Janie has never been afraid of anything I know of," I said, thinking that Jan was most likely to be another impressive woman, as she had the same heroic spirit.

"She'll be groggy for another two hours and sore for a few days," Jan told us. "When she wakes up, give her some water, and she'll tell you when she's hungry." Putting a hand on my shoulder, she added, "I'm going to get out my dog book and see what it has to say about Jack Russell terriers."

"You've met the best of the Russells in Janie Russell," Dick said, stepping forward to pay the bill at the counter. Sandy came from the back, wiping Janie's collar and bell on more ducky paper towels, and tallied up the cost for Dick. Her gory clinic jacket made me shudder.

"I feel privileged to have met her. Let's hope our next visit isn't as bloody," Jan said, taking off her jacket, revealing an amazing Barbie doll body. When Dick turned around, his eyes almost popped out of his head.

"I can't thank you enough," I muttered, enthralled by the transformation from efficient vet heroine to knockout pinup girl. I was afraid to look back and see if a similar alteration had taken place in Sandy. It didn't seem likely.

"Thank you, Jan," Dick said, puffed up like a frigate bird and beaming like a pervert, his eyes all sparkly and bright. Although he was never a man to cause me to be jealous, I still thought it wise to shove him out the door.

In the car, the other dogs paid homage to Janie's debilitated body, like she was the godfather. She acknowledged each one with a growl, curling her lip momentarily, then appearing to get dizzy, she lay quietly on the seat between Dick and me, twitching slightly as we drove back to the ranch.

The day was grand. Infinite blue sky, marvelously mild for late summer, the very air seemed tonic and my dog was going to live. As Dick slowed down to turn in the gate, a roadrunner dashed across in front of the van. I knew we wouldn't hit it. In all my time on the roads, I had yet to see a dead roadrunner. Skunk, deer, armadillo, opossum, raccoon, squirrel, an array of birds, but never a roadrunner. I thought of the Roadrunner cartoons and wondered if roadrunners were really smart; always outsmarting Coyote, never run over by a car. Nifty little birds.

Janie did not move when I got out to open the gates and since she wasn't instigating some death-defying act, Dustin and Tarzan only sat up and gazed calmly at the passing countryside. Lillet slept in Dick's lap while he scratched her ears.

The sun was blistering away when we pulled up at the house and stopped the van. I got out and turned to reach for dear little Janie's drugged body. She was sitting bolt upright.

"Hello there, Janie. You can't be coming around already," I said, with hope. She wiggled her nose at me like Samantha in "Bewitched," and turned her attention over my shoulder to the mountain behind the house. I squinted up the hill, and Dick followed her stare.

"Whatever you're looking at, Janie, forget it," I said.

Dick took his binoculars off the dashboard and looked up the mountain. "I'll be damned," he said. "Goats! She's looking at twenty goats about 200 yards up." He handed me the binoculars. The goats were bounding up the cliffs, their pendulous udders swinging loosely like bagpipes as they moved along the steep path.

"Don't even think about it!" I shook a finger in Janie's face. She looked like she was wearing a bra with yellow iodine stains and splotches of dried blood. She swayed to the side, off balance. "That's better," I said. As I handed the binoculars back to Dick, Janie shot out of the van.

"Janie!" I roared. "Dick, do something!"

"About Janie?" he laughed.

Janie scrambled wildly up the hill. Dustin and Tarzan jumped out of the back windows to follow her. Lillet stayed back, watching them with us.

"I'm getting a gun," I screamed. "I'm going to pick you off at about 100 yards, scattering your bodies all over this hillside!" I threatened the three dogs who had taken off like bank robbers heading for Mexico. I shook my fist. Janie's war whoop pierced the air. Stomping inside the house, from the gun case inside the front door I snatched up a telescope-sighted .270 Winchester and went back out. Resting it on the hood of the car, I got Janie's bandaged body in my sights. Dick watched in cool amusement as she made it half way up the mountain.

"Why hasn't the climb killed her?" I asked Dick. He shook his head proudly, like a father when his kid hits a home run.

"She hasn't even slowed down," he remarked.

I got Dustin in my sights, then Tar. They stopped and waited for Janie's orders. I sighted back in on her and felt the unsettling cold trigger in my finger. "I'm gonna drop you, Janie," I said and held my breath.

She paused for a moment to look up at the goats who sneered arrogantly down at her from a sheer cliff. Swaying ever so slightly, she turned and started back down the hill, the others falling in step behind her. I lowered the rifle and breathed out, dropping my head on my arm.

"I can't take much more," I stated.

With a humorous pleat at the corner of his mouth, Dick put two cone-shaped cartridges in my hand. "It wasn't loaded," he said.

In no mood to be triumphed over, I stood up and wanted to pistol whip him.

"I wasn't gonna let you shoot my dog," he said, leaning closer and winking at me.

Twenty-Two

By the mid seventies, Pete was living in Golden, Colorado, working for SERI, Solar Energy Research Institute. He was the proud owner of a golden retriever named Soccer, he was happy in the mountains, he was happy in his life.

Mom was still living in New York and published her first book, *The Dream Boats*, about "beautiful people on their beautiful yachts." I was very proud of her. Inside the cover, it read, "For Peter and Brooke. I finished something." We had teased her mercilessly for years, saying that she was always jet-setting around the world, giddy on life, never finishing anything. Without ever meeting Pete and me, Shakespeare had written: "Ingratitude, thou marble-hearted fiend, more hideous when thou showest thee in a child." Too right. But we *were* getting better.

Dick renewed his subscriptions to *Shooter's Bible*, *Gun Digest*, *Guns and Ammo*, and *Field and Stream*, along with several others, and enjoyed running his sporting goods store. He was an accomplished and avid sportsman, a crack shot, and he played fair. He was meticulous in how he cleaned his guns, loaded his own shells, sighted-in rifles, and patterned shotguns. He never missed an opportunity to go hunting with male friends, of which he had many. He was a man's man, and a good one. A philosopher of sorts, he generally spoke well of people and harbored a very private system of opinions. Even though he looked people straight in the eyes, it was hard to tell whether he was serious or not since he handled all personal interactions with few words and a wide grin. He was a man with distance in him. He never imposed his will other than pointing out how important it was to roll up the car windows at night, in case it rained, and he cringed if he heard the words, "I'm bored." He was not an asking man, but he was a wanting man. I simply did not know what it was he wanted. We lived in a Lambert green-and-white, three-bedroom house on Dover Road in Terrell Hills, San Antonio, built on a rise with a big fenced-in yard. I had decorated the house in quasi-Ralph Lauren style and landscaped the yard with mostly native plants and flowers. I was an accomplished cook of quail, dove, turkey, duck, goose, redfish, trout, and salmon. My life seemed to be in order.

On July 1, 1974, we had our first child, a daughter we named Emily after Dick's grandmother, Emy Brown. I was three weeks late in producing her, and Dick was home between fishing trips. But our second daughter, Nancy, named for my mother, was born on January 30, 1976, and Dick was not as thrilled because there was one hunting day left in quail season. For a man who had so much difficulty understanding women, maybe even in liking them, I found it odd that God had played such a trick on him. He continued reloading and reading and often I wondered was this guy never gonna change and become part of our bigger, expanding life? But he loved the girls and he was a proud daddy. Never once did he complain about anything. We had two beautiful, healthy girls who were growing up with minimal assembly required, and they added nicely to the pack.

As for the dogs, I kept them current on their shots and heartworm prevention, saw to it that they got daily exercise, and that their teeth were clean. Dustin took up protective custody of Emily and Nancy, making sure they were going in the right direction when they each learned to walk, applying himself as a crutch. Tarzan became attached to Emily, and would sit quietly with her in a big wingback chair in front of the fire as she twirled his long white hair with her fingers. Emily's other hand was occupied with thumb sucking and holding onto her blanket. Tarzan started going into Emily's room when she went to bed, to say goodnight, but eventually he slept on her bed, and that was his lot in life. Having him look after Emily was better than hiring a know-it-all German nanny. Lillet and Janie were not as interested in the girls unless it meant we would be taking our daily strolls or going to ranches for weekends. Janie did like the girls, but she was too busy to concentrate on them. Life was still out there and *big*, and she wanted to live it. Lillet was like me in that she wanted to please her mother, but at the same time, she loved to roll on the grass with Nancy, licking her face, dragging her around by her clothes, nibbling on her fingers. I understood my dogs and I understood my children. I would possibly never understand Dick, but in my complete happiness with our life, I found and had more than enough. It was a time when my earthly portion was to live with a husband, two daughters, and four good dogs who were all doing their best. It was quite a heavenly atmosphere.

One week after Christmas, 1976, during cool and seasonal weather, we packed up the van, the children, the dogs, and went to Spicewood. Dick looked forward to deer season and I looked forward to six days exploring and collecting. The girls and dogs looked forward to life in general.

In a state where seasons commingle almost by whim, once more I was deprived of finding an Ariocarpus Fissuratus because the very afternoon we arrived there was a furious storm. The wind rocked the juniper trees and piñon pines and ransacked the little hills, the sun went out and gray clouds dumped *six inches* of beautiful clean snow—the likes of which I hadn't seen since Gstaad—all over the plains and mountains, giving us an exquisite winter wonderland. The whole Marathon Basin—an area geologists call a window since the entire geological history of Texas lies at its surface—lay under a most unseemly layer of snow. The girls were enchanted. The dogs were sorry we weren't going out to find that mother javelina and beat her up. We holed up in the house with a fierce fire, as the girls ran around the living room with the dogs, pausing to press their noses against the glass doors, trying to see how much more snow had fallen since they last looked. The dogs were mostly interested in the Zwieback biscuits the girls ate, and when there were no more, they all sat by Dick as he read to them from *Precision Shooting*, something about shooting groups where the bullets all ended up in one hole of the target or some such weird nonsense. I thanked heavens he was telling the girls and the dogs about it and not me. I would have been forced to retaliate by reading crochet patterns to him.

In the morning, we dressed as awkwardly as we had at Swanlake, with thick boots and socks, hats and scarves, heavy sweaters and coats. By the time we got the girls wrapped in thermal blankets and stuck them in carriers on our backs, we looked like astronauts walking on the moon. We walked away from the house, down the arroyo, and found ourselves shuffling through deep, slippery snow. Dustin and Janie moved fast, dashing here and there, back over the same paths again and again, fascinated with the snow and making crazy tracks. When their feet froze and ice stuck in their pads, Tarzan and Lillet barred our way, asking that we carry them. Tarzan's bushy black, tan, and gray eyebrows were caked with ice, and he shivered and groaned in Dick's arms. Emily handed her blanket over Dick's shoulder and asked him to cover Tar. I put Lillet in my jacket and could feel her little frozen paws against me. All four dogs had ice straws frozen to their whiskers. Emmo and Nanny (of course we had to give them nicknames) chattered and questioned us about everything. Screaming and laughing at Dustin and Janie toiling in the snow, the girls wanted to get down and run with them.

During our walk, small white clouds started their winter parade, soft and chubby, light as down. The sharp cold wind blew from the north. We were out for about an hour hardly getting anywhere before turning back, wet and cold. No animals were moving, no birds were flying. It was a wild sight, Texas in snow. The girls never complained about the cold, or anything, because, like their parents, they loved the great outdoors.

Back at the house, Efren, red-cheeked and jolly as ever, had built up the fire, and brought one of his eight children, his daughter Hortencia, to clean the house and help us with the girls if we needed her. Hortencia was fourteen years old, with too many teeth and timid as a mouse. She had made the beds and cleaned up the kitchen and was ready to take on the children. Within moments, Emmo and Nanny were sitting with her in front of the fire, holding up wet socks to dry. The dogs were sprawled around them, thawing out.

We dressed again and took one short afternoon walk, watching the sky clear and turn denim blue and the land stand still, locked in a frozen grip for the night. As the sun set on my family, it occurred to me that my life was filled with outstanding sunrises and sunsets, harvest moons, blue moons, full moons. Heaven on earth.

By morning, the sun came out boldly and the melting process lasted less than two hours. We got the girls to make a snowman quickly with the snow around the patio. He wasn't big but he was a cowboy, wearing a big, black hat, a gun belt and pistol, with a corn-cob pipe in his charcoal mouth and red bandanna around his neck. By noon he was gone.

Hortencia stayed at the house when the girls took their afternoon nap, and Dick and I started out together, but as he wanted to look for elk and mule deer and I wanted to check out the stream running through the arroyo, he went one way, I went the other. We agreed to meet back at the house around four. The dogs went with me and I was to wish he had taken them.

I had been walking for fifteen minutes when I heard thrashing and barking ahead but recognized this as searching noise, not mass murder noise. Janie was bell-less because it didn't make any difference—I could have put a Swiss cow bell on her and she would still have found her way to trouble.

Lillet did not like having her little speckled belly wet and cold, so she hung back with me until she couldn't stand it any more and begged me to pick her up. I rubbed her tummy and listened for the others. "Sounds like they've treed something, Lillet." She kissed me.

They were not barking hysterically; they were barking respectfully, like they weren't sure what they were doing but egging each other on nonetheless. I headed for the interspersed barking and occasional howls.

"They're not moving on. So they're not chasing anything. It must be up a tree," I told Lillet. I put her down and she trotted daintily, lifting her little wet cold paws as she followed me.

Arriving at the scene, I said, "Thank heavens. It's just a porcupine." The nasty animal was up in a small tree, unshaken by the commotion. "Forget it, you idiot dogs," I told them. "You can't climb trees and he'll just wait there until you go away."

At the base of the tree, the three sat, open-mouthed, tongues hanging out like big pink noodles.

"Leave him alone! Can't you see he's armed and dangerous?" The dogs stared happily as I spoke to them. "Come on, maybe you'll find a rabbit. That'll be fun." I tried to tempt them. No reaction. "Don't you remember what Dick told you about POR-CU-PINES?" I dragged out the word. Zip from them.

I knew the rules: shoot porcupines on sight. They killed trees, they hurt the animals . . . horses, cattle, deer . . . all I could think of was how unusual it was to find one down in the flats since the pine trees were in the mountains. I got up close to have a better look.

The dogs got more excited, thinking I was coming to help them. Dustin stood up against the tree, while Janie popped up two or three times against the trunk. Tarzan watched Dustin and Janie. Lillet stayed with me. The porcupine was very relaxed. His quills seemed to have a yellow glow, all the way up to his eyebrows.

"He smells," I said to my captive audience. "Ya'll know I could never shoot even this ugly monster."

The porcupine scrutinized me smugly, his nasty toes clutching the limb. He was about two feet above my head, and I wondered if, like I'd heard, he could throw the quills at me. I backed away just in case.

"Come on, you dumb dogs! That porcupine is gonna come down out of that tree and turn every one of you into a pin cushion!"

Like Colonel Travis at the Alamo, but with a stick, I drew a line in the sand dramatically, and said, "Those of you who want to live, cross this line and come with me." Lillet was already by my side but the others looked at me, looked at the line, then looked back at the porcupine where their sights remained. I guess they liked Dick's stories better. I walked away, "I'm warning you for the last time . . ."

From fifty paces, I turned to see the porcupine descending the tree.

"You have GOT to be joking," I snorted.

One butt-ugly, slow-moving porcupine, three delirious dogs, and silly little me with a loaded .38 that was going to remain in my holster. We all moved through the scene in slow motion. By the time I got there and could have taken a shot anyway, the porcupine had come all the way down the tree. With my luck I would have shot a dog instead.

The dogs watched his movement stupefied. My sense of impending injury grew deeper, especially since I could only hold two of them off at a time. Janie bit me once and Dustin almost choked himself. Tarzan all but flipped inside out, Lillet mostly supervised. For about four seconds, the dogs tried to kill the porcupine, but did not. The porcupine, never skipping a step, began to waddle up the creek bed, lighter by some sixty quills.

Instantly, the uncontrolled pandemonium turned into funereal silence. I looked at each dog and saw that we had suffered heavy damages. Neither Tarzan nor Dustin could close their mouths, nor could Janie even blink with the quills stuck in her eyelids.

"Oh, swell!" I said, burdened with responsibility. Staring at them, heartsick, I wondered whether I could possibly save them this time.

Reaching down to pick up Janie, I got lightheaded just looking at her. She was in agony and mighty sorry. None of them could close their mouths over the quills in their tongues. They made no noise.

That would have hurt. Lillet was standing behind me confused.

The dogs followed me back to the house like they were made of glass, silent as church mice and dazed. It was too early for Dick to be back, and the girls were still asleep, so I told Hortencia I was going to have to take the dogs into Alpine to the veterinarian's and to please tell Dick. She yelped when she looked at the dogs. I left Lillet in her arms.

The snow had pretty much melted and the roads were mushy but passable, and I drove as gently as I could in to Alpine.

It was Saturday, and Jan, who could handle a good dramatic situation as well as anyone, saw all three dogs following me unquestionably along the sidewalk to the hospital. She greeted our arrival as if it was the most normal thing in the world. Calling over her shoulder for Sandy, she turned to me and said, "I see we have a bigger crowd this time. Who's this?"

"Dustin. All the way from England to get into this mess."

"You, my boy, should have stayed in England. Or do they also have nasty porcupines?" Jan said, fondling his quill-free ears.

The dogs followed us like little lambs into an examining room, and quickly Jan gave Tarzan an injection. She laughed when I told her his name, saying, "Tarzan and Jane. How romantic!" She instructed Sandy to take him into the other room and pull the quills out when he dropped off. To me, she said, "If you can hold Dustin, I can pull his quills out. I hate to put him out if I don't have to."

I nodded. I felt a lot more helpful now that it was Jan's problem to fix them up.

Sizing up Janie, she added, "First, though, I think I'd better put her out for a while." She carried Janie into the adjoining room and gave her a shot. When she lost consciousness, Jan pried open her mouth and called me to look. I left Dustin sitting on the floor, ever patient, always willing to let the lady go first.

There were quills all the way down Janie's throat as far as I could see. We left her on the table. I grabbed a towel and covered her, thinking it was awfully cold on that stainless steel top, then followed Jan back to Dust.

Shaking her head, Jan spoke to him, "Come on, Dustin, we'll get you fixed up."

I took his front end, Jan took his rear, and we heaved him up onto the table. She looked carefully at the quills closest to his eyes. He sat there chivalrously, believing in her entirely. She opened a drawer in the counter and took out a pair of pliers, asking me to embrace Dustin's head, just in case, so he wouldn't bite us in pain. She then yanked three easy quills out of his muzzle as he yelped and I winced. Jan plucked two more out, dangerously close to his eyes. I could not watch and turned my head, feeling Dustin's body jerk each time as he whimpered in pain. Jan handed me a towel, opened Dustin's mouth, and told me to wrap one end around his upper jaw, the other around his lower jaw, and to keep his mouth propped open. If he bit down while she was working on his tongue he would get the towel, not our hands or fingers. Jan snapped eight more from his tongue and the roof of his mouth. By the time he had slumped over on his side and Jan was trying to reach four more down his throat, she had to get Sandy in to help her. I could not take any more. I felt lightheaded and ready to try gerbils for pets.

When Jan yelled, "Done," I looked up to see Dustin in a cheery state, standing up on the table, wagging his tail. What a great gentleman he was.

I hugged my brave man and escorted him out to the car as he pranced along beside me. When I returned, Jan was leaning over Janie's pincushion-looking body. She was out cold, but her eyes were stuck open. As gently as possible, Jan pulled a quill out of the upper lid of Janie's left eye and held it up, squinting at it in the overhead light.

"Don't worry," she said, "She won't lose her eyesight. These quills are all stuck in her lids. See the barb on the end? Nasty little things." Curiosity overwhelmed me and I looked. But as Jan extracted the next one, I lost any rampant desire of becoming a veterinarian that I'd ever entertained.

"Look down here," Jan said, pointing at her throat. "She's a mess. Didn't you have a gun?"

"I did," I said, guilty as hell.

"Brooke, we all know about the porcupine problem here. You shoot them on sight! No questions asked, no trials, no hangings, no problem." Jan was apparently a frustrated Annie Oakley. She worked busily before Janie came to, concentrating, but talking vaguely. "Never, EVER eat them. They taste like turpentine."

Had I heard her correctly? I had not paid complete attention to her rambling as I was trying to keep my breakfast down while watching little red blood splotches appear each time a quill came out of Janie. I absorbed Jan's line about turpentine and had an instant flashback to Edwig, our Swiss maid. She drank lighter fluid; Jan knew what turpentine tasted like.

I said, "Now, wait a minute. Are you telling me that you have killed, cleaned, and cooked a porcupine?"

"Yes, well, we've all tried to find out if they're good for anything." She pulled quill after quill out of Janie and as I looked closely, I thought I was seeing bits of flesh on each barb's end. Jan went on, "And we have come to the conclusion that they aren't good for anything."

Ah ha! We, who? I couldn't wait to tell Dick that Jan was the exalted emperor of some satanic cult. Barbie doll or not.

"Well, I want to thank you for that information. Just this morning we were trying to figure out what to have for dinner. Guess we'll go with the rattlesnake," I said.

"Okay. My work is done here," Jan straightened up, put her hands behind her and leaned back, stretching out her back. "They are all going to be mighty sore for a day or two. Janie should be the groggiest." I interrupted to tell her the story about Janie and the goats the last time.

"I stand corrected. She would be groggy if she were a normal dog," she added.

"Thank you again, Jan," I said. "We're very lucky you're always here."

"I'm not here tomorrow. I have a day off. If you've planned another day of adventure, save it. I'll be back Monday."

"Well then, tomorrow we're staying home and I'll lock the dogs in a closet!" I said.

"Want any of the quills to make a necklace?" Jan asked.

Another cult ritual? "No," I declined, "But tell me how in the world those quills got so far down Janie's throat?"

Jan knew the answer, "When she swallowed, they upended and stuck into her all the way down. Porcupines are awful on animals."

"What happens to cows, or horses, or deer?"

"Well, sometimes you'll see a few deer and cattle blinded, but normally they have a good natural instinct to stay away. Except the occasional coyote pup. They'll get in a fix like Janie. They starve."

"Man, this is rough country," I said.

Janie stirred on the table.

"She's coming out."

Janie sat bolt upright on the table.

"There you are, you little terrorist. That's what these dogs are! Not terriers, terrorists," Jan said, tickled with herself.

Sandy brought Tarzan from the other room. He was so drugged and lifeless he would have made a cute sandbag.

"Okay, kids, see you Monday," Jan said, slapping my back.

I paid the bill and Jan and Sandy carried Tarzan and Jane to the van. Dustin's face was starting to swell and he whined when we got in. Jan scratched his head and said good-bye.

By the time I got back to the ranch, the three punctured pooches were swollen up and miserable, looking like teenagers who'd had their wisdom teeth out.

Dick, Emmo, Nanny, and Lillet ran out of the house to greet us. Hortencia had told Dick what had happened, and he was laughing at the dogs' appearance. Still smiling, he asked how good old Jan was. I broke the news to him that she despised men, belonged to a cult of Alpine women who felt the same way, and that they believed in human sacrifice, male mostly, if cutting off parts didn't satisfy them. I don't think he believed me but it wiped the supercilious grin off his face. Emmo and Nanny jumped into action playing nurses for the injured hounds, patting their muzzles gently, and kissing their faces so tenderly I knew then and there their "dog person" choices had been made.

Sore, my foot! The next morning, Janie taught Lillet how to kill big game. With no backup help from Dustin or Tarzan, Janie lured Lillet up the mountain behind the house and the two of them brought down a nanny goat. Lillet lashed its throat. Dick and I heard it, but could do nothing unless we shot the dogs. Again Dick declined. Just as I had back at the border in Del Rio, I found myself looking up to the sky for a big idea, thinking things were more out of hand than usual. Janie, of course, always was a lot of trouble. But now she had Lillet following in her footsteps.

Efren didn't mind the killing at all. He good-naturedly dug a deep hole in the ground outside his house, and filled it with chunks of mesquite soaked in kerosene. He lit the wood, placed the cleaned goat in the pit, covered it with huge palm leaves and a wood plank, and cooked it all afternoon. With Efren's family, we sat around the fire as sunset gloried the west in a final fanfare of orange and crimson and the stars twinkled brightly down on us. We had a late supper of cabrito and Mexican rice, stewed with tomatoes and cilantro from Maria's garden. The pit was now our only source of heat and Efren and Dick had built it up to a huge bonfire. Our two girls and four dogs played with Efren and Maria's eight children until it got too cold, and we headed back to the house.

At the end of the week, we packed up and went home. There had been no further bloodlettings, even though I think Dick would have enjoyed seeing Jan again, in spite of my warning. As Janie got in the van and took up her position on Dick's lap so she could look out the window, scouting till the end, I could swear I heard the jungle drums beating across the land . . . "She's gone, she's gone."

Twenty-Three

A simple morning, a beautiful morning, with fat clouds, white as shaving cream, piled high, and fresh air blown in with a cool front during the night. March. A month to blatantly remind me how lucky I was to live in Texas. The third morning in a row starting at eight that a young mockingbird took up in a persimmon tree in the back yard. I read in a butterfly chair on the patio, drinking hot tea, with the girls playing in a sand box and the dogs napping in the rising sun. In the cool wind, the mockingbird sat proudly in the tree with the wind chimes, using them for background music. He started slowly, like he was getting in voice, then began to chirp and chatter incessantly, screeching and clucking, bobbing and flapping, synchronizing with the wind chimes' clanging crescendos and climaxes in the gusts of wind, swelling to such a racket I thought he was losing his mind. I could hardly read with such a performance going on and I started giggling. The girls ran to me and listened, swaying and bouncing around trying to imitate him. Janie got annoyed that he was disturbing her nap and went to sit at the bottom of the tree, not wagging her tail. If she could have thrown a rock she would have.

"How long will you be performing?" I asked the bird. He shut his beak for a moment, listening to me. The girls were startled, thinking I was communicating with the bird. My voice always took on a kinder tone, a higher pitch, when I talked to animals, birds, children. The bird said something to me that I tried to imitate, then Emmo tried, but laughed too much. Nanny clucked and chortled, spinning in place. Janie was the only one to look at him dangerously, licking her lips like she could imagine "mockingbird in a light alfredo sauce."

But none of us could make the same noise . . . he was, after all, a master of languages, stealing from other birds or imitating their songs. If I'd come near to getting the tune right, he would have switched to another. I attempted it again. Dustin raised his head and looked at me, wagging his tail like he was saying "nice try."

"Why can't you sing like that?" I said to the audience of girls and dogs. Tarzan stretched over to me, dragging his tummy on the new, Kelly-green grass. When I looked at the bird, I swear he bowed.

"Bravo!" I complimented him.

"Bravo!" sang Emmo and Nanny, finding me easier to copy.

"We should see if our little bird could perform at the Majestic Theatre. Then we'll get our doggies in a Muppet movie!" Everyone was wiggling, wagging, and clapping, except Lillet. She just slept peacefully in the sun, about two weeks away from having puppies. Trying to get a good strain going, we had bred her to a handsome broken-coated male named Gangster, in Lampasas, owned by friends of John Karger. John was still working at Broadway Animal Hospital and also putting together a new nonprofit organization called Last Chance Forever, saving birds of prey. He still had Harmony, one of Tarzan and Jane's pups, who had been leading a much more impressive life than any of mine ever would, in that she was a drug sniffer at the airport and was even part of John's bird show. John visited us once on Dover Road, driving his pickup. In the front seat, on a perch, sat a lovely golden eagle named Golda, and in the seat beside her was Harmony. They were pals. John told me hunting with a hawk and a Jack Russell was quite an experience. I envisioned Harmony flying with the hawk.

With Lillet's puppies, we were hoping to get another unique chocolate-colored Russell. Years before, Janie had told us and Tarzan in no uncertain terms that she was not going to dip into the puppy pool ever again, and we had respected her wishes. Janie's face was silvered over now at the muzzle and around her alert brown eyes. She had aged well. Like Dustin. His soft muzzle was whitish, and so was the hair around his black eyes. I smiled at the dogs, thinking what an enlightening life they had given me unknowingly. What a grand family we were.

After the mockingbird flew off to regale others, I finished my tea and went in to dress, realizing it was already getting too warm for a terrycloth bathrobe at nine in the morning. My fuzzy green slippers, like floor mops, were a catchall for dog hair, leaves, and bright blue yarn from a current crochet project. I looked like Pig Pen. No wonder Dick had gone to the shooting range so early on a Sunday morning.

The girls coaxed Tarzan into the sandbox and buried him. Janie went out to lie down in the yard next to Dustin, in the sun. She yawned a big yawn and lay on her side, her back against Dustin's. Lillet came inside with me, looking for food.

When Dick got back, we took the girls out for pizza and by early afternoon they were all ready for their naps, Dick included.

Wanting to take a little walk around the neighborhood to see what trees and flowers were coming out, I gently picked up Lillet. She seemed restless and probably needed a little exercise, whereas Dustin was sleeping peacefully in the sun and Tarzan was inside curled up on a pillow next to Em. Janie was nowhere to be seen and I thought it best to sneak out as the pace always changed when she was present. Lillet didn't need any hysteria for the moment.

At the corner of Geneseo and Dover Road, Janie fell in beside me.

"Where did you come from?" She glared at me and I added, "Janie, I looked for you. Honest. You know I wouldn't have left you." The dog saw through me like I was a legislator. "Okay, okay," I broke down, "I promise I'll never do that again!" She drove a hard bargain.

Janie and Lillet trotted together. Janie, so svelte and athletic, cruising with a bounce, moving with grace, watching the world through big, sharp, interested eyes. Lillet, so bulky and packed, unsure of herself and dependent on me. I wondered if she would have her puppies in the closet. I could hardly wait to see what they looked like.

We went up Geneseo and back down, with the median being one of their favorite spots to inspect. We were gone half an hour. Redbud trees bloomed with bright fuschia flowers before the leaves came out, just as wisteria did. Mountain laurels produced fat, grape-like lavender flowers, smelling so sweet I was sorry I hadn't waited for the girls and Dick to walk with, someone to share these wonders. I never noticed anything unusual until we got home. But when I put the two dogs out in the back yard, Lillet dropped on the warm wood steps. I opened the bottom of the Dutch door and leaned down to her. She looked as though she had fainted. I'd never known a dog to faint. I picked her up. She was limp, like an old carrot.

Jumping to the conclusion that it had to be a heart attack from the puppies and the weight, I ran to the car with her floppy body, placed her in my lap, and drove like a bat out of hell for the Broadway Animal Hospital. I hadn't even stopped to tell Dick where I was going, but I thought he would still be asleep anyway. Lillet's head rolled around each time I hit a curve in the road, but I made myself believe that if I got her to the vet's they would save her. They always had saved my best friends. They were my only hope. But things were starting to not make sense. Stroking Lillet's chocolate head, tickling her chocolate ears, I recalled her questioning eyes, matching her dark coat exactly. Lillet, the baby in the family. I had a horrid feeling she was dying. I was not ready to let her go.

Mary Mainster took Lillet from me right away. I waited in the front room, no normal thoughts going through my head. Just stupid things, like I should have known not to walk her so far. But actually it wasn't that far. Probably I should have never let her have puppies. But she was young and healthy, and I knew of no danger. Like how could it be a heart attack when I was sure she had had her heartworm preventative?

I looked at my bitten fingernails and promised I wouldn't bite them again if Lillet lived. That was so stupid a thought, I looked around for something else to stabilize me. Mr. Magoo had been replaced by another pretty bird who was staring at me like he knew what had happened. He cocked his head and snapped his beak, but said nothing. I felt like nothing was normal, everything was off.

I heard someone coming down the hall and rose from my chair..

"I couldn't save her," Mary said, looking at me gravely, wiping her hands on a clean towel. It had no ducks. I wished it had had ducks and that I was back in Alpine with Jan and Sandy pulling out porcupine quills.

I sat down.

"I tried to save the puppies but they were gone, too."

I didn't move, I couldn't speak. Mary sat down beside me.

"What happened?" I asked dully.

"Where are the other dogs?" Mary asked.

"Was it a heart attack?" I asked back.

"Brookie, were the other dogs with you?" she demanded.

Why wouldn't Mary answer me? I wanted her to answer me first. To hell with it, I told myself drearily, and answered, "Janie was with me. Just Janie and Lillet." I gasped when I said Lillet's name.

"Is Dick at home?" Mary asked, but then she must have realized I was slipping away, and she asked firmly, grabbing my arm, "Where's Janie now?"

"How many puppies were there?" I heard myself ask. What did it matter?

"Brookie," Mary said my name sternly, standing me up. "I'm going to send John home with you."

"Don't be ridiculous," I said. I wanted to be alone because I had no idea how this was going to hit me when I caught the full impact. "I'll be all right," I mumbled. Maybe I could just sleep it off. I felt so tired and hungry. If I ate, if I slept, I'd wake up and Lillet would be asleep on my pillow next to me. Alive.

Mary turned and called for John. She put a hand on my arm and I looked down at it. Strong, harsh hands, freckled with liver spots and raised blue veins. My dogs' lives were written on those hands. Those hands that had saved my dogs so many times over for the last nine years. But those hands hadn't saved Lillet.

John Karger stood in front of me, his eyes so sad, and he said, "I'll drive."

Even in my stupor, I was kind of insulted. "Mary, John, you know I'm all right. I just need to get home."

Mary coaxed me towards the door. I took the keys from my back pocket and held them up for John, thinking this must be a new policy at Broadway Animal Hospital: when your animals die, someone drives you home. It all made very little sense to me.

On the way home, I had nothing to say to John and he had nothing to say back. I wouldn't have gone the way he went, but he drove well. And what the hell did it matter anyway?

As we pulled into the driveway, I looked at the house. Lillet would never come home to this house again. She would never eat, she would never sleep on the bed. I would never pat her happy head again. She was gone.

John got out of the car and came around to open my door. He gave me his hand and helped me out.

"I'll just see you in," he said. I was kind of concerned how he was going to get back to the clinic but I was too tired to worry now. I wanted to get Janie, Tarzan, and Dustin on the bed with me and take a nap.

Unlocking the door, I wondered what I would say to Dick and the girls. It was still quiet in the house and I wanted to leave them asleep as long as I could so I wouldn't have to tell them. Maybe I could get John to tell Janie about her daughter?

John followed me in and asked, "Where's Janie?"

I pointed to the Dutch door and patio. Hearing us, Tarzan rushed out of Emmo's room to greet me, sliding on the slick wood floor. Picking him up, I buried my face in his soft white coat.

I looked up as John came back in the house with Dustin at his side. Dustin kept sniffing at Janie's wooden body in John's big arms. She was dead. I looked into John's eyes and just stared at him until he had to say, "Brookie, they were poisoned."

To try to keep Emmo and Nanny's lives normal, I made maca-roni and cheese with hot dogs cut up in it and put them in our bed, let-ting them watch television. But later that evening, when a handsome young police officer, chewing gum, came to the house to ask ques-tions about the incident, the girls ran to the door, probably expecting Janie and Lillet to come home. Not seeing the dogs, they ran back to the bedroom, not at all interested in the officer. They were, luckily for them, too little to understand the tragedy.

I stood like a zombie with Dick by my side, waiting to hear what the officer had to say. I couldn't even remember the last thing that Dick and I said to each other after John told him the story. I had lost a whole day.

"There have been poisonings in the neighborhood," the officer reported.

I had to sit. Dustin and Tarzan got on the couch with me. I gazed miserably at the officer, thinking it was neat that a Texas policeman wore nice, shiny black cowboy boots.

"Who is doing it?"

"A young man who lives on Geneseo has been putting strych-nine in hamburger meat and placing it on the median, in the middle. He's poisoned eighteen dogs so far. Yours included." His gum popped, after which there was a slight silence.

I said, "You knew about it?"

The officer looked up from his pad and pencil, chewing, and said, "Yes, ma'am, for about two weeks."

"You have known for two weeks?" I stood, shaking like a leaf, and my head went light. Wobbling, I approached the officer. Dick stepped in to block me.

"And you didn't warn anyone!" I stated, not a question.

"He puts the hamburger on that median on Geneseo," he said, acting like I was a dumb broad since he had to repeat it. He smiled at Dick as though *he* would understand. His gum popped again. My mind reeled.

Putting his hands on my shoulders, Dick forced me to look into his red-rimmed eyes as he said, "It's not his fault."

The officer backed two steps towards the front door.

"Dick, they knew . . ." I said, weakly.

Dick moved facilely to the front door to get the officer out.

"That seems an odd way to handle the situation," Dick said, speaking slowly and with an unaccustomed vehemence.

As the officer hectored, "We wanted to catch him red-handed," Dick slammed the door in his face.

That night as I tried to sleep, tossing and turning, through spurts of anger and waves of frustrated tears, I reached way back into my memory and recalled sadly that one of Mom's dogs, a dachshund named Bruno, had been poisoned, also in Terrell Hills. I could not remember the details, just her long-term sorrow and vow to never get another dog. But she did get another dog. Janie. And now Janie had been poisoned. My heart hit bottom. How could I tell Mom?

Much later, I got out of bed and made my way in the dark, down to the basement, and found an old suitcase full of dog towels and blankets. Feeling around in the dark, I knew it the minute my hands felt it. I went back upstairs and got back in bed.

I finally fell asleep holding Janie's red cashmere sweater close to me.

Twenty-Four

In the morning, the mockingbird came back. I sat with my cup of tea, swollen eyes, and halfmasted heart, listening as the bird reached his highest pitch. At the finale, he tipped his head to me, acting slightly confused this time when I didn't cheer for him. He would never have to know what happened. He would never have to suffer like I was suffering.

Dick, deeply stunned and unsure how to handle my grief much less his own, sat out with me drinking coffee and reading *Shooter's Bible*. For once, I realized how lucky he was to have his reading to escape into and I was glad for him. I had always found my escapes in the children and the dogs. Dick and I were comfortable enough sitting quietly.

Emmo and Nanny were playing in their sandbox again, with Tarzan buried up to his neck. Dustin lay asleep in the sun. Two dogs seemed so few.

I wished for one wish . . . just one: to make this morning yesterday morning and start all over again . . . with Janie sitting huffily below the noisy mockingbird and Lillet asleep in the sun. This time I wouldn't take them walking and they wouldn't eat the poison.

Janie had been part of my life for nine years. Hell, she had made life happen. There would never be another like her and if there was, I probably wouldn't be able to handle it. The more I thought of it, the more surprised I was she ate the poison. She was too smart to go that way. But the clever young man had laced hamburger meat with strychnine. No dog could resist fresh raw meat. It hurt my heart to think of what he did, not just to me, but to the other dog owners, too.

As much as I despised him, I hated, even more, the heads of the police for not putting notices in the paper or on the neighborhood phone poles, for not warning the pet owners. Sure, their great plan was to catch him red-handed. But at the expense of eighteen dogs? I wished I could find out who was heading up the investigation, to tell him how much a dog suffers when he has been poisoned by strychnine, how he dies in excruciating pain. In my eyes, the fact that they had been so inefficient in their approach was as bad as poisoning the dogs themselves. My blood turned cold.

As the day plodded by, the only thought that cheered me up was of Len Woods, my savior with the explosive chicken. I imagined how he would have handled the situation, conjuring him up in camouflage pants and turtleneck, combat boots, and gloves, peering around from a house on Geneseo. Unbeknownst to the young murderer, Len would plant land mines in the median, and when the boy attempted to leave the poisoned meat, he would be blown to hell!

Otherwise, I foundered in mercurial self-pity as thoughts of Janie and Lillet swirled around in my head, some making me laugh, others making me break down. I went back to the beginning, to Devon, when Mom, David, and I first saw Janie at the farm, how tiny she was, how courageous, how obnoxious. In Switzerland, barking daftly at dull cows, Len and the exploding chicken, in the Alps with marmots. Then her adventures in Texas with squirrels, armadillos, porcupines, javelinas. And her love for Dustin. Enter Tarzan and Mischief. Oh no, not Mischief. And then the birth of Lillet. Her sweet face and kind nature, her need to be loved, her sincerity. It dawned on me that we were a lot alike with such strong mothers. But I, at least, was old enough to stand on my own and survive. Since Janie's strong suit was independence, Lillet needed guidance and protection, and she had turned to me for it. I could imagine Lillet's big, coffee-colored eyes begging, pleading with me: show me the way, protect me. I had let her down. Lillet was only four. And now Lillet and Janie were both dead. They would never hear that crazy mockingbird again. Each time I looked at Dustin, my sweet gentleman, I wondered, would he miss Janie? Tarzan, darling Tarzan. Did he understand? Janie was gone, Lillet was gone.

Mom dropped everything and flew in from New York in the afternoon two days later. As always, she looked elegant and accomplished, hiding her red-rimmed eyes behind a large pair of tortoiseshell dark glasses. And was I just imagining something, or was her blue-and-green Hermes scarf draping limply around her neck? Could a scarf be sad? In Mom's devastation she showed her strength, picking up the pieces, organizing meals, cleaning the kitchen, rehanging pictures. Emmo and Nanny loved having her there because she, at least, did not cry all day like I did.

Pete flew in from Colorado and hardly knew what to do. Crying women gave him the chills, so he kept busy playing with the girls, walking them around the block since I had given it up. I wouldn't let Dustin or Tarzan out of the house as I was afraid the police were still scratching their heads trying to figure out how to handle the killer. I had not heard of any more deaths, and I could only hope the young man was dead himself.

Dick, poor Dick, a private man, a man who loved animals as much as I did, continued to keep his agony hidden behind magazines.

One evening, Mom made a meal of her famous curried chicken, new potatoes, and salad. As we sat silently over delicious peach cobbler, she showed a little necessary impatience with me, pointing out that it was not the end of the world and that life was going to go on even though I morbidly acted like I didn't care. This was a woman who had out-argued, out-fought, and out-done her entire generation and now was even out-living some of them. And she had survived the time so many years ago when her dog was poisoned. I hated when she got mad at me, but deep down I knew she was right. I forced a smile. Emmo and Nanny crawled into my lap and hugged me. My God, I had so much. How much longer was I going to let my life unravel? Again, as I had learned after Mischief's death, life goes on.

Life did go on. Mom took off for Nepal on a shoot for a Tiffany book. Hugging me tight, she told me she was proud of me, that I was the kind of mother she wished she had been for me and Pete. And then she really broke me up by saying she couldn't have picked a better person to have taken care of her Janie. Janie had had a wonderful full life because of me.

Pete returned to Colorado, saying if he stayed any longer he would become a "maniac depressive" . . . like me. He also told us he was thinking of moving back to Texas, he wanted to be closer to his family. When he said that, I wished I had never come back from Europe. None of this would have happened.

Dick, Emmo and Nanny, Dustin, Tarzan, and I went to KWW, the family's ranch in the Hill Country, the following weekend to get away from our sad home. In the evening, we walked the girls down to the Guadalupe River, with Tarzan and Dustin attempting to scour the countryside for sport but ending up close to us, like what was the point? We sat on the rock bank and skipped rocks across to the other side. The girls, dashing around and giggling, were the light spot of my life for the moment, and I had to be careful to keep my spirits up for them.

The cold air stung my face. Gray clouds tumbling and rolling overhead were uncovering patches of blue and the sunset filtered into a multicolored finale, lighting up the cypresses on the river banks.

Tarzan and Dustin seemed so quiet, as if the wind was out of their sails with Janie and Lillet gone. Squirrels and armadillos were living normal lives around us and I resented them. Janie had known no half measures, and Tarzan and Dustin were never called to glory that way again.

Five Mexican tree ducks flew over our heads, their long necks stretched out, quacking to each other busily like a big Italian family communicating over a spaghetti dinner. I looked at my family in front of me. Dick, throwing rocks with the girls, enjoyed his life. He didn't ask for anything more, but then again, he didn't ask for anything at all of anyone. He was doing everything he wanted to do in life, hunting and fishing any time he wanted, reading the rest of the time. I could not fathom how to get him to do things with us. He saw life through his eyes and made decisions accordingly. If we could go along, fine, if we couldn't, fine. It made me feel unimportant, and it made me mad. I felt incompetent in the marriage. But I looked at the girls, their unconditional happiness, their absolute ease. They watched the tree ducks, pointing and flapping their arms in simulation, quacking and running. Two brown-haired, dark-eyed girls who had the vicissitudes of life in front of them. I hoped I could teach them to believe in themselves, not wait for approval, to take responsibility for their actions, not throw the blame somewhere, and especially, I hoped I could teach them not to chew gum in public. These were important issues to me. Maybe Mom was right. Maybe I *was* a good mother.

Tarzan came over and got in my lap, content with me patting his head and scratching his big pink ears. "Tar, the sun is setting in your ears," I smiled.

As Dustin, who was eight years old, an emblem of aging dignity, lay down beside me and licked my hand, I wondered how much longer I had with either one of these two dogs. Life seemed more unpredictable than I had ever imagined, but suddenly that made it more special to me. I had chosen this life, or I had chosen my dogs, and they had given me a life of sunrises and sunsets, of living and learning, of happiness and now much sorrow. I had not bargained for how hard it would be to lose my two little dogs, but I had to believe no defeat was ever final. I knew then, sitting in the Hill Country with my wits about me, that I would forever be grateful to Tarzan, Jane, Mischief, Dustin, and Lillet, for making it such a life.

In the summer of 1979, Dick and I with girls and dogs were at his father's house at Port Aransas, two weeks away from the due date of our third child. Dick was convinced it was a boy. I wanted a boy simply because with scrutiny and early examination maybe I could learn to understand the human male. I could hope for it.

Midmorning Sunday, as Dick came in from fishing alone, I told him I wanted to go home after lunch, that I was feeling funny. He said he couldn't go then because he had seen a "hog" of a redfish over in the flats at Lydia Ann and he could catch it if he went that afternoon. It was one of the classic moments in our marriage when I had no clue how to tell him we were leaving after lunch or I would divorce his ass and take the dogs with me. So, after his lunch and nap, he left in his flat-bottomed boat to catch his redfish.

By four o'clock, my instincts told me to get myself home. I flagged down Pamela Howard, Dick's stepsister, who was leaving the island for San Antonio right away. She was in her brand new black Jeep but was a good sport and agreed to take me, two children, and two dogs home. She, unlike Dick, detected something in my eyes and was concerned for me. During the entire bumpy three-hour drive, I felt like my stomach was a cracking watermelon, and held it firmly in my arms. It was like cargo trying to break free.

At seven in the evening, my first call was to a neighbor to please come over and watch Emmo and Nanny, the second call was for a cab. My water had broken. As the Black Cat cab driver noticed my condition and panicked, I jumped in his cab and bellowed, "Methodist Hospital or else." I was breathing at a rate of knots.

Dick drove in the driveway as we were driving out. I paid the driver and jumped into Dick's car and almost vomited on the spot as the combined smells of fish, WD-40, and sweat hit me.

"Do I have time for a shower?" he asked.

"You'll have time when we're divorced," I said hysterically. Dick put the car in gear.

I got my breathing under control and was feeling optimistically secure with Dick there. But as he swerved around, trying to remember which hospital we went to for the birth of our children, I sadly realized he was only adept at getting to the Broadway Lockers, his favorite spot for game processing, or Nagel Gun Shop, and started directing him to the Methodist Hospital. We were not current on our Lamaze methods, as we had been for the birth of Emily, so I was breathing the best way I remembered, slow and controlled, short pants, long countdowns. Preparing for Nancy's birth, I recalled our third Lamaze class fondly, as Sister Christina cleared her throat and, interrupting all the couples working together, said *real* loud, "Mr. Negley? Would you put the book down and help your wife?" We cut the rest of the classes and did not attempt any joint effort to prepare for our third child's birth.

Sydney, our beautiful and last daughter, was born shortly after we got to the hospital. She was blond and so blue-eyed her nickname would be "Blue."

The doctor announced, "She weighs 7 pounds 11 ounces."

Dick hooted and hollered, saying, "My redfish was bigger!"

After a life with Jack Russell terriers that began with Janie, I have never attempted to live a day without one. Dustin and Tarzan had good lives, remaining in mine long enough to teach me that male dogs were easier for me to cope with than male humans. Dick and I were amicably divorced when the girls were young and we are still friends today. He has been a wonderful father and a good friend to our three exceptional girls. And now, of course, I find him funny.

Mom lives in New York half the year, the other half in San Antonio, and is editor-at-large of three magazines. She's still traveling all over the world, she's still sending postcards with big red lips. Mom's on the brink of getting a new dog, as she just lost her precious Cavalier King Charles, Ritz.

Pete returned to Texas years ago, after a very abrupt yet civilized two-year marriage, and runs the water ski program at Lake Breeze Ski Lodge, at McQueeney. He had a beautiful golden retriever named Soccer who is buried in his yard—nearby forever.

We all feel blessed to have grown up in the company of dogs. None of us, not even Dick, is married at present, but we all have dogs. I do not find that odd.

Since 1977, roll call would sound like: Trapper, Fred, Max, Puddin', Gangster, Morty, Abi, Hubbell, and Banjo; a mixed bag of purebred golden retrievers, Jack Russells, and mutts. Right now I live with Goose, a big-eared, crooked-legged, part-Corgi mutt I saved twelve years ago; Sealy, a tri-colored, eight-year-old Jack Russell, similar to Janie physically in every way except she is half the size; Cody, a big, black, handsome four-year-old mutt abandoned in my neighborhood with his four littermates; and Ciancy, a one-year-old wild and enthusiastic Jack Russell who climbs trees. Each day I take the dogs out for a walk and in my neighborhood I am known as the "dog lady," often mistaken for a dog walker. On my fiftieth birthday, as many dogs came to my party as people. I go to bed at night with Elizabeth Arden Eight-Hour Cream on my face and four dogs on the bed sandbagging me, and I wake up in the morning with dog hair stuck to my face and a smile. I wouldn't have it any other way. I think of the dogs that have passed through my life, and I am constantly amazed how much they have meant to me. As Elizabeth von Arnim wrote, "Once dogs love, they love steadily, unchangingly, until their last breath. That is how I like to be loved."

For Mom, Pete, and me, marriages have come and gone. Dogs have come and gone, too. But our hearts and family have stayed intact. Emily, Nancy, and Sydney have grown up to become three of the best people I have ever known. In law school and colleges here and yon, they have moved out, but come home often to a house full of wagging tails and trusting eyes, and we all have each other. The dogs and their love have always been there for all of us. And that is how I like to love and be loved. My choice was made many, many years ago, starting with little Miss Jane Russell. I am proud to be a dog person.

Acknowledgements

This little book has come as a surprise to many of us.

First, I would like to thank my mother who believed in the book immediately, gave it a spank of approval, and supported me throughout the venture.

To Ray Corliss—a big kiss and hug for helping it through its teen years with his belief and kindness.

And I'd like to thank Norton Mockridge, who came along when the book was somewhat dormant, picked it up and read it, loved it and nurtured it until it could leave home.

I express my gratitude to all and BRAVO!